The Supermarketers

RECENT BOOKS BY ROBERT HELLER

The Supermanagers
The Pocket Manager
The Naked Manager

The Supe

E. P. DUTTON   NEW YORK

ROBERT HELLER

marketers

Marketing for Success, Rules of The Master Marketers, The Naked Marketplace

T·T
A TRUMAN TALLEY BOOK

Published in the United States by
Truman Talley Books • E. P. Dutton,
a division of NAL Penguin Inc.,
2 Park Avenue, New York, N.Y. 10016.

Library of Congress Cataloging-in-Publication Data
Heller, Robert, 1932–
The supermarketers.
Truman Talley Books
Includes index.
1. Marketing—Case studies. 2. Success in business—Case studies. I. Title. II. Title: Supermarketers.
HF5415.H374 1987   658.8   86-23977
ISBN 0-525-24520-0

Published simultaneously in Canada by
Fitzhenry & Whiteside Limited, Toronto

COBE

DESIGNED BY MARK O'CONNOR

TO RACHEL

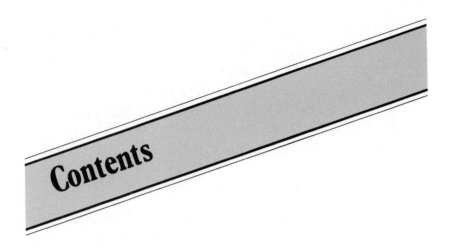

Contents

CONTENTS

CONTENTS

xii

The Supermarketers

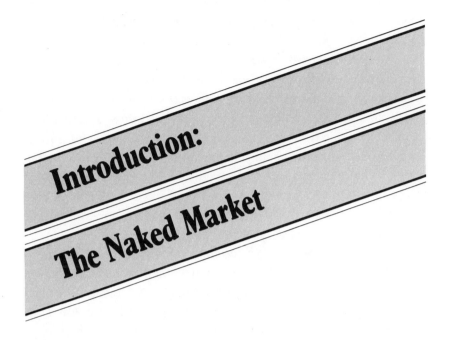

Introduction:
The Naked Market

The years since 1973 have been a marvelous economic era, believe it or not—even though the oil price explosion did end general rapid Western economic expansion, for too long a while. The marvel is that the same dismal years saw the creation of more companies, more self-made fortunes, and more revolutionary product successes than any such period in history. In the last quarter of the twentieth century world markets are being split wide open, old-line companies are being torn apart, and new-style entrepreneurs are pouring through the openings.

The opportunities have been created partly by the new technologies, which have opened up new industrial avenues, often whole vistas of change and wealth. But even in old markets, where microcircuits, genetic engineering, and other such scientific marvels have worked no wonders (and never will), new market opportunities have multiplied. Businesses that miss these boats will—as many already have—perish on the shore.

As always, the iron hand of economics rules. The new technologies are breaking through because of plain, clear economic superiority. Take an aged market such as cameras (George Eastman invented the Kodak in 1895). Electronics has performed three amazing feats at once: lowering the manufacturing cost of the camera while raising its reliability and richly enhancing its appeal through detailed innovation. That enhancement of desirability is the key. In a saturated world marketplace, growth in general demand would have been slow, even without world recessions. Marketing once meant the marketing of need; today, it means the marketing of desire.

Creating and satisfying a specific, optional desire, or defining a new market, makes vastly more money than merely meeting an established human need. In 1984 Intel made 85 percent of General Mills' net income, although the flour giant's sales were three and one half times higher. Specialization, not just of dedicated high-technology firms like Intel but also within old homogeneous markets like bread, is one reason for the magnified role of genuine marketing expertise in today's successes; but even more important is simple ease of entry. In some new boom areas, such as personal and other small-scale computing, entry has been even simpler than it was for the automobile pioneers before World War I. As recently as 1976, the Apple computer firm was begun on $1,500. In many fields now, the well-positioned, small specialist can break in before the big market leaders even realize the risk—if, that is, they are asleep at the switch.

As Apple's own tumultuous experiences have shown, being unprepared is an even greater danger for the upstart that has turned into a substantial competitor. Only a couple of years after the impact of IBM had utterly changed its market, Apple underwent a traumatic top-management upheaval, saw sky-high hopes for its Macintosh computer brought down to earth, moved into and out of heavy loss, closed plants, changed its marketing strategy at least twice— and the saga is surely not over. These days, there is no safety in innovation, no security even in billion-dollar scale—a status that Apple had achieved in record time.

At any point along the spectrum of corporate might, the ferocious competition created by differentiated, easy-to-enter, and desire-driven markets means that a moment's marketing slumber can easily become the Big Sleep. The market has become naked for many reasons: because there's no protection against its forces (even if a government temporarily bails out the feeble, fate nearly always gets them in the end); because changes in management's own world (the job hopping, the market research explosion, even downright theft) mean that few markets hold any secrets anymore—secrets, that is, that can be kept for long; and because most marketplaces are now arenas for naked aggression. Above all ages, this is the Age of Competition.

In such a situation, which won't change before the end of this century, success goes to those who combine the highest degree of aggression with the fullest application of intelligence. It's a combination that only the best people and the greatest firms manage to keep working effectively over the years. This book shows how and why these Supermarketers succeed and, just as important, how their victims, time and again, die from self-inflicted wounds.

Yet, as these pages tell, failures can be turned into successes by following the courses of action, simple in concept but tough to execute, that constitute the creed of the Supermarketers.

1. Concentrate on building winning products, services, and brands—and drop losers.

2. Use corporate organization as a deliberate means of achieving marketing objectives—and change it at will.

3. Stay close to the market at all times, listen to what it says, and act on what you hear.

4. Aim at all times for the optimum returns on sales and investment and never settle for less.

5. Make marketing miracles by turning the impossible into the possible—and achieving it.

6. Scale each activity to the needs of its markets and never be impressed by anybody's size, including your own.

7. Use every aspect of the business to stress its marketing message and make sure that the message gets across.

8. Employ honest means and honest words to achieve your targets—and honest measures to prove it.

9. See diversification, including acquisition, only as another route to organic growth—and insist on getting it.

10. Know that turbulence in technology and markets increases opportunity—and ruthlessly exploit the discontinuities.

11. Pursue growth, not as an end in itself, but as the result of excellent marketing and concentrate on that excellence.

12. Build on the past to achieve success in the present that will guarantee the future—and never neglect the future.

These are the twelve steps, described in this book, that will take the Supermarketer forward in the years leading up to 2000. Every factor that created the extraordinary triumphs of the years since 1973 will become still more intense, from the multiplication of markets to the proliferation of new technology. The stunning collapse of oil prices in the mid-1980s, though, has set these forces against the background of a distinctly different world economy. The opportunities for true marketers who know their nakedness and then don the right clothes will still be lucrative. This book is their guide.

Step One: The Creation of Market Leadership

1. THE CLASSIC CASE OF COKE

No company should be more strongly placed to reap the harvest, as opposed to the whirlwind, of the late twentieth century's marketing turbulence than Coca-Cola. That's why the most significant event in recent marketing history, the equivalent of President's Nixon's taking the dollar off the gold standard, was Coke's bombshell in the spring of 1985. Suddenly, Coke announced that it was changing its famous secret formula 7X: the recipe that had peopled Atlanta with Coke millionaires, spread the symbol of American civilization around the globe, and created one of the world's most triumphant marketing machines. No single event better epitomizes the violence and depth of the change that has swept across world markets in the Age of Competition.

On the face of it, Coca-Cola had no more reason to tamper with its formula than Michael Jackson has to grow a beard. Not only was "flagship" Coke the most popular soft drink in the world, but Coke the company, under a vigorous new broom, Roberto C. Goizueta, had been innovating as never before. One week earlier, Minute Maid orange soda and a reformulated Fresca had gone into test markets, joining other wonders, such as Diet Coke, which had catapulted to instant success. From one point of view, Diet Coke's success was a convincing demonstration of the company's newfound prowess; from another, there was the rub.

As Diet Coke cannibalized Coke sales—down by 4 percent in U.S. supermarkets since 1981—so Pepsi crept nearer and nearer, thanks largely to brilliant ads featuring the aforementioned Michael Jackson. Pepsi had advanced to an 18.8 percent share, against Coke's 21.7 percent, at the time of the birth of the new Coke formula. As Coke had no distinct taste advantage over Pepsi, leaving well enough alone must have seemed a greater danger than striking out boldly with a new formulation—though the latter route carried risks of its own. To begin with, it implied (as Pepsi promptly noted with delight) that the old Coke was imperfect. At one hundred years of age, that would have been excusable, but Coke was paying the price not of its product's antiquity, which didn't matter, but of the antiquated Atlanta management of the recent past, which did.

For too many years, the old kings of Coke had let Pepsi set the pace. Real Supermarketers know better than to leave things alone. Even if their product is supreme, with all competition lost to sight, the investment in better marketing, in research, in management talent, and in technology is constantly being reinforced, partly for self-protection, partly because no other way exists of making an organization successful—not only fat with wealth but also lean with ambition and primed for competition.

The company's latter-day burst of innovation was a kind of catching up, without which the Coke formula couldn't, in fact, have been changed: the magic new "smooth" syrup came to light during the high-tech R & D work required for Diet Coke. The diet formula was an indispensable development—not so the new formula. To quote my prediction of the time: "Almost certainly the promotional value of the switch will be greater than the immediate sales benefit from the difference in taste, which only 55 percent of Coke lovers apparently prefer." As events proved, 55 percent was on the high side —far too high.

Throughout the subsequent embarrassments, as vociferous public demand forced Coke to bring back the old flavor as "Classic" Coke, nobody could tell how far the great company's losses had outweighed its gains. But one thing is certain: the Coke saga shows that, in times that are turbulent in terms of both technology and markets, yesterday's supremacy is today's vulnerability. There is only one protection, in good times and in bad, and it doesn't lie in technology alone, or even mainly. Play consistently to your strengths and invest consistently in them and you won't need to change your flavor—maybe.

2. PULLING THE TECHNOLOGY

One plausible answer to the billion-dollar, much debated question, Why did Coke do it?, lies in the company's technology. Its boss, Roberto Goizueta, comes from a technological rather than a marketing background and, it is said, was so fascinated by the technological breakthrough that he couldn't resist modernizing the taste of the world's favorite soft drink. Whether it is true or false, the story has a cogent moral: Technological leadership is important, often crucially so, but being led by technology is generally fatal.

The lessons of the late twentieth century teach that the more miraculous technology becomes, the more those who manage it depend for success on entirely nontechnical skills: above all, those of marketing. This essential truth of the Age of Competition was symbolized in unmistakable terms when John Sculley, a marketing man from PepsiCo, was appointed president of Apple: the warmest seat in the hottest high-tech market. In fact, throughout its astonishing growth to a billion dollars of sales in half-a-dozen years, Apple had flourished partly because of marketing "smarts," but that was when the gee-whiz company had much of the personal computer market to itself. With that security destroyed, primarily by the invasion of IBM, Apple had no option but to raise its sights several notches: hence Supermarketer Sculley.

Hence, too, the heavy bet on the Macintosh computer, a major advance in technology, but also a step forward in marketing because the new computer's main attraction—one bound, it seemed, to make sales easier—was that a novice could master it in twenty minutes. The trouble was that this proved to be no great asset in a business market dominated by IBM and IBM compatibility. In other words, high technology is itself a marketing tool and may well be entirely useless if it isn't geared closely and powerfully to a marketing need that can be economically serviced. (By definition, a marketing need that can't be economically serviced might as well not exist.)

No more striking proof of this point will ever be provided than that of the supersonic airliner Concorde. Forgetting its relatively cramped interior, this is plainly a superior product, delivering its service (air travel) in far more acceptable form, that is, faster. Real product superiority invariably has the sublime virtue of attracting a premium price. But the premium can't be scaled up indefinitely. Nor will it necessarily reach a level at which prices cover the costs of the superiority. Believe that it will, and you're liable to end up with a Concorde—a product whose real, unsubsidized costs are simply too large ever to be matched by the revenue available at any imaginable price.

There's no true marketing "pull" in such a situation: the product may be desirable, but not at any price. You can usually tell when irreversible errors of this kind have been committed. The proponents of the mistake produce extraneous arguments to prove that it wasn't a fiasco after all, but a masterstroke of management. Thus Concorde's defenders claim that the superjet is a flagship for the conventional flights of British Airways, and that its long and costly genesis produced spin-offs for the more humdrum products of British and French industry.

Even if £900 million were a sensible price to pay for a mere flagship, there was no evidence, either from British Airways' financial results for many years or its seat occupancy figures, that the airline had any image advantage over its competitors. Nor does anything confirm the notion that factors that have nothing to do with the actual product or service offered ever help build sales. Thus the brilliantly cultivated branding of an IBM or a Mercedes-Benz is certainly a most powerful tool but only in the service of powerful products. Bad IBM products (such as its first stab at copiers, or the PC jr computer) fare like anybody else's bad products: they flop.

The second argument, the spin-off one, is equally feeble. It would make no sense to build a supersonic airliner if the actual intention had been to make something else. It's also quite misguided to pursue the technology-push policy—or, to phrase it another way, the Technological Mousetrap Myth—a delusion with much industrial blood on its hands. The myth goes that if you make a better mousetrap the world will beat a path to your door. It is venerable to the point of decrepitude and has been disproved again and again, never more comprehensively than by the total defeat of competitors who had genuinely stolen technological marches on IBM in mainframe computers. It didn't matter: IBM was still incomparably stronger in the only place that counts, the marketplace. Despite all such evidence, many allegedly marketing-oriented companies still operate on the mousetrap principle: improve the product, they think, and technology push will create the sales.

Unfortunately, a few successful cases encourage managements in this delusion. For example, managers from Michelin, when it achieved wonders of penetration in the tire market in both the United States and Europe, had been heard to say that the company had no marketing. According to this interpretation, the French firm merely concentrated on technological superiority and raked in the sales as

9

inventions such as its steel-radial tire inflicted torture on its competitors.

Examine the case more carefully, though, and it's clear that Michelin had plenty of marketing—and excellent marketing at that. The Michelin tire man, the guidebooks, and so on are only a minor, though valuable, part of the mix. The main thrust through the decades has been the deliberate and consistent association of Michelin with the idea of product superiority. In its policies on pricing, distribution, advertising, and everything else, Michelin preserved the image of premium supplier. And the product was genuinely superior. The actual technology was part of this marketing package, a weapon that was used to achieve great force at the point of consumer impact.

When managements deny their own strengths, though, something is awry. Doing well by accident means that events can with equal accident undermine the magic—as happened with Michelin. When competitors caught up with its marvels, Michelin's product superiority was no longer genuine; thus the inadvertent effect of its other excellent policies on its marketing no longer had the same force. Without transcendent product advantage, Michelin was revealed as naked in the naked market, with consequent great damage to its profits. Maintain your strengths deliberately and in full knowledge of their nature and you won't have to deny them. More important, they won't suddenly disappear.

3. THE WONDER DRUG OF SMITHKLINE

Pharmaceutical companies have long demonstrated the underlying principles of technological marketing. It isn't simply a question of developing a new and more powerful or efficacious drug—that is only the first name of the game. The second is marketing, pure and not so simple—achieving the maximum impact on the medical profession in the minimum time, in the sure knowledge that, sooner rather than later, heavy competition will arrive on the scene. What the drug companies have experienced ever since chemotherapy got into its wondrous postwar stride is now common to most industries: a desperate competitive scramble to catch up (and if possible overtake) whenever a genuine innovation appears on the market.

In some cases the competition takes desperate measures even before it has a weapon in hand. When SmithKline launched its anti-ulcer drug, Tagamet, in the West German market, it found that its guns had been temporarily spiked. A competitor had rushed out a heavy advertising campaign giving the impression that its modified existing product was the wonder drug for which German doctors and their ulcer patients had been waiting. It took great effort, much money, and much time before the company recovered from a weak German start with one of the strongest products the industry has ever seen.

This single wonder drug (developed at SmithKline's British offshoot) transformed the Philadelphia firm into a wonder company. Over the decade to 1984, its earnings per share rose by 20.4 percent annually, its deliriously happy investors reaped a total reward of 19.94 percent compound. The ulcer relief that Tagamet provides spun so much money (SmithKline's 17.1 percent net return on sales was third highest of the top 500 U.S. companies) that it underpinned a largely new, immensely successful worldwide marketing operation.

Yet drug company managers are wiser, perforce, than those in most other businesses. In pharmaceuticals, even if competition and lapsed patents don't, one day, make their eggs less golden, sudden disaster can always turn a dream product into a nightmare. As soon as grave safety doubts appear, companies, wriggle though they may, have no real option: the curtain must be rung down, no matter what the cost. Eli Lilly, during a run of appallingly bad publicity, actually had no choice when deaths were shown to result from its bestselling antiarthritis drug, Oraflex. It put off its evil day as long as possible, which proved to be far too long.

It's not hard to see why any marketer would be reluctant to stop a smash hit in its tracks. Consider what must have gone through the minds of SmithKline's managers when confronted, not with the type of hard and ineluctable facts that torpedoed Opren, but with a scare —raised by some medical experts—that their beloved Tagamet might carry a risk of cancer, and at a time when other medical opinion was swinging toward the newly arrived Zantac from Glaxo. The first scare blew over; the second did not. Zantac has come to stay, and Tagamet's pot, while still full of honey, now has to be shared.

So SmithKline was wise to diversify (though not wise in the buy itself), purchasing the Beckman Instruments business while its own honey was at its sweetest. True, development of a second wonder drug would have been a far better use of SmithKline's new wealth. But the odds on developing a once-in-a-generation product like Tagamet are far, far too long. They barred SmithKline from the correct response of any firm blessed or cursed with a wonder product: building a wonder portfolio.

4. PRODUCING THE PORTFOLIO

The wonder company that relies on one technological wonder product, no matter how superb, is on fundamentally unsafe ground. The best consumer marketers have long known that safety lies not in products but in portfolios of products. That defense was what enabled Procter & Gamble to ride through the withdrawal (on grounds of medical danger) of its Rely tampons, and Johnson & Johnson to survive with remarkable ease (the first time around) the disaster of having to withdraw and then relaunch its Tylenol capsules when some of the supply had been poisoned.

The idea isn't to diversify for its own sake. Successful exploitation of the wonder product necessarily involves the development of many corporate strengths other than the technology itself. The brilliant marketing company exploits both its technology and its essential strengths; in marketing, these should always include branding and distribution. Thus Canon has very sensibly sold all its nonphotographic developments under the brand name it has so deliberately built up in cameras. The success of the copiers reinforces that of the cameras and vice versa—while it also happens to be true that the image technology built up in cameras has direct relevance to copying. Copying, in turn, rubs off on typewriters, and so on.

In contrast, Konishiroku, one of Canon's rivals, sold its film under the Sakura brand name, its cameras under the Konica banner, its plain paper copiers as U-Bix, and absolutely nothing under the name of the company itself. However excellent its technology (and Konishiroku has many innovations to its credit), that policy tied a hand behind the company's back in all three markets and helps explain why, despite huge sales of film, in which Canon does not compete, the firm is less than half Canon's size. Significantly, in 1983 the Sakura film brand name was changed—to Konica.

The portfolio principle rests on the certainty that channels of distribution, communication, and very often production can carry more than one vessel along them. The wise company, high tech or low, adds to that knowledge the equal certainty that, since competition always overtakes an innovation, the first public appearance of the latter must always be seen, within the company, as the prelude to the next innovation—the development that will always give the company's portfolio its market edge.

When the Walkman personal cassette player appeared, Sony knew that it had only six months before competition would arrive, so the first enhancement of the Walkman had to be completely ready at the time of the original launch. Any honeypot will attract other, maybe bigger, bears. That is one unavoidable risk of being best. But not being best carries even greater risks. The best companies have mastered the trick of minimizing the dangers that technological triumph may be transient by the nontechnical management and marketing successes that, in contrast, last for a corporate lifetime—and may make that life, for all practical purposes, everlasting.

To a Japanese company the principle of everlasting life is fundamental to its corporate philosophy. That's why observers of Sony's slide from grace, caused mostly by its great gaffe of backing an inferior technology in videocassette recorders, had to expect that a climb-back would follow. It came with startling speed; after an earnings decline of 50 percent in 1983, Sony reached a new profit high of $291.6 million the next year. Booming VCR demand, largely in the United States, helped even Sony's long-lagging Betamax business. But the true explanation lay in Sony's portfolio—notoriously limited though it is by a grave shortage of nonconsumer offerings.

Add to that deficiency the floundering in VCRs (market share down from 13 percent to 7 percent in two horrible years) and the slowdown of the Walkman to an amble, and Sony should have been in a sorry state. Its portfolio rescued it; laser audio discs took up the slack, while 8-millimeter video developed into a strong contender for future supergrowth. Beyond that, Sony is pushing for a 50–50 breakdown between consumer and industrial products by 1990, compared with a miserable 80–20 at present. To Western observers, that looks like baying for the moon; even to Sony's boss, Akio Morita, it sounds a bit farfetched. But the history of Japanese firms attempting the apparently impossible and achieving it doesn't encourage heavy bets against Sony's chances.

The same industrial route has already achieved wonders of portfolio planning for other Japanese companies with hot but cooling consumer markets. Olympus, for example, shrugged off a bad patch in camera sales with some ease—because they now account for only a third of its total turnover. Compared to the top camera firms, Sony has been a conspicuous industrial laggard—partly, no doubt, because of the very same presumption that created its VCR vicissitudes. Given its stupendous record of invention and innovation in consumer products from the first tape recorders onward, Sony proudly took it for granted that consumer supremacy would carry it through all circumstances, just as it arrogantly assumed that its rivals would fall meekly into line with the Betamax system.

As Morita told *Fortune* magazine much later, "We didn't put enough effort into making a family." When JVC came out with the incompatible and superior VHS, it overcame the disadvantage of a two-year time lag to sweep past Betamax, along with a large and growing family of fellow manufacturers. That stunning upset makes it clear that no company, not even a Sony, can any longer base its portfolio on one or two consumer triumphs. Future innovations, in any event, are highly unlikely to be allowed a two-year period of monopolistic grace.

Yet simply ask this question: What fate would attend a typical Western company that, having pioneered a market, lost 83 percent of its share and left itself painfully overdependent on a consumer products sector where it had just been comprehensively worsted? Having answered that question, ask another: What is the value of building a portfolio not just of products but of technological capacities, and using them to create a larder of potential winners from which, in time of need, new market entrants can be taken off the shelf? The answer is the difference between destruction and salvation.

5. THE MAGIC OF MERC

Genuine top quality that generates genuine top prestige reinforces its owner by creating something else: top branding. The car industry provides classic proof, both negative and positive, of the role of the brand in markets. Long-running failures (although by definition they don't run forever) have failed brand policies. No long-running market success demonstrates more convincingly the vital relationship between product, image, label, and marketing performance than the might of Mercedes-Benz. In the post–1973 decade, even in West Germany where manufacturers were mostly sunk in shocked gloom, which recession usually produces in their unaccustomed minds, Mercedes drove further ahead. Its continuing rise in sales and output, even in 1982, an awful year for cars, was the stuff of which most other car groups' dreams were made. In following years, the company grew still further, proving again the power of a formula strong in its very simplicity.

Once it had reestablished its technical reputation after World War II with a famous string of racing triumphs, Mercedes consolidated its position at the top of the market. It has concentrated on making up-market machines that are consistent in performance and image: solid, reliable, fast, comfortable, and unmistakably Mercedes in style down to the last knob. Subordinate branding of individual models has been minimal. For example, a new range in the early 1980s incorporated enough engineering improvements to excite experts and had also been given a significant facelift (by restrained Mercedes standards), but it wasn't even granted a series letter to itself—it was the *new* S series.

The company's novel introductions come at rare intervals, which helps confirm the image of stability and consistency. Coupled with methodical and highly effective buildup of distribution, the steadiness has brought Mercedes unrivaled volume for a luxury producer. In 1982 and 1983, its worldwide sales were over two-thirds those of all British-made cars on the UK market: it turned out more than 450,000 motors in the two years combined. American and British firms in many industries have shunned volume business to go after up-market segments with higher added value and higher quality. But they may be barking up the wrong tree; the great Japanese success stories (just like Mercedes) achieve those triumphs by *combining* quality and volume.

Another lesson is that building on an established segment (like luxury executive transport) is as important as finding it in the first place. Mercedes had its strokes of good fortune here—such as being the leading maker of diesel cars when the oil crisis struck—but it also surmounted in a masterly fashion its apparent vulnerability, as a company making only gas guzzlers in a fuel-economy era. And that was before the appearance of the down-sized range that was its main innovation of the early 1980s and the latest, most severe challenge to its marketing skills—a test triumphantly passed.

But what are those skills? They don't lie in the aggressive promotion and clever identification of "niches" that have made BMW another fine example of German marketing power in the same industry. The Mercedes skill rests on the persistent projection and reinforcement of a high-quality, one-brand product line—and nothing in marketing works better. The brand is the brilliance, and the brilliance is the brand.

6. BUILDING THE BRAND

The essentials of a product/brand policy are probably easier to apply if product, brand, and company are one and the same. In that respect, an IBM has the edge over a GM. It's far harder to maintain corporate branding over a widely diverse product range, or one in which (as with GM) the company competes with itself. In such cases, the brand becomes in effect a separate firm, which may have unfortunate results.

This kind of misfortune explains why GM started reshaping itself, in its most radical revision since the prewar, founding days of Alfred P. Sloan. Its existing brand pattern simply didn't fit the evolution of its markets, for which read "the rise of the Japanese." Without the challenge from the East, the GM organization might well have lasted to the end of the century. But even with stiff quota restrictions, the Japanese share of the U.S. market had risen to about 21 percent. While GM dominated sales of U.S.–made cars almost as never before (with around three-fifths of the market), not only was it unable to roll back the Eastern tide of small cars by straight competition but it couldn't even come near the costs in Toyota City.

In 1983 both Toyota and Nissan had U.S. sales comfortably over the half-million mark where VW peaked. The Germans were selling only a third of these Japanese figures, having staged one of the more sensational sales collapses in car history. GM hadn't done

17

likewise, but its small cars had limped in the Japanese wake, partly because all five famous brand divisions (Chevrolet, Buick, Pontiac, Oldsmobile, and even Cadillac) had covered the waterfront, from full-size to down-size. In the process, GM moved nearer and nearer to what the British deprecate as "badge engineering," with different names on more or less identical cars.

GM's real engineering was all done centrally, anyway; until previous reforms, under the long-running GM rethink and fight-back, the divisional marketers had no real responsibility for the models they had to sell. This, of course, is marketing nonsense of the first order. The further stage of GM's revolution meant bifurcating the colossus, with Chevrolet and Pontiac forming a subcompany (still of gigantic size) to look after smaller cars from conception to consummation, leaving the larger models to the other brands and starting—abortively, as it turned out—a whole new Saturn division to compete head-on with the Japanese subcompacts.

GM's marketing managements face a formidable task in preserving their branding (and dealer networks) while reshuffling the products that they support. GM has been put under real pressure: even if your resources are gigantic, these days they have to be concentrated to guarantee, not success, but the possibility of success in an environment where branding weakness of any kind may be fatal.

More successful multibrand strategies than GM's abound in fast-moving consumer goods. Thus Beecham's corporate name is carried by only a single product line among many; Procter & Gamble doesn't sell any Procters or Gambles. But Macleans, a major toothpaste for decades, was one of the original constituents in the Beecham's merger, and its marketing management has missed very few tricks in updating the brand to match the twists and turns of the market, even while launching (with Aqua Fresh) an entirely new brand in both Britain and the United States. Innovating assaults such as Aqua Fresh capture the imagination as they make their initial penetration, but launch (as Beecham discovered painfully in the United States) is only a start. The race is won not by speed off the mark but by staying power, one reason why companies with the most established market leaders are also those that win prizes for new product development—companies such as Mars, 3M, Kellogg's, and P&G. These Supermarketers adhere to what the great management prophet, Lyndall F. Urwick, set out as marketing catechism in 1933: pay attention to things like "constant and systematic study of the products and methods of competitors, the development of new methods and avenues of distribution, and the supply of new products . . . to secure the established markets and the winning of new markets." Follow that advice and both the product line and the business should be well protected—even in the naked market.

7. THE PROOF IN SCOTCH

Scotch whisky may be the perfect product: homogeneous, and thus simple to manage, yet capable of endless brand differentiation; cheap to produce, but capable of commanding premium prices. Also, it's a product in which strength should go to the strong. The ability to produce consistent high quality in large volume depends on vast and costly reserves of aging whisky. Equally important, the bigger the brand, the higher the advertising budget that can be lavished on its support.

So what explains the strange fate of the Distillers Company, Limited (DCL)? This crowned king of Scotch became a great mystery over the wasted years that led to its nemesis in 1986: first attacked by a far smaller company, it next abjectly surrendered its independence to Guinness, a company with half its own stock-exchange valuation. That was the price of market loss after market loss. The rot started in the crucial U.S. arena, where the DCL brands lost their lead abysmally to J&B and Cutty Sark—both owned by St. James's Street wine merchants who hardly made up in social distinction for what they lacked in marketing muscle and smarts.

J&B and Cutty Sark are so-called light Scotches, which DCL

didn't then deign to produce. The market might have wanted it, but the company's Scotch barons didn't. In the English market, where DCL's central control (or uncontrol) resided, the lead was lost with equal humiliation to a "heavy" Scotch—Teacher's—whose producer was another dwarf compared to the collapsing king.

Uncoordinated, undermanaged, and undermarketed, the once-great and all-conquering DCL brands—Johnnie Walker, Haig, Black & White, VAT 69, and Dewar's, each run by independent baronies—failed to exploit their innate and historical strengths in competitive markets. DCL even contrived to lose leadership in the most embarrassing place of all: Scotland, the heart of the industry. Once again, the winner was a less-than-middling firm, this time Arthur Bell & Sons. As recently as 1974 this small company was turning over only $90 million, a mere ninth of DCL's total. In 1982–83, after multiplying fourfold, Bell's had reached a fifth of DCL's sales. The discrepancy in profits, although less marked, was still great: the one-time tot had increased its net earnings by 832 percent over a period in which DCL's had only tripled. Yet as that tripling shows, despite the erosion of its share in key markets by essentially one-product companies such as Bell's, DCL still had a formidable portfolio of brands that, given aggressive and ambitious modern marketing, could have wreaked on its smaller rivals the same kind of havoc that IBM has visited on its lesser foes—hence DCL's own attraction as a takeover target.

Considering Bell's fairly primitive beginnings—it originally launched its sensational rise on the slogans "Afore ye go" and "Have a ting-a-ling"—DCL's directors must have been fast asleep at the switch. They woke up in 1985, launching a great shake-up, even before the bid battle, in a belated, uphill struggle to drag the whisky barons out of feudal marketing and into some semblance of modern times. This move roughly coincided with General Motors's decision to set in motion the greatest reshuffle in its history in order to sharpen its fight-back against the Japanese and recover its lost brand identity. The analogies between Scotch and cars in this instance are obvious.

20

Whatever DCL's brands had once stood for was gone; whatever sense it had once made to have separate companies marketing separate, ill-differentiated brands in all geographical markets no longer applied. Hence the necessity for a clear split between overseas and home trade. Hence, too, the eminently sound $250 million bid for Somerset, the distributor of Johnnie Walker in the United States. There the Scotch business had suffered general reversals partly because the distillers didn't control their own distribution, a defect that has become increasingly deadly in the battle among U.S. brands (and not just in liquor). Above all, though, DCL's neglect of basic marketing for fifty years explains its brands' loss of eminence and demonstrates that quality and prestige alone cannot support a brand. The vital task of brand support demands three other essentials: organization, governing will, and dominating purpose.

8. PRODUCT DEATH CYCLES

The lack of security in old, established product ranges is one compelling reason why the conventional wisdom is now so keen on new product development, innovation, R & D. Call it what you will, the innovative process is a matter of life and death in today's markets —mostly, alas, death. Attrition rates in new products, especially in fast-moving consumer goods, are awful enough to make the most ambitious marketers quake in their Gucci shoes.

For every pearl of a new product, there are a dozen swine that either never reach the shelves or perish on them. Nearly all so-called new products carry no hope of brand leadership in the years to come, polish your crystal ball as you may. Most will be line extensions or gap fillers rather than product breakthroughs.

Renewals of product lines are not the same as innovation. They are, however, essential for corporate and brand survival. Their success helps explain why, if you survey the list of brand leaders in any

21

market, their sheer longevity leaps off the page. The dozen top U.S. brands of 1923 still lead markets as diverse as chewing gum (Wrigley's) and batteries (Eveready). In Britain the dominant dozen of 1933 still lord it over everything from cornflakes (Kellogg's) to vacuum cleaners (Hoover) and razors (Gillette).

The dominance of these long-lived British brands has to be qualified, though. Half the British dozen are actually U.S. (or, if you prefer, global) subbrands; of the remainder, all have been merged or acquired in recent times. Before leaping to the conclusion that this is the inevitable consequence of the high worth and rarity of durable, lushly profitable brands, consider that in case after case (Gillette, Kodak, Hoover, Singer) the golden oldies have come under increasing, often unprecedented, pressure. Old product development in these cases has become as high a priority as new, because leadership nowadays may simply make the company (like Distillers) a sitting target.

This analysis may not be helpful, however. Commonsense realism dictates that you never change a winning formula, or product, or marketing method, unless and until it ceases to win. The reason is self-evident: you risk alienating old customers and can't be sure of attracting new ones, not if you already have, say, over a fifth of the market, which was the case with the previously mentioned Coke brand. Yet there is equal danger in sitting still while watching a powerful competitor like PepsiCo come up on the outside.

Actually Coke formulated the perfect response to the threat, diversifying its portfolio with new brands, including variants, that handsomely outsold Pepsi's rival entries. As a result, the king's all-product share in 1984, the year before it changed the formula, was 39.2 percent—up from 36.7 percent in 1976. What, you may ask, is wrong with that? Only that Pepsi had been closing the gap: one of its several concoctions to 1.6 of Coke's became 1 to 1.4 over the same period.

Wisdom and experience suggest that, in any competitive market, a vigorous and effective opponent will take its natural share. The underdog has one advantage, too: a point of share, which is no harder to gain (possibly easier, since the challenger is farther from saturation), must represent a greater percentage advantage. In fact, Pepsi gained five overall points from 1976 to 1984, Coke only 2.5. But all Pepsi's gains were in the first three years; the onslaught had been slowing in the face of Coke's renewed vigor and Pepsi's own increasing penetration of the American soft-drink market.

Coke was a victim, however, of the logic of variants: you must always expect to lose some sales of the parent brand to the baby. From that angle, Diet Coke in particular has been too successful. Essentially, defending the market share of really big winners is a no-win game. However brilliant the defensive moves, the attackers are bound to cause some brand erosion over time. This fact of market life must also raise the premium on aggressive innovation. Far better to erode somebody else's market than your own. But that is often the game at which the proud possessors of golden oldies have least skill —and consequently least success (witness all the new-product failures).

Companies are unlikely to get smash hits in new markets unless the corporate way of life is geared to genuine innovation. This quite certainly means moving away from the tyranny of new-product development committees and the like, and breaking into a new world where real innovation is one of the line manager's prime responsibilities—a matter, figuratively speaking, of his own life or death. Nor is this simply a matter of organization. It demands a whole new culture of the corporation in general and its product philosophy in particular.

9. THE IMPROBABILITY OF PERDUE

When is a product not a product? When it's a commodity, of course. Once upon a time, in most markets, the best product was the one that everybody needed—nuts and bolts, say, or fertilizers and textiles. So greatly have market conditions changed that today the fate all companies should fear is when a product becomes a commodity—meaning (as in the above examples) that everybody uses it but also that too many people sell it, so that prices are held down and nobody earns much from an offering that accounts for too much turnover to be easily abandoned.

Nuts and bolts and fertilizers have long since crossed the dividing line between product and commodity, though exactly where that great divide comes is difficult to say. Like being in love, it's a situation you recognize at once when it arrives; or perhaps the condition is more like falling out of love. For the achievement of commodity status is a terrible letdown. The beloved product, with a price that could be managed and massaged and with profits that rose as the learning curve worked its magic, reducing costs as cumulative production increased, suddenly becomes, at worst, a license to lose money and, at best, a cash cow, to be milked as long as there's anything in the udder.

More often than not, the great divide is crossed because of overcapacity, sometimes created by a fall in demand but frequently the result of the rubber-type market. Rubber type is what journalists in the old days of hot-metal type wished they had when a favorite headline failed to fit in the allotted space. The rubber-type market is identified by the fact that, when all the market shares of all the producers, as reported by the said producers, are added together, they come to considerably more than 100 percent. Extrapolate this endearing tendency into the future, and you can easily arrive at 200 percent—and that may, alas, turn out to be 100 percent more than actual demand: and that is the birth of a commodity.

Everyone knows that a commodity is a commodity is a commodity. The market price determines what anybody can charge, and all the huffing and puffing in the marketing world won't alter that price or the basic considerations that govern market share—for instance, the number and desirability of gas station sites. Everyone knows these intractable facts. Everybody, that is, except Supermarketers such as Frank Perdue.

Marketing expert John Guineven writes: "Ten years ago, chickens had as strong a claim to commodity status as pork bellies or crude oil. . . . But the chicken world has undergone a revolution in the United States thanks to the remarkable success of an improbable character. . . ." That improbability was Perdue. His success demonstrates that the ancient truths of branding apply as strongly to ancient products as to new. The key is differentiation, and the key to that is knowledge of what the customer really wants.

Whether there is any virtue in a chicken being fat and yellow (the desired qualities thrown up by Perdue's research) is beside the point. He was able to satisfy customers' perceived wants by the intelligent use of farming technology, which he didn't so much supplement as magnify by persuasive promotion ("It takes a tough man to make a tender chicken" and "You get an extra bite in every breast"). Every aspect of the operation, including the individual inspection of every chicken, because that's how the customer inspects them, reinforces what is, as Perdue himself emphasizes, a highly lucrative message: "Customers will go out of their way to buy a superior product, and you can charge them a toll for the trip."

If you can perform that trick with a dead chicken, as Guineven notes, you can perform it with anything; anything, that is, where better characteristics of service or product can distinguish and differentiate your offering. And that covers nearly everything—even, no doubt, nuts and bolts and fertilizers.

10. COUNTERING THE COMMODITY

The power of retailers vis-à-vis manufacturers has increased and continues to increase. And nobody knows how to stop them. The great retail chains have two potent weapons in their armory: their vast buying power, which confronts many, fragmented suppliers with a few, concentrated purchasers; and their handsomely exploited

25

ability to create brands of their own that have all the power of the great retail name behind them.

The manufacturer has one weapon and one weapon only: the customer franchise created by years of product acceptance and heavy promotion. This isn't an armament for which storekeepers show much respect anymore. At one conference in 1984, a retailer was moved to ask, "Who needs brands? We certainly don't. The customers don't; so why should they exist?"

This argument is only partly true (fortunately for brand owners). For, as the astonishing impact of the IBM brand in personal computers shows, customers *do* like brands; they like everything about them, even their advertising. It's not only the implicit guarantee provided by the manufacturer, or the reliability and consistency of the brand—these are qualities that own-label products can match. The brand, as an academic expert, Geoffrey Randall, wrote in *Management Today,* has something all its own: "as marketing people and researchers know, buyers perceive that brands . . . have a personality to which they can relate, and which adds something to their satisfaction in purchase and use."

The further the product is from commodity status, the easier it is to establish and promote that personality. Instant coffee is an example of extreme difficulty—easy to imitate, tough to differentiate —but that doesn't stop Maxwell House from trying. Perdue's chickens are one example of strong branding making a silk purse out of a sow's ear, or a chicken's breast. Manufacturers have alternative strategies to backing the brand up to the hilt, but listing the options shows their relative weakness: forward integration into owning your own stores; making own-label products yourself (if you can't beat 'em, supply 'em); and cooperation with retailers—a strategy, naturally, that the latter loves.

As one adman quoted by Randall observed, the cooperation retailers seek is "the cooperation the rabbit gives the stoat." How to escape rabbit status is well known and much more easily (and cheaply) said than done: maintain product leadership, maximize production efficiency while minimizing cost, market intensively with

26

all available tools and skills. But there's a catch-22, as Randall notes: "Not all manufacturers can have brand leaders, and not all the brands of any one firm will be strong enough to survive in all circumstances."

This uncomfortable truth helps explain the rush to purchase, for billions of dollars, repositories of great brands in the mid-1980s. The name of the game has suddenly changed. Big independent brands have long been sitting ducks for the attacks of the multiproduct mammoths once memorably embraced by a *New Yorker* cartoonist under the corporate name of Engulf and Devour, Inc. But the big-brand biters have been bitten, engulfed, and devoured in turn. If a Chesebrough-Pond's (not to mention a General Foods) isn't safe, who is?

The automatic answer to that agonized question appears to be: if colossal size is no protection, try supercolossal. In other words, marketing considerations are only part of the deal. The activities of free-lance corporate raiders, coupled with the eagerness of greedy bankers to finance once-unthinkable megadeals, reinforced by the investment community's shortsighted lust for birds in the hand, have opened the floodgates to the greatest reshaping of the corporate map since the trustbusters started busting. Now the busting has all but stopped; leaving companies sitting on invaluable, superior brands as potential victims of the corporate strategy logic.

Only market-leading brands can withstand waxing retailer power, runs the argument. Because developing or redeveloping brands to achieve leadership is now phenomenally costly and risky, even for experts, why not buy a ready-made basket of leading goodies? Certainly nobody on Wall Street will raise any objections to a timely bid by some superstrategists who can boast a better record, however marginal. For instance, which of the two new, huge partners, Philip Morris or General Foods, provided the best return to investors during the decade before the former swallowed the latter?

The answer is not the conqueror, but the conquered (it was 16.38 percent for Philip Morris, against 18.22 percent for General Foods). It's true that the winner who took all did better on all other

27

counts, such as annual growth in earnings per share (16.48 percent versus 9.78 percent, according to *Fortune*) and returns on both sales and equity. But the latter lead is partly a function of the inherently high margins on the demon tobacco rather than a reflection of demon management. All the same, General Foods did lack luster for the proud possessor of so many gorgeous brands—and there is a reason.

No doubt, the mediocre performance reflects the difficulty of maintaining momentum behind a widely diversified collection of major products. Making the collections still vaster doesn't seem a promising approach to resolving that problem. Could the rise in retailer power partly reflect undermanagement of major brands by businesses that had the resources available to manage far better but couldn't apply those resources effectively? After all, even the largest retailers have only a fraction of the outlets available to a national brand name. Those with strong brands are stronger than they sometimes think.

So goes the argument of management consultant Martin van Mesdag, whose advice to suppliers applies to businesses great and small: "A brand is the commercial strongbox in which a manager holds his investments, from which the worth of the company stems. Brands are the best guarantee of continued profitability, and must be freed. . . ." Freed from what? From managements that don't understand their fundamental importance.

11. THE BOX OF WINE

Success as well as failure can sometimes drop from the skies on the undeserving. For example, there was (and is) a large brewery of no great marketing distinction that suddenly found itself with a smash hit, a product called the Wine Box, a minor marvel of modern technology that was developed in Australia. The story goes that success caught the brewery unaware. Having bought the necessary machinery, the brewery's wine and spirit men presented their small ad agency with a plain white box, in which the wine was packaged without benefit of bottle.

No marketing budget or idea of the market potential were communicated to the creative people at the agency. Their clever design, however, treated the box as a poster, which is how it worked when gracing the company's liquor stores. Initially, that's all the box did grace; there was no promotion expenditure. Only as the box took off into the marketing blue (thus proving, incidentally, the sadly underrated power of packaging) was the marketing budget lifted with it. Honest marketing managers can produce many such examples of triumphs, which look in hindsight like marvels of mental might and rational decisions but which actually swooped down on them unaware.

But the company itself didn't capture the public imagination: that was done by the product concept, *wine-in-a-box,* promptly copied with exemplary speed by those competitors with the necessary wit and resources. The innovator had missed the chance of killing two birds with one stone: winning both market leadership for its boxed wines and a huge leap in recognition of the company itself as both a brand and a retail chain. Few customers knew that it was the wine and spirits outlet of the giant brewery, which deliberately used a wine name as far removed from beer as possible.

The object of innovation and diversification is not just to give the company another line of business but to help generate the dynamic, organic growth of the whole company that will result from any marketing strategy worth the name. Plainly, this can never be achieved from a base product that, like many beers, has become a near-commodity. It can be only imperfectly achieved by an innovation, such as the Wine Box, that is treated merely as an add-on to the basic business.

Most companies fall into the trap of reasoning that the strength of the business will be automatically increased by the very acts of innovation or diversifying. Buying into another unrelated trade or pulling off a single act of innovation, like the Wine Box, are never

29

enough in themselves. Time and time again, new entrants into new markets succeed only in demonstrating that they are hopelessly ill equipped to exploit their rare successes in these new competitive wars. It's vital to learn just where weakness in such combats proves so killing.

12. TRIUMPHS OF INNOVATION

The answer to the question just posed, and the solution to the commodity threat, have been carefully documented by an expert from the A. C. Nielsen company, studying success and failure of new products introduced into the grocery trade. The failure rate is notorious—well over 90 percent—but the majority of the rare large successes come from the largest companies, which, of course, is why they stay the largest. Part of the reason for their dominance, no doubt, is pure muscle: financial and distributing might that gives an enormous advantage in developing and putting across something new to the consumer and the trade. But another reason is pure management: the giants simply take more care over their new product programs. Above all, they *have* them.

If the Nielsen guru is correct, products that weren't around ten years ago always account for about a quarter of sales in any sector. Thus any company not developing wonders that will stay the course must eventually be shut out from more and more of its market segment. This doesn't mean developing mere line extensions or relaunches, however. These are the expedients—often very necessary —that persuade noninnovators that they are innovative.

Whether markets are fast- or slow-growing, the companies in search of higher profits and real corporate expansion are going to carry on competing, fighting the packaged goods fight with all their might. At the end of the day, global market shares may be little changed by all the moiling and toiling, though the incomes of advertising agencies, media, marketing men, and others will be merrily inflated along the way. It would be a mistake, however, to suppose that brilliant marketing and advertising alone will win the day. The race will go to the manufacturer who can produce the genuine blockbuster innovation.

Yet, to take the grocery trade as an example again, in the 1980s innovations have been sparser on the ground, or the shelf, than usual —witness any list of top new products in the 1980s. In the main, they are no more than extensions of the product line. Many of them must have cheerfully cannibalized sales from the main product lines from whose wombs they sprang—a constant danger that, in overcrowded markets, will destroy many future efforts to steal a competitive march. Indeed, the prospect yawns of generation after generation of "me-too" and "me-me-too-too" products.

The yawn will no doubt be shared by the consumer. The signs are that supermarket shoppers are getting more selective, more bored with sameness. "Me too" is a sure way of guaranteeing that products will turn into commodities. "Me different" is the only hope for any company that wishes to win markets worth the victory. The more markets are saturated, the more consumers are driven by stimulated desire, the more powerful and insistent this truth must become. To prove the point, look only at *Fortune*'s list of the superstar products of 1986.

There's a live superstar (Bruce Springsteen) and his latest, red-hot, five-disc album; the American rival to the banned krugerrand gold coin; and a dead cheap Korean car. Those apart, the winners are all truly innovative—and most have already reaped huge commercial success. They consist of the "biggest advance" in consumer batteries "in twenty years" (Kodak); a "vastly improved" Spectra instant camera that, thanks to a patent suit against Kodak, is now unique (Polaroid); another unique offering, an antiplaque dental rinse (Plax); the first possibly effective anti-AIDS drug (AZT); a toy gun that zaps 'em with light emission (Lazer Tag); the very first superpowered personal computer (Compaq); and Pepsi Slice, the first soft drink to add multiflavors of fruit juice.

31

The lesson is unmistakable and should be unforgettable. The future rests firmly and fully not only on efficiently exploiting the old (if it is viable) but on genuine triumphs with the genuinely new.

To summarize some of the important points I've mentioned in Step One:

1. Play consistently to your strengths and invest consistently in them.

2. Seek technological leadership, by all means, but never be led by technology.

3. Wonder products are wonderful, but wonder portfolios of products are much better.

4. Build product portfolios by first establishing two other portfolios—of technological strength and marketing capability.

5. Nothing in marketing works better than the persistent projection and reinforcement of a high-quality, one-brand product line.

6. To protect the product line, know your competitors, develop new ways of distribution—and develop new products.

7. Brand support demands more than strong products—give it organization, governing will, and dominating purpose.

8. You're unlikely to get smash hits in new markets unless the entire corporate way of life, and line managers' jobs, are geared to genuine innovation.

9. Better characteristics of service or product can distinguish and differentiate almost anything in almost any market.

10. You can best resist retailer pressure by understanding and exploiting the fundamental importance of the brand.

11. You'll never get innovation and diversification to yield their maximum contribution if they're treated as add-ons to the basic business.

12. "Me too" is a sure way of turning products into commodities; "me different" offers the best hope of substantial victories.

Step Two: The Keys to Marketing Management

1. THE TIMEX TIME BOMB

When Timex signed up the Sinclair computer for manufacture in Scotland and marketing in the United States, it must have seemed one of the sweetest deals in history. The midget computer's sales rose to world record numbers, soaring past the Pets and Tandys to lead in the American market as in Britain. The comparison needs to be qualified by the fact that the Sinclair/Timex machine was much, much cheaper than its rivals. But that too was a tribute to maestro Sir Clive Sinclair, who correctly saw that a little (some would say itsy-bitsy) computer priced at $199 would be irresistible to many Americans—even though it couldn't do much in the way of serious computing.

The initial success in the States belonged as much to Timex as to Sinclair, of course. The machine carried the manufacturer's name in the United States, and it's doubtful whether without that marketing (and manufacturing) power Sinclair could have survived the onslaught of the ambitious American competitors alerted by his successes in the new growth market. They promptly left no trick unplayed in striving to steal Sinclair's (and Timex's) clothes. Nowhere has there been a more striking demonstration of the speed with which today's naked markets change and weaken.

There was a time bomb ticking away under Timex. A scant two years after the Sinclair machine had so surprisingly cracked the U.S. market, machine and marketer were caught in a ferocious price war. The $199 tag became a fond memory. The next level of $99.95 gave way to $29.97, then to an astonishing $15 in a market where two far more powerful competitors (Texas Instruments and Atari) had already been forced into grievous loss. As sales continued to plummet despite the price cuts and TI's undignified withdrawal from the market, the time bomb exploded. Timex was forced to withdraw from the U.S. home computer market in its turn for underlying reasons that form the foundation of modern marketing.

2. COMPANYWIDE MARKETING

The marketing on which companies are now forced to depend differs in kind, scope, and power from that which reigned in the better-protected markets of the postwar seller's paradise. One critical difference is that marketing is now seen in proper perspective: neither as an add-on to boost corporate selling power nor as a wonderful new discipline about to swamp the entire company, sweeping all before it. Today's marketing is indeed companywide, but it's an integrating, animating force that binds together the other functions rather than subjugating them.

The relationship can be seen clearly from what happened at

GM's British subsidiary, Vauxhall Motors, when Australian John Bagshaw was brought in as marketing director. Bagshaw found that vitally important fleet orders had been lost by failure to meet delivery promises. He got back to the production people, and they improved their performance so sharply that Bagshaw could keep his promises to the letter. This improvement helped greatly to propel the company's market share from 8 to 12 and then to 18 percent and to push Bagshaw into responsibility for production and next to still higher things in General Motors.

The connection between manufacturing performance and marketing capability is too obvious to be ignored—but that doesn't stop people from ignoring it. Delivery and quality are the two touchstones. The saving grace for management is that the revolution in production technology and methods (as the Japanese have shown) has made it much easier to reach and maintain proper standards. Without that improvement, for instance, Sir Clive Sinclair would never have been able to succeed in computers where he had failed in calculators. His brilliant pioneering thrust into the calculator market foundered on quality problems so awful that they have passed into industrial legend.

His misadventure proved that even a man like Sinclair, with innovative prowess of almost Mozartian proportions, needs more, much more. Getting the goods to the market isn't enough, nor is having them lapped up by the paying customers. Administrative and productive capacity has to match inventive brilliance if a calculator-style comeuppance is to be avoided.

A marketer who cheerfully admits that he has no great interest in management, like Sinclair, thus has an Achilles heel which is bound to prove fatal—as Sinclair's did in the spring of 1986 when, crippled by continuing losses, he sold his computer business, patents and all, for a mere $7.5 million to stronger hands and vacated the scene. The fundamental principle is that business is an indivisible whole. Before Sinclair's calculator breakthrough aborted, one marketing consultant sought to argue, though, that the inventor had disproved the above tenet: by splitting manufacture from marketing, subcontracting all production to several suppliers, Sinclair had made a world-shattering business breakthrough as well. Who needs manufacture?

The answer, most of the time, is that marketers do. True, subcontracting did work better for Sinclair the second time around, first because of the change in technology mentioned above: the very same integrated circuitry that enabled Sinclair to bring the machines out so cheaply also reduced the room for sloppy production. A second factor was that Sinclair chose in Timex a single, much more powerful supplier for his computers.

Actually, in the crisis of the home-computer market, Sinclair was probably lucky not to have built the integrated, fully managed organizational machine that meeting the marketing challenge demands. That machine, with its inevitable overhead costs, would surely have failed, if not when the U.S. market collapsed, certainly when the same recession hit Britain. As it was, Sinclair Research nearly disappeared from sight a year before the eventual sale. Its resident genius compounded already grave problems by cutting prices after a disastrous Christmas sales season. This sabotaged the value of his own grossly excessive inventory and everybody else's.

For a managerial mugwump like Sir Clive, that's par for the course. But the managerial maestros of IBM made exactly the same error, lowering the price of the PC to try to stimulate a demand that never materialized. The titan suffered the indignity of profit forecasts —and, still worse, profits—running awry amid a market setback of such proportions that Apple had to close two plants for keeps. Yet apart from the hard, special case of the British home-computer market, the slump had one curious aspect: it hardly existed. Forecasters in the United States in mid-1985 were expecting computer sales to show a double-figure rise for the year: that could only be called a slump in an industry where 25 percent per annum has been the norm.

Like little Sinclair Research, the whole great worldwide industry had geared up for expected supergrowth and was caught redhanded and red-faced when the norms changed. The shortfall in demand shouldn't have caught the industry by surprise, though. It had happened even in premicro days, and it happens everywhere. All "inexhaustible" booms are exhausted sooner rather than later. Greed, ambition, and unfilled orders create overabundant supply, and even small shifts in the demand curve are enough to convert the production surplus into a stock mountain of Common Market proportions.

But there was a deeper, more worrying, and more instructive explanation in the computer crisis. *Business Week* listed five causes at the time, including ballyhoo over pending new models that stopped customers from buying old ones; that most PCs are "ornery and too hard to use"; that the technology doesn't allow computers to communicate as customers want; that many companies are stuck with several different makes of "computers that can't understand each other"; that customers are confused by too much choice and want time to digest their purchases.

Look carefully at these five factors and a strong common theme leaps to the fore, highlighted by the recurrence of the key word *customer.* All five represent basic marketing errors of exactly the same nature as those that typify production-led companies. Anybody who has ever picked up (or thrown away) a PC manual knows that, for all their protestations about being "customer-led" or "marketing-led," the manufacturers have largely ignored all customers except those who speak their own jargon, and have even failed the latter where computer speaketh not to computer.

In the wake of the slump, or slowdown, the wiser computer managements have been trying to mend their ways, although it goes against the cultural grain. There couldn't be a stronger demonstration of the necessity of companywide marketing than its absence in a business that had every incentive and every resource available to apply every tool of the marketing trade. What Sinclair simply ignored, for reasons of temperament, the giants missed by equally culpable neglect. There is, however, one saving grace: the omissions are incredibly easy to rectify—for those, that is, who survive the failures of the past.

3. THE INSTANT ERROR OF POLAROID

The degree of corporate risk in the naked market is shown by the strange events at Polaroid. This great innovative multinational, famous for its marketing and its technology alike, suffered declines in sales for four consecutive years. Companies with billion-dollar turnovers in markets that are still growing hardly ever lose sales in a single year, let alone four. Polaroid's experience showed that management mistakes can undermine even a classic position of marketing strength. But in naked markets, what used to take many years has been speeded up, like slapstick chases in Mack Sennett movies: the time span of destruction has been telescoped.

It isn't simply that Polaroid was too much of a one-product company, although that was the diagnosis proffered by chief executive William J. McCune, Jr., the first successor to the legendary Edwin Land. The fact that McCune was in his mid-sixties when Land left the scene drops a strong hint: the great businessman/inventor had stayed on too long—and by leaving a veteran of his own regime in charge, Land stacked the odds heavily against the company's striking out in *any* new directions, let alone the right ones.

McCune saw Polaroid's problem as overdependence on instant photography: ergo, it had to diversify into noncamera, nonconsumer markets. It's an old, sad story. A company whose basic business is faltering blames the trouble not on mismanagement of the base activity it knows and loves but on lack of new markets it knows nothing about. Yet Polaroid's critical threat was basic: the coming of competition in instant photography coincided with a fall in instant's market share. This happened largely because orthodox camera firms had been breathtakingly innovative—what with endless single-lens reflexes, compacts, and now discs and videos, Polaroid was being attacked from all sides.

To make matters worse, conventional color film has been improved to startling degrees, with one-hour processing on tap—while the filmless camera is on the horizon as yet another threat. The competitive catalogue shows that Polaroid committed the classic error immortalized by that great guru of marketing, Professor Ted Levitt: it saw itself in the business of *instant* photography—not of photography, whatever its nature. The narrow-front strategy had kept it well away from the powerful Eastman Kodak for the years of supergrowth. Eventually expansion and product maturity always demand a switch to a broader concept. The main broadening at Polaroid was to make its own film (it had previously been contracted out to Kodak). That only precipitated the Goliath's competition in instant cameras: Land and McCune's diversifications, which only generated a third of sales in 1982, could give little protection against that. The courts could, forcing Kodak out, but not until 1986.

Fully exposed, Polaroid's picture plainly needed merger and/or partnership as the right strategic choice. Having roused the not-so-sleeping Kodak giant, Polaroid should have gone the whole way and bought into conventional film and cameras. There were, after all, plenty of possible partners—not only Japanese, but German and even American (3M, for one, has been striving to break Kodak's stranglehold on film). Products such as Polaroid's computer-linked printers, whatever their commercial virtues, are no answer to a problem of such strategic magnitude. As one Polaroid executive told *Business Week,* "You can't stay on this path and assume it's going to be OK." In the naked market, no position is secure. Even Kodak has avoided Polaroid's trap only by means of a phenomenal pace of innovation in the 1970s and 1980s—and even that didn't save it from a heavy fall in profits as Japanese competition bit deeply into margins.

Polaroid has been innovative all its life and has by no means slackened its own pace; indeed, its fortunes turned in 1986 as the brand-new, vastly better Spectra range wowed the market—like Spectra, all the photographic innovations have been instant (including the ill-fated instant home-movie venture, Land's last fling, which coincided fatally with the coming of video). The tragedy is that the old management, which was powerful enough to carry Polaroid through the growth era of instant photography, proved inadequate

39

to meet the challenge of a market where instant was no longer enough for supergrowth—or growth of any kind.

4. MEETING MARKET THREATS

One company's innovation is another's poison. Even a longtime market leader can be killed off by a new technology that brings an unexpected threat. The exploitation of xerography by a firm outside the traditional copying industry (Haloid, later Xerox) sounded the death knell to the giants of duplicating. They took a long time a-dying. Today the technological leaps are longer and faster: the deaths of those left behind are no longer lingering. Like so many little old Swiss watchmakers stranded hopelessly by the electronic watch, even the mighty and modern and prestigious are vulnerable.

It's difficult, of course, for one's heart to bleed for a company so massively successful for so many years as Kodak. After absorbing the onslaught from Polaroid, and long putting off the evil day when it had to compete in instant photography itself, Kodak has been challenged from another and far more threatening great leap forward in technology. Before long the filmless camera, having already cornered the home-movie market, will emerge in still photography, as Sony, Canon, and others keep their promises (or threats). What will Kodak do about that?

Kodak will not be alone in seeking the answer to one of marketing's most atrocious questions. The several high-prestige, high-quality camera firms in Japan that lack the necessary expertise must be wondering how the new technology will (or won't) affect them. The strategic choices start with the do-nothing deal, otherwise known as the ostrich theory: if you shut your eyes Sony will go away, or its Mavica camera won't work well (at the initial stage, apparently, the color version didn't), or people won't want to buy it. The trouble with this head-in-the-sand approach is that, although it is easy and involves no capital expenditure, it may be fatally wrong.

A more sophisticated version is to do nothing, but get some hasty research and development under way, so that if the new competitor does take off you can dive in before all the water has been drained from the pool. In Kodak's case, the problem is not that camera sales will be lost (since Kodak serves the mass market, and the filmless starting price is high) but that film sales might be threatened. When Polaroid came along, it was easier for Kodak to hedge its bets, because it made the film for its new rival—until the latter unwisely pulled the plug. But if it doesn't have Sony's technology in-house already, what are Kodak's hopes as it strives to catch up in so advanced a field as electronics?

A similar question hangs ominously over the reverse of do-nothing, throwing every available resource into beating the competitor to the punch. The chances of success are so remote that it makes more sense to follow the General Motors example and buy rights to a new wonder (as it did with the Wankel engine) in order to protect your flanks. You then run the risk of finding out expensively and too late, as did GM, that do-nothing would have worked best, because the enemy did in fact disappear before your very eyes.

In other words, there is no easy solution. But there is a certainty: no company occupying an important position in any market should neglect any challenge, trivial or tremendous, that threatens any part of its market stature. In Kodak's case, it would certainly have been unwise to take much notice of Sony's Akio Morita when he said his system was unlikely to replace conventional photography. No doubt that's what they said about valves when the first transistor radio was launched.

One leading U.S. manufacturer, Zenith, even used its old-fashioned design as a selling point for a while—none of this newfangled nonsense. But newfangledness tends not only to win but to take bread from the mouths of the oldfangled. Thus RCA, which dominated the vacuum tube business, missed the transistor boat and never got back on board. Kodak is trying desperately not to repeat an error that would be fatal to a company that is much less diversified than RCA. Hence the massive research effort to turn the Rochester stalwart into an electronic-based rather than a film-based company.

In other words, Kodak cannot live off its technological past if it wants to have a future—even if the future is problematical. After all, nobody could have known that instant photography would be contained by developments in conventional cameras. The battle might have gone the other way, and so might have Kodak: down.

5. THE BEAUTY OF BANG & OLUFSEN

By what seems a curious paradox, the actual design of Polaroid's products, cumbersome and unlovely in the years of supergrowth, became elegant and brilliant in the period of mounting problems. The paradox disappears when a few more examples of the same phenomenon are noted, such as those contained in a report in the *Financial Times* just before the Car of the Year was to be named one recent time. The reporter noted that Rover (the 3500), Porsche (the 928), and Lancia (the Delta) had each won the prize in previous years but had received no prizes in the marketplace. "Yet cars that were voted into second place—the Ford Fiesta and Opel Kadett, to name but two—have sold like hotcakes."

The observation should give the marketing-minded food for some fairly furious thought, and not just about cars. The same thought occurred to a company chairman contemplating a faulty electric razor: he grumbled, fairly or unfairly, that companies with immaculate reputations for aesthetic and exemplary design, such as Braun, Bang & Olufsen, and Olivetti, never made products with a performance to match the beauty of their packaging.

The proposition is not likely to appeal to the managements concerned. But if you ask a stereo buff about Bang & Olufsen, you observe a distinct curl of the lip. And the bestselling Lettera 22, a world-famous design, was heavy and not particularly pleasant to operate. Unlike Bang & Olufsen, Olivetti was not appealing to the well-heeled, upper-crust market to which appearance matters more than function. The Olivetti range was for the general public, and the typewriter's weaknesses in this respect, in hindsight, appear to reflect the general debilities that once almost bankrupted the great Italian company.

The distinction between form and function neatly illustrates why marketing needs management. It explains why, even though the winners of the Car of the Year award both gain and exploit the prize's considerable publicity value in the marketplace, the better-managed runners-up win the glittering commercial prizes. Critics who confer awards and write about design are inevitably most impressed by form, while motoring journalists (who judge this particular prize) are by definition enthusiasts, people who don't approach a set of wheels with the same attitudes as does the family motorist.

Managers are in neither position—not if they're doing their duty by the market and their customers. The true hotcake cars are designed with the functional market requirement as the starting point: the contents, in a sense, determine the package. A result that is still good enough to earn second place from the professionals must be a highly successful compromise—and the dimensions of compromise are determined mostly by trade-offs between cost and price.

Give the designer his head, however, and his natural response will be to place the package first and foremost. As noted in contrasting Bang & Olufsen with Olivetti, the manager may have good reason to go along with this policy. If the goal is to sell expensive stereos to the average pair of ears, or costly luggage to an expensive pair of hands, that makes magnificent sense; the visual excellence, like the high price, reassures customers that they are buying top functional quality as well—even if they aren't.

The rationale, though, is exactly the same as that which produced the little, Spanish-made Ford Fiesta: the design must suit the marketing purposes of the product. But a high-design, low-function strategy carries higher risks than a low-design, high-function one.

43

That's because the former implies a high price, which leaves plenty of room in terms of cost for a competitor to attack, tempting the top of the market with quality that goes more than skin-deep.

Not only that: the high-design company also faces a rude awakening if the performance doesn't match the package and the promise. That happened with the three prizewinning cars mentioned above. For the Rover 3500, the Porsche 928, and the Lancia Delta, a miss was even worse than a mile. In the demanding, capricious naked market of today, it's not the applause of the critics but the roar of the crowd that must be earned.

6. MANAGING BY DESIGN

The fate of the Cars of the Year doesn't imply that managers and marketers should ignore design. Far from it—refusal by management to admit design into the important processes of the firm is pernicious in the extreme.

The truth is that there can't be design, good or bad, without management—even if it is only management by abdication. The decision to do nothing about design or to let a bad design run is a decision about design, and a rotten one. Good design includes performance, technology, image, cost, manufacturing method, and development potential. Thus, whatever aspect management wears, design is included in it or includes it. Unfortunately, the tendency has been for both management and the design world to think of design almost as aesthetics, as something added on. Hence the "chairman's wife syndrome," in which an important corporate design decision is relegated to the status of choosing chintz curtains.

The new Age of Competition does not allow for such disregard of design systems. Even if growth gets faster the affluent societies of the West, saturated with consumer and industrial goods, will be dominated by a trend that has become ineluctable: the great switch to specialized, smart, differentiated markets. In satisfying the markets of desire, rather than those of need, design must be paramount.

Thus, in world markets, the hallmark of the Japanese approach has been consistency and competition, with continuous upgrading of rival designs. The pace of Japanese innovations is so bewildering by Western standards that it tends to obscure the great cleverness with which the novelties are packaged. In cars, where Japanese products didn't rank in the forefront of design, the offerings were continually being improved. For a long time, too, the Japanese car has met the basic requirement of any design: to give the consumer a perceived high value for money.

That is good management and true marketing. The task is to direct the efforts of the design team toward areas where high pay-off can be achieved—and then management must see that it *is* achieved. A perfectly designed product that doesn't sell is a contradiction in terms. In this age, the income of the designer and the manager alike depends on maintaining a flow of highly marketable and profitable products. The work of the designer has a vital contribution to make to both parts of the equation: marketability and profits. The alleged dualism or dichotomy between management and design is thus as totally false as that between sales and production. Either they all go hand in hand or, in the Age of Competition, none will go at all. Production is sales is design is marketing—and they all add up to, and need, management.

Thus there is no excuse for regarding design as a luxury, an optional extra, something in a different category from unit labor costs, stock control, machine and material utilization, market penetration, or profit margins. That attitude has become increasingly untenable for overwhelming reasons, which have their roots in the close analogy between design and quality: two functions that are truly aspects of each other.

Without design for efficient manufacture, Japanese standards of quality control can't be achieved. The customer's perception of quality, too, is vitally affected by the whole design process. In saturated

45

markets, where competitive products of equal virtue are in abundance, desirability is crucial, which is why Japanese camera and audio firms strive not only for the latest electronic leapfrog and the highest quality but also for the look and feel that will convey the idea of modern technological excellence.

Fall behind in design and you fall behind in both quality and perceived quality—and thus in competitive power in the marketplace. And then, in the conditions of the 1980s, with most markets both oversupplied and highly competitive, the business must eventually fail. Do the opposite, and the business must surely succeed—and that applies just as forcefully to a service company as to a manufacturer, to a fashion chain as to a maker of construction equipment.

At J. C. Bamford, a family-owned engineering company in Britain, tiny in comparison with the giants in its industry (such as Caterpillar Tractor and Komatsu), prosperity rests on an astonishing lead in over fifty countries for a single product: the backhoe loader, which accounts for 70 percent of its sales ($270 million for 1986). The design of this Sitemaster success, a one-machine alternative to all the other equipment used on a construction site, was crucial to its market penetration. As chairman Anthony Bamford says, with typical British understatement, "Good design doesn't guarantee success, but it is certainly a very considerable element in achieving it."

Another British Supermarketer, Ralph Halpern, expresses the same point more sharply: "People only used to be concerned about price. Now they have aspirations and want to know how it performs, how it looks, what it can do for them—and that means it has to be well designed. Poor design means poor profits." Halpern took charge of a men's clothing chain, the Burton Group, at a time when nobody believed that dynamism could be injected into a business that had lagged behind for what seemed like living memory. His answer lay in design management, in identifying specific customer "life-style" groups, male and female, and meeting their distinct needs with textile products ranging from the conventional to the ultrafashionable.

The results of this careful design targeting, aimed at price bands as well as customer profiles, were spectacular. Burton profits rose fivefold from $24 million to $120 million between 1981 and 1985, as sales multiplied 2.5 times. The transformation embodied the same truth as that in Olivetti's latter years. Its design excellence couldn't save the company from near-collapse in a period when it was making the wrong products for an office market being revolutionized by the microchip. But when Carlo de Benedetti moved in, at a time of apparently bottomless financial crisis, he could draw on the company's design strengths in his total, and totally successful, revamping of the product line.

The value of design in a case like Olivetti's lies not only in generating products that are conceived for economical manufacture, that work efficiently and look functional and desirable at the same time but also in the overall image of the corporation. For example, at IBM every detail of the world's most successful manufacturing (and marketing) business is embraced by an overall design policy, right down to the "big blue" corporate color scheme. The importance of design runs so deep at IBM that the marketing management responsible for a new product works alongside the designers, to be joined when needed by the engineers who will put the latest gizmo into production.

IBM is one company that works hard, and (like everybody) not always successfully, to stay alert to change, to welcome and master it. Such firms, however far short they fall of the ideal, have been making rapid inroads in most markets. Their characteristics include an integrated, aggressive, profit-oriented design policy. And those who don't join 'em in this commitment aren't winning: they're being beaten, and will go on being defeated.

7. THE DREAM OF DE LOREAN

A marvelous design (marvelous, that is, in the eyes of the designer and possibly the beholder) can flop. The same fate can also overtake a magnificent market hit—that is, a product that achieves maximum recognition in the marketplace, enormous word-of-mouth advertising (the best and cheapest kind), and a high level of consumer desirability. These are among the characteristics of a superbly successful launch but, as every launcher knows, the launch isn't even half the battle.

Few initial marketing operations have ever been handled with such impressive skill, such remarkable éclat, as the launch of the De Lorean car. The same question is raised by the cases of con men down the ages: Why didn't John Z. De Lorean concentrate where he was brilliant (promotion and publicity) and make millions thereby, instead of losing a fortune by doing what he was bad at—making and selling a marketable product?

The invariable answer is that the same faults of character that generate public impact lead their possessor toward deception. The De Loreans of this world represent in extreme form an archetypal marketing menace: the fellow with the flamboyant manner and technique who operates to immense public effect, but whose ultimate impression on the public (in the only terms that count, those of sales and profits) falls far short of the image or, as De Lorean called it, "the Dream."

This dreamer's professional weaknesses were evident long before he and his gull-wing car came to grief in one of the strangest business sagas of the late twentieth century. The weakness was evident from a glance at a typical De Lorean ad in *The New Yorker*. Risks shriek out from the purple prose: "Your eyes skim the sleek, sensuous steel body, and all your senses tell you 'I've got to have it.' . . . It all began with one man's vision of the perfect personal luxury car. . . . Of course, everyone stares as you drive by. . . . After all, you're the one Living the Dream."

Clearly, the "one man" (whose visionary face stuck out from under the gull-wing doors in the ad) was living, or at any rate advertising, in a bygone Detroit age, the one in which he grew up and whose death left even his former employer, General Motors, struggling to get on technical and financial terms with the new era. In a day when function rather than form dominated consumer choice, miles per gallon outweighed dreams of glory, and keeping up with, or ahead of, the Joneses was less enrapturing than it used to be, De Lorean and his dream were obsolete.

But putting that aside, the De Lorean case is a perfect example, because of its flamboyance and exaggeration, of the dangers that haunt new projects. All of them contain an element of dream, the necessary enthusiasm that explains such unnecessary phenomena as overoptimistic interpretation of initial sales data. Early sales, hyped up by the sheer pressure of the launch, are very often misleading. Quite possibly, the tales of De Lorean's dream car selling like hotcakes and fetching a colossal premium may even have been true, but they told absolutely nothing about the real impact of the car in the market. It takes a long time and careful analysis before confident assessments of underlying demand can be made and secure increases in production authorized.

It wasn't surprising that half the cars ever made in Belfast ended up in stock. To anyone who protests that you can't draw any lessons from a strange character like De Lorean, or from a project backed by a foolish government with taxpayers' money, the answer is that many an honest marketer and many a decent corporate backer have ended up in exactly the same hole.

Enthusiasm is a prerequisite of successful marketing, and enthusiasm is difficult to contain within bounds—especially if the management desperately needs the project, as did the Northern Ireland government. Those who desperately want something to come true soon start to believe that it is true, and the very marketing razzmatazz that is supposed to seduce the public seduces the backers. Often the seduction is so powerful that the financing executives lock themselves into a most painful position: damned to huge losses if they cut off the pet project and probably damned to even bigger ones if it carries on.

Yet marketing analysis should have shown De Lorean's backers that the Dream was doomed, long before they threw out the baby with the bathwater. One of the oldest and soundest adages in advertising is that the product must match the promise. Exactly the same must be true of the rest of the marketing process. The De Lorean car lacked the distribution, quality, cost structure, marketing universe, engineering, and so on that were required to make any kind of reality out of the Dream. Against those deficiencies, a spectacularly high level of market recognition makes little difference.

8. PROFITING FROM PIMS

De Lorean (or his backers, at least) might have avoided disaster had he answered this questionnaire: Are the following propositions true or false?

1. Business situations are usually regular and predictable.

2. Business situations are basically alike in that they all obey the same "laws of the marketplace."

3. These laws of the marketplace determine about 80 percent of the observed profit results, even across different businesses.

4. There are nine major groups of influence on business return on investment and cash flow:

    a) investment intensity

    b) market position

    c) relative product/service quality

    d) productivity

    e) market growth

    f) innovation, differentiation

    g) vertical integration

    h) cost push

    i) current strategic effort

5. The combined operation of these nine factors is very complex.

6. Product characteristics don't matter, because the laws of the marketplace operate in all markets, regardless of product or industry.

7. The impact of the strategic characteristics of a business asserts itself over time—that is, you can disobey the laws of the marketplace only for a limited period.

8. Business strategies are successful if their strategic fundamentals are good, unsuccessful if they are unsound.

9. Most clear strategic signals are robust, meaning that if a business move looks really good it won't be negated by a moderate error in your sums.

If your answers are nearly all "true," then you agree with the basic propositions of Profit Impact of Market Strategy (PIMS). It stems from a detailed study of at least five years of results reported to computers by some 3,000 business units. No business should ignore what PIMS has to say for many reasons, not the least of which is because much of it is self-evidently true.

PIMS teaches that the key thing you need to know is *relative market share* (RMS). RMS is your market share divided by the combined share of your three biggest competitors. In other words, if your market share is 30 percent and the combined share of your three biggest competitors is 45 percent, your RMS is 66 percent. RMS strongly influences *profitability* (defined as profit before interest and tax, divided by working capital and fixed investment). According to PIMS, profitability works out roughly the same as relative market share. If the latter is 13 percent, your *return on investment* (ROI) is likely to be the same.

A second truth (or truism) is that heavy marketing devastates the profits of low-market-share businesses. Equally obvious, but equally important, high R & D expenditure also zaps the profits of businesses with low market share. Then, expensive capital investment programs can cripple businesses with low shares. The moral is clear: you must try and break out of a low share posture—but not through buying your way out. Look first at the other factors, starting with *relative product quality* (RPQ).

This means no dreams of glory. It means taking the customer's view, not your own; looking at both the product and the associated services; looking at how your product relates to other competitors in the served market—but excluding price from the analysis. You measure RPQ subjectively, looking at, say, product attributes such as consistency, durability, and variety, and service attributes such as delivery efficiency and technical advice.

To get an RPQ score, assign a weight to each attribute according to the importance you give it (adding up to 100 percent). On a scale of zero to ten, score your major competitors' average performance on each attribute. Score your own performance on each attribute as well. Finally, indicate whether you're "superior," "equivalent," or "inferior." If you're not sure whether the business is clearly superior or inferior on any point, then treat it as equivalent.

Now for the numbers. If you're superior, for example, in attributes weighted 15 percent and 5 percent, that's a score of 20 percent. Any attributes on which you're equivalent don't count. If you're inferior, say, on two attributes weighted 30 percent and 10 percent, that's 40 percent. To get your RPQ, subtract the sum of your inferior attributes from your superior attributes. In this case it would be 20 percent minus 40 percent, which is −20 percent. This business is trailing major competitors on two major product factors that are important to customers. As Irish expert Charles Carroll says (mildly enough, in the circumstances) this places the business "at a severe disadvantage in the market."

Other important characteristics of RPQ are:
1. RPQ promotes profitability.
2. High RPQ is a partial substitute for market share.
3. Heavy marketing does not compensate for poor RPQ.
4. A poor reputation for quality (De Lorean again) can cripple innovation.
5. When market growth slows, quality becomes even more important.

Avoid the investment intensity trap at all costs (De Lorean didn't). Look at your investment (both fixed and working capital at book value) as a percentage of sales and as a percentage of value added (defined as sales minus purchases of raw materials, energy, and components). The fact is that whether high fixed capital or high working capital is to blame, investment-intensive businesses need a strong market position to offset the consequent profit damage. Heavy marketing efforts do not provide that escape.

Don't fall into the trap, either, of believing that the amount of investment per employee is the most significant determinant of increased productivity. It's only one among ten major factors that influence the level of productivity in a business:

1. Market share
2. Relative market share (RMS)
3. Relative product quality (RPQ)
4. Investment per employee
5. Real market growth rate
6. Percentage of employees unionized
7. Level of marketing expenditure in relation to sales
8. Order size
9. Fixed assets in proportion to total investment
10. R & D as a percentage of sales.

The PIMS conclusions on all the above are clear. High productivity obtained through investment boosts profitability, but not dramatically. Both fixed and working capital raise productivity, and a strong market position further enhances it. But since profits inevitably suffer badly when productivity is bought with too much investment, the answer is to go for labor quality—that is, to manage better so that you can get improved employee effectiveness, which has a powerful and positive effect on profitability. How much of an effect? It can be as much as from 6 to 39 percent in ROI.

With that information behind them, would-be De Loreans know how to become winners and avoid being losers. The recipe is simple.

53

1. Look at the overall growth in your served market. If you want to win, it should be modest to high (but not *too* high). In a stagnant or declining market you're apt to lose.

2. Your market share should be adequate to strong, meaning greater than 20 percent. A weak position of under 10 percent will probably prove fatal.

3. Keep your product quality high and well differentiated from competitors. Similar, imitative, commodity-type, inferior products are doomed.

4. In investment, be as parsimonious as possible. High and increasing capital intensity is a losing position.

5. In productivity, seek balanced growth through investment and people. If secured at high investment cost, your productivity won't prevent you from losing.

6. Your marketing effort should be deployed to meet strategic objectives. Sales desperation in search of "volume" will be fatal.

Carroll concludes that it is probably impossible for the loser to be profitable, just as it is nearly impossible for the winner to be unprofitable. That's the reality. Everything else is a dream.

9. THE HAWK THAT FLEW AWAY

Once upon a time, there was a large engineering company in England that saw one of its most prized products land an order worth hundreds of millions from the richest customer in the United States. Another of its masterpieces had already satisfied the same mighty customer. And it had participated in the only airliner project offering serious competition to Boeing. The company's cup should have been flowing over. Actually, it was empty.

The company was Hawker-Siddeley, and the Pentagon's huge order for the Hawk jet trainer—like the sales of the Harrier jump-jet

to the Marines and the building of the wings for the A300 Airbus
—was lost to its progenitor when the House of Commons (by a single
vote) nationalized its aircraft interests. This passing into government
possession was particularly painful and ironic for Hawker-Siddeley,
because all three projects had been launched as private ventures, or
PVs. Hawker was not at all averse to public money, but in all three
cases the government originally didn't want to know.

For instance, the whole concept of the Hawk, the insistence that
it be a tactical aircraft as well as a trainer, was the manufacturer's
idea of what the customer needed, not the customer's notion. Why
is this particular customer nearly always wrong? The record of ventures backed by British politicians and civil servants, in aerospace or
anything else, is one of failure so nearly complete as to defy the law
of averages. Add to the sins of commission those of omission (such
as the obtuse decision not to back the three Hawker PVs), and there
is apparently a great mystery to be resolved. It can't simply be that
government is offered only the duff projects that nobody else will
finance; the Hawker PVs alone contradict that thesis.

The question is better approached the other way around: Why
did Hawker get it right? The answer establishes the essential platform of effective marketing management: the identification of manager with market.

10. MAKING MARKETERS RESPONSIBLE

Very few markets can support much more than three richly profitable entrants. Of those that can, most are not in heaven but in the
suspended hell of warfare. When the hellishness becomes real, as in
Vietnam or the Falklands, the market test for military procurement
is never the price tag, the bang per buck, but the effectiveness of the
bang. In the aftermath of actual conflict, in fact, spending is apt to

get a boost, not only from replacement but from remedy of any ineffectiveness laid bare.

True, there have been times, as under President Carter or the Labour party in Britain, when cutbacks in defense spending for budgetary reasons have wreaked some havoc among the marketers of death. But in both countries, new governments dedicated to defense hastened to raise the ante: the Reagan bounty, for example, at first added up to a deeply gratifying annual boost in spending as far as the eye could see, or the missile could fly. So why aren't the recipients of these riches, the makers of these market hits, the rulers of the economy?

The explanation is the same as that for another phenomenon: the world growth stakes have been led not by the high-defense spending superpowers, the United States and the USSR, but by the defense niggards such as Japan and West Germany. At the level of the firm, as of the nation, military business in general leads only to more military business. True, there have been some spectacular spin-offs from defense billions in the United States, notably the original impetus to the silicon chip. But who landed the largest bonanzas? Not the defense moguls. The big winners have been people like the Microsoft PC software wizard, Bill Gates, who were barely born when the Apollo program blasted off.

By the same token, as noted in Step One, if the technological spin-off exists that was originally supposed to justify the ruinous expense of the Concorde, it has been remarkably well concealed. The truth is that developing specific products, priced on a cost-plus basis, for the military or the government bears no useful relationship to making multicopy models for the masses—which is where the world markets lie. It may well be that the wonders created in the military zone have miraculous application in ordinary life. But effectively the transfer is no easier than translating any scientific or technological breakthrough into an economic one.

The process is certainly not facilitated by the fact that the markets of death are, on the whole, far more profitable than those of peace—with the vast added advantage in cash flow terms that the

56

military customer pays up front, and thereafter on some basis that usually adds up to cost-plus. Civilian markets offer few such parallels, which is why the habits encouraged by dealing with military customers cut so little ice in civilian commerce.

The moral is exactly the same as that of the De Lorean Dream: the true measure of marketing success isn't public impact and awareness. Neither is it the established past strength and superiority of the product and its market position. And it certainly isn't the ability to serve customers who don't have to count the cost with what they imagine to be their hearts' desire—fondly and maybe foolishly. Hawker got its three private ventures right because the company's future in the aviation industry depended absolutely on correct market predictions and projections. On the customer's side, the mistakes didn't matter. Nobody's future in government would have suffered if Britain had missed the Airbus entirely, or if the jump-jet had been permanently grounded, or if the Hawker management hadn't launched the Hawk.

In the most modern of industries and markets, the most ancient management truths apply. You get the best performance only where those responsible for policy are also responsible for its execution, and where their own futures are linked with the results. No doubt the bureaucrats who turned thumbs down on the three PVs took some view of the future markets for British aerospace products. But they weren't properly equipped to do that, and so they got it wrong. No doubt the great defense contractors can see the need for nondefense success as clearly as anybody else can—but they see the peculiar requirements of the peculiarly profitable Pentagon business with even greater clarity; and that orientation governs their achievements, and lack of them.

The true test of marketing management is providing people who have the option to refuse your offer with a product or service that they want to buy at a price they can afford and that offers a large margin over cost—large enough to finance the investment and improvement that will undoubtedly be required. It's a sad reflection that the British economy would be far better off had the country, instead of building the Concorde, given birth (as its French supersonic partners did) to Baron Marcel Bich. His products? The ballpoint pen and the disposable razor.

11. THE SAVOY OPERAS

Different companies under attack often turn to a similar defense. From Zenith to the big old Swiss watchmakers such as Omega, Rolex, and Patek Philippe, they cling to the life raft of high quality and high prestige. It can be a bumpy ride. In 1982 Zenith took a $22 million loss, having given shareholders a 4 percent decline in their investment annually since 1972. The truth is that superiority in technology and prestige cannot be divorced for more than a moment; nor prestige from prestigious management.

To put it another way, if higher prestige doesn't pay off in higher profits, it isn't worth much. The essence of the situation was made clear when Lord Forte's effort to capture Savoy Hotels was at its most intense. The Savoy directors may have known more than Forte (the maestro of Trusthouse Forte, owners of the Plaza Athénée in Paris, the Grosvenor House in London, the Ritz in Madrid, and the new Plaza Athénée in New York) about running deluxe hotels— though you wouldn't have bet on it—but when it came to managing a business, the record spoke, or rather whimpered, for itself. In 1979 the Savoy Hotels produced half the profit it had made in 1970, when turnover was two-thirds lower. If Forte's Waldorf, just across the Strand in London, had performed so feebly, either the hotel or its managers would have been put out to pasture long before.

To the then chairman, Sir Hugh Wontner, for whom the Savoy was "an historic part of London that it is my duty to preserve," that may have been beside the point. Prestige, however, isn't its own reward, even though the managers of prestige products do commonly behave as though high prestige necessarily equates with low profits—if any. No doubt that thought consoled the managers of the Rolls-Royce car division during the dozen years of losses before their large and mounting profits, as an independent company, exposed the unflattering truth about the previous incompetence.

Of course, prestige in itself is a mighty marketing asset. The money-losing Rolls-Royce still commanded the reputation of making "the best car in the world," even after auto aficionados had long ceased to think it anything of the sort. But if management itself still believes in the former glories, great danger threatens.

Indeed, Rolls-Royce sales did drop alarmingly, especially in the key U.S. market, when the buyers who made that market decided that the machine was too little car for the money, thus forcing the company into the unprecedented step of slashing its prices to salvage sales. Prestige, like advertising, is ultimately only as good as the product. And like any other factor in management, prestige is not without cost. That cost must be abundantly covered by the returns. Otherwise you stumble into the Savoy syndrome: losses in four of the ten years 1973–82 and post-tax returns on capital never out of (usually low) single figures.

The larger the loveliness of the product looms in the managerial minds, the greater the chance that nonprestigious, mundane matters will be ignored—such as the management, control, and marketing systems in which Forte is expert. Those proficient systems explain partly why Forte, who was once "practically nothing," as Wontner said, came to control a group with, at the time of the initial onslaught, some 27 times the sales and 133 times the profits of the Savoy Hotels. That's really something.

Prestige implies premium quality and premium prices—and, from the latter, the well-managed company should derive a premium profit. That trick in turn demands, in some respects, even tighter, tougher management than does serving the mass market, because the prestige business is vulnerable not only to lower-priced or more efficient competition (witness the Japanese camera firms that undercut and overtook the lordly Leica) but to management's own potentially poor sense of priorities. Often, prestige goeth before a fall. True prestige lies in truly being number one—and that demands primacy in all respects. In that position, a company has options. Once primacy is lost, in technology or anything else, the options rapidly begin to disappear.

12. PRESTIGE EQUALS PRIMACY

The decline in the engineering supremacy and reputation of Rolls-Royce, however imperceptible to the eye of its typical purchaser, carries with it the threat of brand obsolescence. People will always pay a premium for the best, or what they believe to be the best. Damage that belief, however slightly, and you mar your chances of preserving the premium. True, factors other than technology may apply—snobbery, pleasure in an object made in small quantities by craftsmen, the aura of a well-nurtured brand—but these days top technology has a cachet of its own. Given the cost of launching a major technical innovation, this is fortunate—but what happens when the rare, expensive technology becomes general and cheap?

When the laser audio disc was unveiled by Sony in conjunction with Philips, it raised a fascinating and fundamental issue for deluxe and mass marketers alike. Would or wouldn't the disc do to the conventional long-playing record and to conventional record players what they had done to the 78 rpm record?

Launching a new technology can carry serious marketing risks. If the revolutionary innovation gets out of hand, it can, like any successful revolutionary innovation, destroy the established order for keeps. The establishment rarely recognizes the danger: there were surely adding machine and slide rule manufacturers that didn't see the first large, expensive electronic calculators as any threat to them —poor fools.

What if the laser disc were to make the long-playing disc as obsolete as the slide rule or the piles of 78s that now litter attics? Would they be joined by moldering turntables, ranging from exclusive, precision-made wonders of Rolls-Royce quality and costing hundreds of dollars, to the down-market machines of Sony and Philips themselves? What would be the impact on record companies and on turntable, arm, and cartridge makers outside the big names backing the compact disc system? And would laser discs bring the relentless advance of the cassette to a juddering halt?

In order for a technological challenge to subvert a market, there must be a real advantage, in price or in use, over the existing product. The discs are not only nearly as compact as cassettes but they lack cassettes' disadvantages of hiss, fragility, and unreliable reproduction. On the other hand, discs (like their first players in comparison to those for LPs) started out very expensive compared to both records and cassettes, which is characteristic of new technologies in their first manifestation.

The cheapness of cassettes, of course, is what damaged record sales so severely—down by 30 percent since 1975—as do-it-yourself pirates taped music off the air or from other people's discs. To that extent, laser discs offered the record industry a golden hope of winning back lost customers. But any bonanza of that kind depended not only on a vast increase in the library of compact discs available but also on contradicting the basic marketing strategy by which innovators try to restrict the damage done by their new technology.

That strategy is to price the miracle product at the very top of the market and then bring the price down gradually as the market widens. So long as costs (thanks to the combined wonders of the learning curve and economies of scale) fall faster than prices, everything is fine. Thus the Philips players weighed in initially at luxury levels of $750; the more sophisticated Sony cost even more; and buying the five-inch discs then available would have cost up to $3,000.

In the past this strategy has worked well, in celebrated examples ranging from nylon stockings to Polaroid cameras. But the pace of technological life has been heating up, as demonstrated by the frenetic multiplication and price falls in microelectronics, in both components and computers. Given that the laser disc really is a great advance in quality, durability, and desirability—a steel radial tire (which stole the market) rather than a Corfam synthetic leather (which flopped)—it's hard to see its exclusivity lasting much longer than that of the first, expensive quartz watches. Somebody, somewhere is going to share the same, sad fate as the prestigious old Swiss watchmakers. Already in 1986, the disc, still relatively expensive, had clearly taken over the market lead; but already, too, its technological lead, and market potential, were under threat from a great leap forward in cassettes.

For purveyors of prestige, the lesson turns out to be the same as for those who peddle near-commodities: the best course is to be best at everything from technology to distribution, from reliability to advertising. Above all, success and survival depend on being best at listening to the signals from the market and reacting to them immediately. There is always a way, as the Swiss watchmakers found when successfully launching the fashion-conscious Swatch timepieces in the face of intense Japanese competition. There was only one problem: Swatch took too long to emerge. In naked markets even the most luxurious of producers can't afford the luxury of delay.

To summarize some of the important points I've mentioned in Step Two:

1. You can't manage well without good marketing—but equally, you can't market well without good management.

2. Marketing only works at its best when it permeates the whole company—meaning its deeds, not just its words.

3. If your basic business is faltering, don't blame the trouble on failure to develop new activities.

4. Never neglect any challenge, trivial or tremendous, that threatens any part of an important market.

5. Go for good design, which is like good advertising: the performance must match the package and the promise.

6. Production is sales is design is marketing—and they all add up to, and need, management.

7. Your dreams can become reality—but only with real backing from the prosaic facts of distribution, quality, cost structure, marketing universe, and so on.

8. It is probably impossible for the loser to be profitable, and nearly impossible for the winner to be unprofitable.

9. Identification of your managers with the market is the best way of identifying what the market wants.

10. You get the best marketing performance where those responsible for policy are also responsible for its execution.

11. If higher prestige doesn't pay off in higher profits, it isn't worth much.

12. True prestige lies in truly being number one; and that demands that you get primacy in all respects—from technology to distribution, from reliability to advertising.

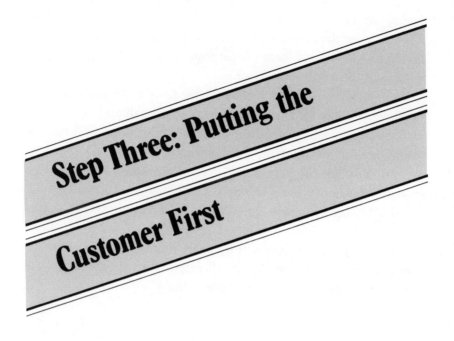

1. THE BRIGHT BUSINESS OF BENETTON

Marketing success often sounds like the art of the impossible. Imagine, for instance, deciding to build a worldwide store chain that sells only one kind of product under a meaningless surname, using as manufacturing and marketing bases a little Italian business run by three brothers and a sister. That apparent nonsense was the real-life success route taken by Benetton, whose woolen knitwear bids fair to become as universal as Levis (another once meaningless surname).

The Benetton fairy tale began as humbly as any Silicon Valley electronics venture born over a garage. Giuliana Benetton sewed sweaters for the large Veneto textile trade. Luciano Benetton, the eldest son of a deceased truck driver, had a job in a menswear store. The Benetton woolens, at first made by Giuliana on a home knitting

64

machine (according to *Time* magazine) and sold by Luciano from shop to shop, grew to the point where they needed first a factory (in 1965) and then a store (1968).

Just twenty years after they began, the Benettons were selling in 3,500 stores in fifty-four countries, opening a new store every day, making 40 million items in ten factories—and had earned $500 million in sales revenue in the previous year. The Benetton Four (Luciano, Giuliana, Gilberto, and Carlo) combined fierce attention to computer-aided productive and distributive efficiency with the power of franchising and advertising. They spend $11 million a year on the universal message, "United Colors of Benetton," which pulls in customers as far apart as the United States (450 stores), South Africa, and Hong Kong.

But neither the computers nor the approved and tightly controlled franchisees nor the advertising nor even the high value for money prices—nor any other of the bright Benetton ideas—truly explain the impossible success. Rather, bright colors are its foundation. They sold Giuliana's first woolens to the first customers in the 1960s and are the prime reason why young people buy Benetton in the 1980s. Like Levis in the long blue-denim boom, Benetton caught the fashion mood of a public that knows no frontiers. And there's another reason why Luciano, Giuliana, Gilberto, and Carlo were able to sense and tap that rich vein of taste. When the first plant opened in Treviso, Italy, they were respectively thirty, twenty-eight, twenty-four, and twenty-two years of age.

2. TIMING AND TASTE

Victory in the naked market demands more organized management, and better managed organizations, than ever before. The necessity of method, however, by no means excludes the primacy of ideas, of inspirations that may well be born not from the intellect but from the gut. Most, if not all, supreme marketing triumphs, from Ford to Sony, have sprung from the particular, instructive, intuitive identification of a taste or interest (usually that of one person, a Henry Ford I or an Akio Morita, or of one family, like the Benettons) with the desires of a great, fat mass market.

Indeed, the most valuable talent in marketing, the one gift the doting marketing parent would wish for an infant, is clearly an unfailing instinct for what the customers want. The licenses to print money go to those who sense or guess consumer tastes before anybody else—and who know how to gratify those tastes—such as, in the world of the media, Canada's late Lord Thomson (commercial TV and newspapers), or Lord Grade, formerly of ACC (which as ATV was the prime mover in British commercial TV).

The trouble with tastes, though, is not only that they change but that the markets in which they are met change as well. Once upon a time ATV and its U.S. equivalents could concentrate on churning out their recipes in a simple mono-product format—network television. Now, in the age of the multimedia conglomerate, with the media still multiplying, nothing is that straightforward. Grade at least had the vision to sense the change—hence his own conglomerate ventures into White Men's Graves like feature films. What he didn't have was one irreplaceable quality: youth.

Precious few cases exist of middle-aged (let alone aged) breakthrough, or of maestros who, like the old man of Spain in the limerick, can do it again and again. Rather, that's what's wrong. They do repeat and repeat the winning formulas of the past, until they arrive at the point where the recipe no longer works. If they stick around, the results for their companies are generally excruciating. The longevity of the Hollywood tycoons, for example, helped ensure that their creations, MGM, Paramount, Twentieth Century–Fox, and so on, all ended up as mere divisions of somebody else's conglomerate.

Taste-making and sensing are really a young person's game. Careers that don't start until middle age (as the above-mentioned Roy Thomson's breakout into Canadian radio) are as rare as the white rhino. The predominance of youth makes it important to have a management structure that allows its young people to take the lead at the right time, like the persistent Sony executive who, in one version of the story, unable to persuade his seniors, got through to president Morita with his marvelous idea of the personal hi-fi.

But it's rare to find a boss of great stature who will listen to and back (against opposition) the inspirations of younger people, and rarer still to find an entrepreneurial tycoon, used to years of applause from the multitude, who can bear to change his own act. The absurd incident at ACC in which an executive committee specifically excluding Lord Grade was formed is reminiscent of other attempts to cope in cases where the tycoon has outlived his touch; the stratagem never works.

The problem (as shown by the events that culminated in ACC's takeover and Grade's ousting) is to deal with the problem before it becomes a crisis. For the flash of the old brilliance (the Muppets, which Lew Grade brilliantly spotted and backed) you pay heavily with the dull thud of the new fallibility (*Raise the Titanic*, one of the movies' mightiest losses). The problem finally gets resolved by failure, but only after enormous damage has been done to the company's image in the marketplace. It makes a strong case for compulsory retirement at sixty-five, if not sixty. After all, at seventy-five a manager is older than most of the market—and anybody who thinks that doesn't matter doesn't know marketing.

It isn't just a question of the much-trumpeted youth market, although fate isn't merely tempted, but positively enticed, by middle-aged executives who think they understand nymphets and moppets. The need is to be in tune with the spirit of the age and the technology of the times. The tender years of people such as Steven Jobs, the Apple computer founder, are no accident. Nor is it an accident that the large companies in the high-technology industries—even Apple itself, after it reached billion-dollar scale—have found it very hard to retain the Jobs-like talents in their suffocating bosoms. Brilliant breakthroughs are more commonly found where the genius not only identifies with a growth market but has the personal motivation to make an idea succeed and personal responsibility for its progress from birth right through to the ultimate realization.

3. THE BRITISH BUNGLE OF GM

An American professor once believed that the manifest destiny of the world economy was to be controlled by 300 multinational giants. Now that he has been proved manifestly wrong, it's important for marketing managements to understand why. The answer lies deeply rooted, not just in the nature of huge corporations but in that of the fast-evolving markets of today.

As a demonstration of the processes at work, take the very strange case of General Motors, the world's greatest manufacturing company. You might suppose that, stuffed with management and money, GM could impose its will on any market it chose—but you would be wrong. In the UK, having first seen its domestic appliance business, the once market-leading Frigidaire, go down the drain, GM proceeded to record nine losses (the ninth a thumping $120 million) in ten years of making a comparable mess of Vauxhall.

Naturally, there are plenty of extenuating circumstances. GM started the decade with too small a share of Europe's most sluggish car market. Since the oil price crisis of 1973, the truck business (where Bedford used to reign supreme, but took its lumps from Ford) has traveled a bumpy road. The car side, anyway, was squeezed between the importers and Ford—and, like the latter, suffered from having its assembly operations divided in two, by government fiat, with one of the plants on Merseyside. But excuses are not explanations.

The underlying truth is that Detroit never allowed Vauxhall to develop its own destiny. It thus lagged fatally behind in producing its first small car (GM didn't then believe in small cars). The independent design and development strength that had given Ford the first Cortina and consolidated its hold on the UK market was never really matched at Vauxhall. When the U.S. management in Dearborn did tighten its grip on UK Ford, it was part of a bold, ultimately successful operation to create a trans-European automotive complex. GM sat on its hands across the ocean.

Then the wheel swung full circle. GM put billions into downsizing its cars; the design capabilities of Opel were called on to help create not just European but worldwide answers to the Japanese challenge; the Vauxhall and Opel ranges were integrated; and a European organization was created in 1986, a couple of decades after Ford's. As that long lag shows, the only thing wrong was that these things should have been done much earlier. Everybody, parent and child included, inevitably suffered from the floundering of the past.

The cost of this sad story is plain—though the £107 million of new equity that GM had to pump into Vauxhall in a single year (and even the $2 billion cost of the total European revamp) was a fleabite in Detroit terms. Vauxhall was too small for Americans to manage from the United States, but at GM, where everybody turns only when Father does, subsidiaries have no option but to wait their turn. What happened, when Father at long last rolled over, demonstrated only how shortsighted previous policy had been. In 1982 British industry offered few contrasts more bizarre than that between Vauxhall, with its 61 percent rise in car output, and Ford and BL, whose production actually fell (by 10.4 percent and 2 percent, respectively).

The reason was not only that GM had followed its Ford leader in having a common car range sold in all the European markets and made in more than one country, nor even that it had possibly gone a decisive stage better by spreading its model ranges across the world. It was also because, descending to the local level, GM had backed the new Vauxhall models with an all-round drive to improve every aspect of performance, from labor discipline to delivering fleet cars on time (as noted earlier). Getting your act together is not only the prerequisite for saving a long-failing company, as Vauxhall was. It is, of course, the true definition of good marketing.

Marketing managers notoriously brought much disillusion

down on their own heads by the original emphasis, as their great day dawned, on marketing as some separate and miraculous management discipline. By the same token many companies, by no means only in cars, wasted their efforts (puny or not) to develop new wonders by failing to ensure that they would be produced to order—or to master the little matter of not having the things fall apart with use. The point is obvious, and crucially important.

So how and why did Vauxhall's lords ignore the imperatives of the factory floor and marketplace for so long? Again, no doubt, because even a $1.1 billion company (1981 figures) was a drop in General Motors' $63 billion ocean. Only when setbacks in the fat and comfortable U.S. market forced GM to see its international business as a whole did Vauxhall fall into its proper place, not as a struggling producer with an uneconomic share of a single market but as an integral part of a broadside attack on the wide, wealthy world. The Detroit bosses had barricaded themselves from reality with fixed ideas such as "There's no future in small cars," and "You can't sell the same car in Britain and Germany" (let alone America). They were wrong.

4. MARKETING SMARTS CALL THE TUNE

One of the strangest reasons for GM's lag behind the world in which its customers lived was a total lack of interest in market research. Its executives thought they knew better than the customers—and certainly better than any research company. Many managers share the benighted belief that such research is futile. When a researcher asks hypothetical questions, like "Would you like such-and-such a product if it existed?" and "What isn't on the market that you'd like?" it is futile. Iffy questions get iffy answers. But research is indispensable for testing a real product concept, or for finding possibly invaluable explanations for market phenomena.

Consider, for example, the boom in compact 35-mm cameras, a sector previously in such sharp decline that manufacturers had given it up for dying. Then somebody in Japan had the wit to ask why sales were falling. The answers (difficult loading, complex operations, the need to focus, and so on) gave birth to the idea of the auto-focus, auto-exposure, auto-loading, auto-wind camera with automatic built-in flash, and—presto!—sales boomed by 50 percent a year, changing the whole shape of the market.

In other words, the manufacturers had gotten out of step with their market. There are rare geniuses who are in constant communion with their customers. These exceptions prove no rules. And in complex, segmented markets this kind of lightning is unlikely to go on striking twice in the same place. Continuous, organized questioning and questing are the indispensable methodology, and variants and variations are the objects of the search. The single-product, single-brand king of the market, its dominance resting on one dominant theme, is obsolete. What an old-line giant like Coca-Cola has been forced to do (proliferate brand variations and innovations to defend its lead against Pepsi) is precisely the same course forced on an indecently young market leader such as Apple.

Against this background, especially after so many years during which anybody with pretensions to management know-how has stressed that marketing washes whitest, you would expect to find marketing's top practitioners high in any business pantheon. But *Business Week*'s 1985 list of "the new corporate elite" had only five categories—none of them marketing. The classes of business supremacy were high-tech entrepreneur (seventeen out of fifty members of the elite), service gurus (nine), corporate rejuvenators (fifteen), financial engineers (six), and a sinister-sounding group labeled "asset shufflers" (three, including T. Boone Pickens, the raider of oil mammoths).

Nobody can produce an elite performance in the first three categories without making some kind of marketing magic, true. But the list contains nobody who—like the late Ray Kroc of McDonald's —has taken a consumer brand and conquered worldwide, or even

America-wide, tastes. And in the dominant high-tech sector marketing has generally come in a limping second after the technology itself. The same issue of *Business Week* reported the trials of Dr. An Wang (one of the elitists) in minicomputers and personal computers, where IBM was outselling Wang to managers by a massive twenty to one. Hewlett-Packard, too, found itself a marketing babe-in-arms when it came up against the same IBM opposition in PCs (or tried to).

As noted in Step One, Apple's Steve Jobs (then a member of the elite, now presumably ousted from it as well as from Apple) had to import marketing talent from PepsiCo, which he did almost too late in the day and in the certain knowledge that without a powerful injection of professional marketing management, his company might well fall victim to a potentially virulent strain of the De Soto disease. If De Soto means nothing to you, that is precisely the point. It was one of the myriad motor companies that boomed in the industry's early days and then disappeared, by amalgamation or death, as the pressure of the heavyweights became inexorable. Apple's hard-pressing mammoth is IBM, the heaviest of them all. Even without the impact of IBM's brand and marketing muscle, which took a third of total personal-computer sales in no time at all, Apple would have been increasingly squeezed. IBM's shock wave has made the pressure triply intense.

Its success also stimulated the second largest computer company, DEC, to intensify its cultivation of Apple's orchard, along with other technological powerhouses such as Hewlett-Packard, Wang, and Data-General. Throw in the fact that the Japanese are thrusting powerfully for sales, and that U.S. rivals who grew spectacularly along with Apple (such as Commodore) are still in business, and you have a marketing maelstrom. De Sotoism has set in, as smaller stars such as Vector and Osborne have dimmed after only a few years of glorious life.

Apple's hope of avoiding similarly inglorious retrenchment can no longer rest on the identification of its founders, Steve Jobs and Steve Wozniak, with a market composed of like-minded computer buffs. Actually, it never did. The key to Apple's triumph was the machine's adoption by managers as a business tool, a development that Jobs and his backers had the wit and wisdom to exploit at full tilt. The exploitation of Apple's friendly name and image was also a highly professional demonstration of the marketing skills that were truly required to turn Jobs's genius into hard sales.

Yet the story became a textbook illustration of the usual fate of the high-tech company, riding high only as long as its technology is unique and powerful. If its microcircuits, computers, or software are leapfrogged by somebody else, or if forceful new competition appears, the company is thrust into an entirely different environment for which, lacking marketing, it is ill-equipped. It is thus set up for the services of a corporate rejuvenator, maybe one of the elite, who in turn may well be a master of marketing smarts (like Lee Iacocca at Chrysler). But the driving force of corporate rejuvenation demands and deploys much, much more.

Great marketing is only one foundation of corporate miracles. For instance, one shining success in the U.S. steel wasteland is based on scrap, financial incentives, new technology, and an organization so flat that only three layers separate the boss from the actual steel-makers. Time and again, it's such organizational drive, not just pure marketing brilliance, that underpins the turnaround triumphs. That's why John Sculley from PepsiCo couldn't make progress so long as Jobs, with his inimical addiction to a different kind and style of management, was in the way at Apple.

The hard truth, even while one Apple II computer was still pouring off the assembly line every fifteen seconds, was that a one-Apple company was no more viable than a one-Coke company. To maintain itself as a billion-dollar business, the infant Apple (b. 1976) had to sell not just a computer but a whole range of products, distributed and supported in the marketplace as impartially as, well, apples—or Pepsi. In today's high-competition markets, high technology is of the highest importance, but it is not the highest protection. The best protection is keeping the two halves of the vital equation, the market and the management, in touch. Getting out of touch is the marketing sin that's unforgivable at any time, difficult to cure

73

most times, and, if unhealed, fatal in these times, when technology may set the tempo but marketing smarts call the tune.

5. THE FOLLY AT PHILIPS

The most conspicuously large companies in the world inevitably provide today's outstanding examples of the difficulties that arise when managers try to make markets behave to suit their (the managers') convenience. The whole point of markets is that they suit nobody's convenience but behave as they wish. Even some highly sophisticated managements appear to miss altogether the direction of markets. It doesn't require much to prove the point; the giants prove it themselves by selling the businesses with whose markets they haven't come to terms.

One such case is the 1981 selloff by the Dutch Philips super-mammoth of Cambridge Electronic Industries. At the time it was fashionable for giants to offload bits and pieces that either were too small for their comfort or didn't fit into market plans. And spunoff groups, forced to concentrate on their own markets without Father watching over them, can show surprising speed. But CEI's twenty-odd companies weren't all that tiny. They shared among them $120 million of sales in markets that were right up Philips's alley—electronics and electrical components, and defense and electronic systems.

Possibly Philips never really wanted these odds and ends that came in with a television and telecommunications company called Pye, whose previous magpie management cared not, apparently, for the economies of scale or the virtues of concentration. From that angle, the selloff was merely the culmination of a takeover that must have given the Dutch at least as much trouble as it was worth. But it seems characteristic of Philips to devote endless time and trouble to its various enterprises without in the end obtaining full payoff from its endeavors.

Just try, for example, to think of any consumer market in which Philips is the undisputed leader. No doubt there are some. In audio and video, however, Philips may be "simply years ahead" in its technology (as its ads claimed), but the Dutch company is certainly years behind in its market impact. The Sony Walkman and the JVC videocassette recorders, to take just two examples, cleaned up while Philips plugged on determinedly with less rewarding adventures. Somehow its technical excellence doesn't seem to get translated into world-beating mass-market products.

According to one informant, the explanation of the failure is simple. Any Philips subsidiary, he says, can generate superb products for local consumption and often conceals their development costs craftily in the accounts. If the official Philips range were to consist of these black market innovations, even the Japanese might tremble. But when the ideas get back to the center in Eindhoven, Father says no—for instance, to a marvelous portable color TV that could have given Sony a run for its money. If this account is correct, then perhaps Eindhoven gave the wrong Philips division its freedom. Maybe all its divisions—not just the Cambridge ragbag—need to be set free.

6. SPEEDY, SPECIALIZED, SIMPLE —AND SOPHISTICATED

Everyone knows that small is beautiful when it comes to growth, partly because tripling a little is much easier than doubling a lot, but also because the small firm has a greater 3S potential than the initiative-crushing corporate elephant. The three Ss stand for *speed, specialization,* and *simplicity,* the basic ingredients of entrepreneurial success. *Business Week*'s 1985 ranking of the 100 "best little growth companies in America" added a fourth *S* to the formula: *sophistication.*

Fully two-thirds of these little lions lived exclusively or essentially in the well-traveled high-tech territories of electronics (overwhelmingly), health care, and defense. Everything else was a feeble also-ran. Consumer goods accounted for only eighteen stars, and that's on a very broad definition that includes Kung Fu movies and stress tests for the coronary-prone. Nine companies were in industrial necessities, ranging from steel bolts to supplying workers for nuclear plants; four were in transportation; and three marketing services firms and a couple of specialized publishers made up most of the remainder.

As for retailing and fast food, the solitary retailer (record, tape, and video stores) was joined by only a single chain of family steakhouses, featuring Hawaiian chicken. Could there have been a massive shift in the location of crocks of gold? Or could it simply be that old-fashioned growth businesses soon cease to be little in a country so lavishly supplied with consumers?

The answer depends partly on whether you think $150 million of sales is little, that being the cutoff point in the *Business Week* exercise. On the assumption that new retailers and other consumer businesses are still coming forward, the magazine's snapshot, picking the small stars on their record over three years, should have frozen more of them on the way up. It is easier to accept that the action really has shifted. That raises two issues. First, those without technological capability need not apply. Second, how much ultimate mileage is there in sperm banks, electronic parts for satellite dishes, and oceanographic instruments? These are not going to provide the foundations of the next General Motors.

The high-tech boom is thus spawning a host of fast-growing mice with four alternatives. One is to sell out, presumably to one of the elephants around which the mice are currently running circles. Another is to become one nucleus of a group with several other like nuclei. A third choice is to diversify, becoming the holding company for a goodly set of wholly owned subsidiaries. Fourth, a firm could continue to paddle its technological canoe and pray for smooth waters. All four alternatives have obvious drawbacks, which means that the 4S firms, with their stunning annual rates of profit growth (79 percent, 115 percent, 93 percent, for example), have a tiger by the tail.

That's much better than having a corporate elephant on your chest. Elephantiasis is a corporate disease that is not confined to elephants, however. The fast-growing 4S firm must multiply as well as magnify, if only because of the necessity to expand geographically. No high-tech company outside the United States, for example, can afford to ignore the American market. But that takes it into a whole new ball game, not only in terms of more intense competition but in matters of organization and control. Neither aspect of the game is easy to win, as the once high-flying British computer firm Apricot found out at a price.

"This is not an industry where you have the opportunity to sit and think," said an official of Apricot, Inc., on the tender subject of the loss of three senior executives, including the chief, from the fledgling outfit. He meant that the Americans were not moving fast enough for a company whose ambition was to win 1 percent of the U.S. market. That's no misprint: the company's share was then put at 0.16 percent, meaning that Apricot was aiming at a 525 percent boost in its penetration—and it was still short of over 200 dealers (out of 250) and running two months behind its own schedule.

The course is tough in a hard, harsh U.S. market where you either get it right—or right in the neck. The foreign managements that have succeeded have done so by resolving two sensitive issues that are central to any U.S. venture—or any parent-child relationship. The first is intervention. The departed Apricot boss, Robert Coolidge, told the *Financial Times:* "I learned very quickly that [the British] wanted a closer hand in the management of the business than I had envisaged." The second management issue is not who (who's in charge?) but how. Coolidge again: "We typically do more research on issues before we make a move." The deliberation of American managers (by no means the trigger-happy, dynamic gunslingers of fiction) can drive Britons to drink; conversely, the pace and devil-may-care dash of British invaders can make Americans' minds boggle (not always with admiration).

Irritation with slow progress and intervention with slow managers tend to go hand in hand. But the larger truth is that you can't build an Apricot, Inc., or any other kind of Inc., by remote control. The secret of the U.S. buildup that turned Hanson Trust from just another conglomerate into an international superstar was that Sir Gordon White moved himself body and soul to the United States. So, in an earlier generation, did Leslie Lazell in creating Beecham, Inc. Whether the chief executive is European or American or Japanese may be irrelevant. But if he isn't really chief, his executive work won't work.

A market that moves as fast as computers (and speeding-up is common to all naked markets) demands swift reaction, just as the man from Apricot said, but it also necessitates more, not less, of the researched information beloved by the company's departed American trio. After all, what happens next, not what's happening now, is what determines the fate of marketing ambitions like Apricot's plan to make its 0.16 percent blossom. For want of sitting and thinking, fools do sometimes rush in where angels fear to tread. That way, even in a 4S company, small can become very, very ugly.

7. THE ROUGH RIDE AT RALEIGH

Sometimes a company just can't seem to win. Raleigh was once the greatest name in bicycles around the world—a name that meant millions in the days when the bike was the universal form of personal transport. Come the car, and the royally rich days were bound to die eventually; in the late 1960s the world market halved. The writing was indelibly on the wall but Raleigh ignored it, largely because of a few years of miniboom, led by the United States.

After the oil crisis, the American bubble burst. Stuck with a gigantic sixty-four-acre main site, six smaller factories, more than that number of brand names, and a docile home market, Raleigh stopped innovating for four whole years and concentrated on churning out existing models, mainly for the Nigerians. It woke up from a 1979 strike to find imports pouring into the home market, export sales drying up, and its parent, the conglomerate Tube Investments, gagging on an unpalatable loss of $21 million.

New management was installed, five plants were closed, and six thousand models were cut down to one thousand. Still dissatisfied, the conglomerate bosses forced another change at Raleigh's top. The *new* new leadership decided to concentrate on the neglected innovation, to cut back on component manufacture, and to say all but good-bye to the little old United States. The Huffy Corporation took over the business of the Raleigh Cycle Company of America and Raleigh, with misplaced relief (at giving away the world's richest market), turned to a massive program of rejuvenation, including one of the most ambitious automation projects of the early 1980s.

That ambition also proved to be misplaced. The automation project, when (ostensibly) completed, refused to operate as planned. The entire plant became hopelessly entangled in one of the most infamous fiascos in factory history. Production came to a full stop, and Raleigh returned to grievous losses that once again placed its parent under heavy financial pressure.

Yet this wasn't a business that an entrepreneur would automatically shun. Bike riding has gained in popularity all over the affluent West. There had to be ways of making the market work, and Raleigh (with its kids' sporting bikes, for example) had found some. But Raleigh as a business didn't work.

In the transformation effort that crashed into the automation fiasco, the latest Raleigh supremo said, "We are now trying to pursue a well-thought-out strategy, one that will stand the test of time. Previous ones didn't." They didn't because the parent had no well-

79

thought-out strategy of its own for a subsidiary whose entrepreneurial needs in a consumer market were as distant from manufacturing steel tubes (TI's base business) as the Tour de France is from a ride through Central Park.

For effective entrepreneurial marketing the manager needs to know three critical things: when to start, when to stick—and when to stop. More often than not, that's what separates the entrepreneurial sheep from the managerial goats. Entrepreneurs know, sometimes by pure instinct, when opportunity has knocked. They also know when to stick it out during the dark hours, days, and years when labor is rewarded with nothing but losses. Finally, they know when to abandon a permanently losing cause. Such decisions usually come more easily to the entrepreneurial soul than to the manager—who, in any event, seldom has the freedom to make the entrepreneurial decision. In the Raleigh case, the entrepreneur might well have concluded that, despite the ecological and exercise boom, the bike business would never see glad confident morning again. He might have preferred to get out altogether.

But Raleigh's business still looked too big and too long-term to abandon, so the entrepreneur might well have kept the bikes, geared down to the scale of his markets, and pushed up those markets, as far away from the low-priced Far Eastern competition as possible. Then he would have bought or built around this base other businesses in which the competitive pressures were lighter and the growth prospects longer—with the sky the only limit on his horizons. But managers buried inside conglomerates, such as Raleigh's TI parent, seldom if ever get that freedom. They can't form the ultimate, optimum strategy. They can only implement tactics that they hope will bring them through into the bright sunlight beyond.

If they succeed, it is a triumph of man over machine—over the corporate engineering that tries, because it must, to make all the parts mesh into a whole. If the cogs and wheels are themselves well engineered, well managed, and financially well nourished in strong markets, the policy naturally works like a charm. The test comes, like all management tests, in adversity. And it is the business under pressure that, above all, can't afford to turn only when Father turns, especially if it was initially Father's fault that the child got into its fix.

8. HOW *INTRA*PRENEURING BECOMES *ENTRE*

Getting out from under Father's feet—that's the secret of the *intrapreneur,* the employee within a company who acts in an entrepreneurial manner and from whom blessings like new products, new markets, and new methods flow. The person who can produce things like Texas Instruments' Speak-n-Spell machine, the IBM Personal Computer, the Ford Mustang, and a worldwide engineering plastics business for General Electric is worth his or her weight in gold—and the book *Intrapreneuring* (1985) is an invaluable guide on how to find and mine that treasure.

Actually, the treasure should find itself, according to a list of ten "freedom factors" set out by author Gifford Pinchot III.

1. Self-selection: "Intrapreneurs appoint themselves to their role and receive the corporation's blessing for their self-appointed task. Despite this, some corporations foolishly try to appoint people to carry out an innovation."

Moral: Encourage the self-appointed intrapreneur.

2. It's important that there be no "handoffs." That means taking the innovation away from the people who started the ball rolling and handing it to somebody else.

Moral: Provide ways for the intrapreneur to stay with his or her own intraprise.

3. You're asking for trouble unless the doer makes the decisions. Pinchot writes: "Some organizations push decisions up through a multi-level approval process so the doers and the deciders never even meet" (especially common and especially deadly in large firms).

Moral: Let people do the job in their own way, and don't

81

constantly make them stop to explain their actions or seek permission.

4. You'll find it difficult to get a true intrapreneurial atmosphere going without corporate slack. That doesn't mean idleness, it means "discretionary resources to explore and develop new ideas. Some companies give employees the freedom to use a percentage of their time on projects of their own choosing, and set aside funds to explore new ideas when they occur."

Moral: Don't control resources so tightly that nothing is available for the new and unexpected. If you do, the result will be nothing new.

5. Make sure there's no jackpot philosophy: you won't hit the jackpot every time, and you shouldn't try. "Today's corporate culture favors a few well-studied, well-planned attempts" to do just that but it's better, suggests Pinchot, to have more ideas going, "with less careful and expensive preparation for each."

Moral: Develop ways to manage many small and experimental products and businesses.

6. As the above implies, you won't get far without tolerance of risk, failure, and mistakes. They're the sine qua non of innovation, even of successful innovation, which "generally begins with blunders and mistakes."

Moral: Set up your system so that it encourages risk taking and tolerates mistakes.

7. You need a special kind of money: *patient* money. Because it takes time to innovate, perhaps decades, you can't confine the process within the annual planning and budgeting rhythm of the company.

Moral: Be prepared to try something and stick with an experiment long enough to see if it works, even if that means a period of years and a succession of false starts.

8. Intrapreneurs can't get going without freedom from "turfiness"—people defending their own interests. "New ideas almost always cross the boundaries of existing patterns or organizations," and that makes people jealous. Their efforts to defend their turf will

block innovation, unless you have developed ways of unblocking it.

Moral: Do just that.

9. Evidence shows that cross-functional teams do the innovative job best, "small teams with full responsibility for developing an intraprise." According to Pinchot, they solve many of the basic problems of innovation. Some companies (all too many, in fact) resist the formation of functionally complete, autonomous teams.

Moral: Don't.

10. Remember that multiple options are as important for the intrapreneur as they are for the entrepreneur. The latter always has plenty of choices, but internal innovators are often told, for example, that "they must have their product made by a certain factory or sold by a specific sales force." Pinchot notes that "too often these groups lack motivation or are simply wrong for the job and a good idea dies an unnecessary death."

Moral: Don't force intrapreneurs in your company to face internal monopolies. Free them to use the resources of other divisions and outside vendors if they choose.

Of course, intrapreneuring is useless unless the ideas fit the market. Ask the following basic questions to find out if they do.

1. Is there a real customer need?

2. Can you get a price that gives you good margins?

3. Would customers believe in the product coming from your company?

4. Does the product or service proposed produce a clearly perceivable customer benefit that is significantly better than that offered by competing ways of satisfying the same basic need?

5. Is there a cost-effective way to get the message and the product to the customers?

The conclusion is obvious: you won't get intrapreneurial wonders without a deliberate effort to seek out people with an abundance of entrepreneurial abilities and also to encourage all executives to develop them. But you won't get an intrapreneur by placing an Organization Man in a new-product development unit. Actually, such units themselves show the Organization Man's mind at work. Taste-making innovation shouldn't be somebody else's job. It should be part and parcel of the work of any manager with profit responsibility. That way the entrepreneurial company blends with its intrapreneurial inhabitants to the benefit and profit of both.

9. THE BEAUTY OF THE BUYOUT

Segmentation has always been a sensible policy, and it has become downright mandatory in markets that have themselves become far more segmented. What BMW exploited so brilliantly, for example, was a mere segment of the car market—the sporty executive sedan, where the sedate models of Mercedes didn't compete. This was a market that Daimler-Benz had ignored and went on ignoring for years. By the same token, once BMW's bite into the overall executive car market had become too big for Daimler's comfort, the leader wisely produced a car positioned as far apart from its existing models as possible, without sacrificing the unique Mercedes attributes. In much the same way, once Apple's segmented bite into total computer sales had become too large for even IBM to stomach, the giant set up a segmented, concentrated group to develop its phenomenally successful counteroffensive.

At the opposite, regressive end of corporate life, the unwanted business, the lesson of the leveraged buyout is much the same. The bought-out business that floundered so miserably inside its parent that the latter wished to be shot of the misery, time and again flourishes when set free, in almost all cases in a segmented market on which its management can concentrate in the sure knowledge that it's a case of develop or die.

The financial legerdemain of the buyout formula is, of course, another powerful motivational factor. For instance, one ancient pottery came into the hands of three managers who put up $60,000 between them for the equity, while the investor who took the rest supplied $270,000 in loan capital (which provided the leverage). All they had to do was continue as they had begun (moving from the hands of the receiver to sales of $1.5 to $2.3 million and profits of $75,000 in the first year), and the equity-owning managers would be certain to clean up.

Such blessings don't come automatically. One of the new management's first acts was to cut the range of patterns from forty to only four. Business history records very few cases in which careful, rational scrutiny of a product range fails to come up with findings that the company is making and marketing too many products or variations, most of which make either no contribution or an actual loss. After analysis and abandonment of these noncontributors, the marketingwise company carefully defines the market sectors at which the remaining products will aim, devotes all its efforts to those sectors and those sectors alone, and builds up the business in each sector. The key words, for a small pottery no less than for a Mercedes or an IBM, are *segment, concentrate,* and *develop,* making a marvelous market acronym: *SCAD.*

10. SEGMENT, CONCENTRATE, AND DEVELOP

How do companies in Japan, the most hierarchical industrial society in the world, manage to escape the deadly hierarchical hand? How have the Japanese equivalents of Raleigh thrived where Western companies have wallowed? The answer is competition—of which the Western world does not have nearly enough. This was true even during the great oil price recession, when prices and profits came under severe pressure as the surviving manufacturers struggled to stay in the game. For price competition isn't the only element in competitiveness—not by any means. And the extent to which Western business is uncompetitive (or rather noncompetitive) can be seen in seemingly minor events, such as Canon's launch of two highly automatic, low-priced 35-mm cameras in 1982.

The significance of Canon's act goes beyond the direct onslaught on a snapshot market that Kodak was trying to tie up still tighter with its new disc system. The real lesson lies in the fact that this top-quality Japanese producer had extended its range downward, with innovative mass-market products, in the teeth of fierce, crowded competition at home. To test this truth, try counting the number of famous Japanese camera firms—you'll need both hands and all digits.

In the durable goods industries of the United States (or of Europe for that matter), two or three fingers are usually all you require. This difference is so striking in the markets where Japan has made its deepest inroads (think only of cars and stereos) as to question the whole galloping Western trend toward monopoly and oligopoly. McKinsey consultant Kenichi Ohmae is plainly right to attribute the competitive power of the Japanese outside Japan to this intense competitiveness inside.

The hustling and bustling seen in Japan are characteristic of all growth industries in their dynamic phase. The great car names that have long been amalgamated in the West were born in an atmosphere of just such cut and thrust. Today's amazing data processing market exhibits just the same effort and proliferation. True, many cooks can all keep alive and well more easily in kitchens that are busy and booming, but it's also true that the strenuous competitive endeavors themselves stimulate demand.

By the same token, the shrinkage of competitors and of competitive ranges in Western industry, and the concentration and reduction of innovative investment that have followed, must have contributed heavily to the prevailing sluggishness. Paradoxically, the antitrust laws that have played a part in keeping Japanese firms at each other's throats, instead of in each other's arms, were wished on the occupied nation by the postwar American military government. As with the single-industry union structure that the British similarly gave the West Germans, the occupiers wrought more wisely than they knew —and far more wisely than they have practiced themselves.

The law, however, is not the only reason that the Japanese invaders outnumber the Western defenders in so spectacular a fashion. Where British, American, German, and French industries have tended to amalgamate and concentrate, the Japanese have been fruitful and multiplied in ways that their cultural norms encourage but that those of the West hardly allow. Thus, even hi-fi aficionados can be forgiven for thinking that Aurex is a Toshiba brand name. Actually, Aurex is a separate part of the Toshiba empire, with a jealously guarded independence. In the same market, Aiwa is half-owned by Sony but is equally jealous and independent, and JVC, the videocassette recorder leader, is a 50 percent interest of the giant Matsushita —again, fierce in its autonomy. Other such cross-relationships abound in Japan. Where Western companies like to crush their domestic competition, the Japanese embrace it.

The result, for the investing company, is to foster a second source of technological and marketing ideas while sharing, as an investor, in its success. The half-child gets the financial backing it requires to develop technical ideas and spread them across world markets. The consumer gets a greater variety of choice. And the Japanese economy gets some protection against the emergence of the bloated, overcentralized, slow-moving giants that have held back progress so visibly in many Western industries. The typical UK or U.S. big (or even middling) company board demands 100 percent even of almost nothing. Far, far better, surely, to have only half of something truly great.

Whether or not the Japanese businessman thinks consciously that way, the subconscious forces run powerfully against true takeovers of any kind. That would mean subjecting the "spirits" of one company to those of another, something as unpleasing to the subjugator as to the victim. The corporate spirits, however, have no objection to beating the hell out of another company if the opportunity arises, which explains the courage and craft Japanese companies bring to attacking any market that seems attractive—even if it is occupied by so powerful a company as Xerox in copiers or Toyota in cars.

But when a Ricoh or a Canon takes deadly aim at Xerox, or a Honda (against the wish of the government agency MITI) decides to break into the car market, the managements are not so foolish as to attack across the board. Typically, they search for the mighty opposition's weak point, the neglected sector where it is vulnerable. To put the process more positively, the company looks for a niche, a segment, which it can profitably exploit.

Time and again, the Japanese have found this segment beneath the colossus (giving an extra dimension of meaning to the phrase "the soft underbelly of the giant"): cheaper and smaller copiers; cheaper and smaller cars; cheaper and smaller TVs. But whatever the actual products, the supersuccessful Japanese have nearly always followed the strategy of SCAD, which works as well for a tiny pottery firm as for a conglomerate giant.

11. THE THREE-RUNNER RULE

Heller's Rule of Markets states that most markets can support (profitably, that is) only one leader, one runner-up, and one specialist. With more, especially more nonspecialists, everybody may suffer —even Number One. But the overcrowding effect isn't inevitable for the leader. The mainframe computer market is a perfect illustration of the Three-Runner Rule: IBM first, Honeywell second, and the rest nowhere, with the specialist role (either in very large and powerful machines or, at the opposite extreme, small to tiny ones) filled at different times and in different circumstances by companies such as Control Data, Amdahl, DEC, Compaq, and Apple—and a host of powerful companies struggling to come in out of the cold.

Yet IBM maintained both its supremacy and its profitability by concentrated marketing management which, even when it missed an opportunity, never lacked the resources to remedy its error, however colossal. By never relaxing its grip, IBM made its main-line, mainframe competitors pay the entire price of overcrowding. They incurred huge losses even though, for a period of several years, the antitrust action brought by the U.S. Justice Department inhibited some, maybe a great deal, of the natural vigor that IBM would otherwise have shown.

Antitrust considerations certainly played a role in another illustration that the price of profitable leadership is eternal vigilance. For decades, the U.S. car market perfectly illustrated Heller's Rule: General Motors was first (by far); Ford, second (but also profitable); Chrysler, third and hopeless; and American Motors only viable in a profitable specialist niche (compact cars for a while, Jeeps before they too died). But the pattern was shattered by the rise of the import tide. Only import quotas on Japanese cars stopped them from driving Chrysler (even after the company's celebrated recovery) and possibly even Ford to the wall.

And what was GM doing all this time? The years of restraining its domestic market ambitions because of antitrust fears saw GM's labor costs rise far above that of non-U.S. competition, its productive efficiency drop far below, its models become uncompetitive, and its innovative ability become stunted. The result, when recession coincided with incompetence, was a massive earnings collapse to a mere .5 percent of sales in 1981—by a company with a dominant market share. Yet, as GM promptly showed with its massive $50 billion comeback drive, the resources required to defend profitable leadership were there all the time. They simply had not been properly deployed.

12. STRATEGIES OF MARKET POWER

In bad hands *strategy* is an excuse for too much turgid talk and too little decisive action. Marketing strategy ought to make all the difference between success and failure by stimulating action, as can be seen from the answers given in crisis by General Motors to the three critical questions that have to be answered by would-be strategists.

1. Should your business conserve resources and retrench, or increase its use of resources and expand its activities? (GM's answer: increase and expand.)

2. Should the strategic positioning of your company in relation to products, markets, and competitors be changed? (GM's answer: yes.)

3. Should the level of resources be changed? For example, should your company invest to improve substantially over the medium term the abilities of the production activity in areas such as productivity, quality, and delivery? Should it invest in seeking a substantial improvement in its labor relations over the medium term? (GM's answer: yes, yes, yes.)

These questions come from an article in *Management Today* by Brian Houlden, professor of business studies at Warwick University. Many managements cannot answer the above questions and, even if they could, wouldn't sufficiently understand the importance of some powerful related concepts, for instance, *strategic analysis* (that's the jargon for what is mostly simple common sense). For example, do you know who your main competitors are and how your *market power* relates to theirs? Even if you do, you're not finished with the concept of power. What about your relationship with your suppliers? Houlden tells the cautionary tale of a firm which in a recession drove down the prices of its two main suppliers, until one went out of business. The surviving supplier then really applied the screws.

90

After power, consider the *radius of competition.* Where is it coming from? In other words, how far away from home is your company trying to compete, and from how far away will competition be coming? If you're supplying components to the British car industry and you ignore the fact that all the major car firms, British and otherwise, are sourcing on either a European or a worldwide basis, you're going to be in deep trouble. As Houlden warns, the "unexpected" overseas competitor can usually be anticipated by anybody whose head isn't in the sand (or the clouds).

Another thing no company can afford to neglect is the division of markets into *segments,* meaning that different groups of customers have different needs—and that companies wanting to win have to adopt appropriately different strategies. You won't get this one right unless you can answer the following questions.

1. What is happening in the market and why?
2. What segments are developing or disappearing?
3. Which segments offer the potential for success in this company?
4. What are the keys to success in this sector—and how can resources be allocated and reallocated to point the company in the right direction?

The above concept, *keys to success,* is strategically vital. In some markets volume and price may be critical; in others the key could be product design, quality, workmanship, after-sales service, or all of them put together, or it could be something else again.

The other crucial matter is corporate direction; that determines whether the abovementioned issues truly transform the company's marketing stance, or lead nowhere:

1. Do the top executives really know what a business strategic issue is?
2. Do they as a group (for example, as a board or management committee) devote time to addressing strategic issues?

3. Do they have a sound conceptual basis for grappling with strategic issues?

4. Do they have sufficient awareness and appropriate sensors of the environment to bring up the strategic issues for consideration?

5. Do they know enough about their main competitors and really understand the keys to success in the areas in which they wish to compete?

6. Are they prepared to face the issues and, when necessary, decide how to change the business?

7. When planning to change strategic direction, will they draw up a suitable action program, including departmental strategies consistent with the overall change desired?

8. Do they have the motivation and ability to implement changes effectively and to verify that the intended results are obtained? If not, can they make the necessary adjustments?

As Houlden observes with self-evident truth, "Experience so far is that in some, mainly small, companies the answer to virtually every question is 'no.' With larger companies it is rare to find 'yes' as the answer to every question." Can you really stand back and honestly say "yes" for your company to all the questions in the checklist? If not, the honest course of action is perfectly plain: turn "no" to "yes"—right away.

As GM's experience shows, however, that's not the end of the story: only the beginning. The 4.7 percent loss of market share that GM suffered in 1986 (meaning an enormous $6.5 billion in sales) was the consequence of leaping ahead of Ford and Chrysler in long-term strategy (or trying to) while falling behind in the not-so-little matter of meeting current market wants. Producing a convincing strategy doesn't lessen the need for staying close to the customer—it intensifies that need, and always will.

To summarize some of the important points I've mentioned in Step Three:

1. Taste-making and sensing are a young person's game; so make sure young people can break though the bureaucracy.

2. Give the breakers-through the personal motivation to succeed—and the responsibility for achieving success.

3. Marketing strategies should be decided in the markets where they will be applied, and by, or with, those who will apply them.

4. Getting out of touch with the market is unforgivable, even in markets where technology sets the tempo: it's marketing that always calls the tune.

5. Don't try to make markets suit your convenience—they suit nobody's convenience but their own.

6. Faster-moving markets demand swifter reactions—but more deliberate and thorough research than ever.

7. For effective entrepreneurial marketing, you need to know three critical things: when to start, when to stick—and when to stop.

8. Pacesetting innovation should be part and parcel of the work of any manager with profit responsibility.

9. Segmentation, always sensible, has become downright mandatory in markets that have become far more segmented.

10. Competition itself, between and within companies, is the most effective means of stimulating competitive prowess.

11. Most markets can support only three profitable firms: one leader, one runner-up, and one specialist.

12. Producing a convincing strategy doesn't lessen the need for staying close to the customer—it intensifies that need.

Step Four: Managing Markets
for Maximum Return

1. THE MAN WHO MISSED *NOW!*

Publishers are particularly prone to the notion that better quality, in and of itself, generates commercial success. Aside from the fact that quality in a magazine or newspaper is subjective, an unmeasurable effect in the eye of the beholder, a major misapprehension about markets is involved. Producing a superior competitor to *Vogue* might not be impossible, but the time and cost that would be involved in overtaking *Vogue*'s sales and attracting its advertisers while simultaneously financing superior quality would be real obstacles.

Even if *Vogue* obligingly did nothing to improve its own quality, the cost of competition would almost certainly be far too high to justify the venture financially. In other words, higher quality is the sine qua non of competition in this context, but it's not the factor that actually determines success. This truth emerged starkly from the dismal story of a magazine called *Now!*, a foolhardy attempt to mimic the success of *Time* in Britain. Its owner, Sir James Goldsmith, shortly to become an outsize U.S. corporate raider, remarked rightly over the corpse that consumer products often fail, but he omitted to add that these failures mostly follow from incorrect assessments of the market.

The crucial point for *Now!* was whether it could attract enough readers of high enough incomes to justify the purchase of advertising space at what were high rates, by the standards of the color supplements of quality Sunday newspapers. In their ideas of what kind of circulation would achieve the desired result, the *Now!* promoters were misled by the seeming modesty of a target like a quarter of a million copies—peanuts by the standard of London's evening newspaper. They overlooked the crucial question that faces any marketer: how to reach the magic numbers.

The only sure way available was TV advertising. For Goldsmith's purposes, though, TV had the well-known defect of delivering far too diluted an audience (all TV, not just the commercial variety, has a low socioeconomic profile) at far too great a cost. *Now!* could indeed have been established by sustained exposure on TV but the expense would have made the $18 million that Goldsmith actually did lose pretax (on turnover that may not have exceeded $15 million) look like starters.

A press campaign could have been more precisely targeted but would have been most unlikely to deliver the required total response, a point that applies very strongly to the third possible course, direct mail. Even with a 2 percent response rate, the mailing operation required to obtain 100,000 subscribers would have been of overwhelmingly daunting proportions—and apparently it was the failure of the final direct mail foray (launched on the strength of a 1.6 percent test response) that hammered the final nail into the *Now!* coffin. The so-called rollout as the rest of the mailing followed is said to have produced only half the test result.

All this elementary analysis could, of course, have been carried out before the baby was conceived. But no doubt its progenitors fell back on the age-old hope that the shining virtues of the product itself would suck in the demand required. That hope is the marketing equivalent of three morbid letters: *RIP.*

2. FOUR QUESTIONS OF QUALITY

No matter how wonderful a product seems, not only to you, but to other people, four penetrating questions always have to be answered in the affirmative before a company can hope to have a success, and not a mere *succès d'estime,* on its hands:

1. Is it the right product, or is there something wrong with it?
2. Are you taking it to the right market, or is there a better way to distribute it?
3. Is the timing right—or off?
4. Is advertising or its equivalent needed to prime the pump?

These questions are adapted from a real-life catechism: the questions asked by one Matt Sanders before he decided to kill a product, his own baby, called the Workslate. The case may be the most intriguing in Gifford Pinchot III's book *Intrapreneuring,* because the lessons of failure should always teach more than those of success. The first Workslate lesson is the one mentioned earlier: a rave reception teaches you nothing except that you've had a rave reception. The Workslate's could hardly have been better.

When finally done the Workslate, a powerful small computer the size of a piece of letter paper and one-inch thick, was enthusiastically greeted. It appeared on the covers of three major computer magazines, was featured in the American Express Christmas catalogue and was touted in a mailing sent to a million of E. F. Hutton's clients. A major computer retailing chain was so impressed, they forecast that they would buy everything Matt's team could make. . . . As they raced to get the capacity ready to meet this burgeoning demand, Matt's team was euphoric. The experts loved their product. Based on this response, Matt's team planned to sell 100,000 units in the first year, a retail value of $90 million. But the experts were wrong.

Experts often are, but that isn't the major moral. Part of the explanation lies in the first phrase of the quotation: "When finally done." The project ran into production difficulties that Sanders hadn't expected, being unused to high-volume production, as was his company, Convergent Technologies, which made an excellent living by manufacturing work stations for large computer suppliers.

The disasters—which included a shipment of components going to Italy instead of California, and a 747 airliner breaking down with vitally needed equipment on board—taught Sanders that "you need direction certainly. You need excellent planning and scheduling. But you also have to be prepared for and supportive of disorder." All true, no doubt, but again not the whole or even the most important lesson. The fact that the factory was about a month behind the production schedule, making it late for the "Christmas window" (getting it into distribution in time for the seasonal rush), wasn't good. But that was far from the worst of it.

"As the orders trickled in behind schedule, it occurred to Matt that something was wrong. For some reason, the customers weren't buying Workslate. With the help of experts, the team had grossly underestimated the missionary selling needed to launch a new computer product. They went through the normal phases of letting go of a dream: confusion, hurt and acceptance"—to which should be added learning. In Sanders's own view, the most important lesson to be drawn from this $15 million disaster is that you must treat failure as a learning experience, not simply by listing your errors and resolving not to repeat them but using them as a stepping-stone to bigger and (you hope) better things.

For that lesson to be effective, however, the failure must be fully and fairly analyzed. It's not often that you see a business story from the two sides that always give a better picture of the truth. But one man who spent six days negotiating (abortively) to buy the Workslate assets learned some interesting things about its failure, things that add a new dimension to the Pinchot account.

First, "the price of the product to the consumer kept changing almost weekly—first $900, then $1,300: when that knocked the enthusiasm of people to buy, it was lowered to $1,100, and so on. The accountants going through the books were the ones responsible for the price hikes. Quite rightly, they discovered that even at optimistic production runs the price of $900 was too low. However, the managers would not cut costs." Apart from other excessive expenses, claims this informant, "they had 50 engineers on R & D."

The killer, though, was that "they used a totally new sales force to go to the consumer and ignored their old sales network of business sales teams and connections. We believed and still do that the product was not a consumer item. While the Christmas rush window might have helped, it was not an ordinary personal computer. If they had stayed with their business connections and distributors, sales, I believe, would have been steady and large." Maybe Sanders and his cohorts would argue with that. But there can't be much arguing with this informant's answers to the four questions posed earlier.

1. *Was it the right machine, or was something wrong with their offering?* It was the right machine.
2. *Were they taking it to the right market, or was there a better way to distribute it?* They took it to the wrong market and distributors.
3. *Was the timing off?* Irrelevant.
4. *Did they need to advertise it to prime the pump?* They needed to advertise and inform the business community vigorously.

Just like Sir James Goldsmith, the Workslate team believed deep in their hearts that the excellence of the product would sell itself. On very rare occasions that may be true. Even companies with good reason to suppose that they have found the crock of gold, though, have even better reason to ask themselves the four questions —and to make absolutely sure they get four right answers.

3. THE KEY TO CHRYSLER

The resurrection of the Chrysler Corporation under Lee Iacocca seems to prove against all the odds and most of the experience that crippled giants can take up their beds and walk. In 1983 Chrysler actually made a profit, repaid a mountain of debt famously early, and again became a serious contender in U.S. markets, with a range of models built around the basic "K" car cleverly enough to compete effectively with Ford and GM. Indeed, in 1985, with profits pouring in, Chrysler was the only one of the three to raise its market share.

True, there were special factors in Chrysler's case. A reluctant Washington guaranteed loans without which the company, down to its very last million on one horrendous day, would have failed. Chrysler was also greatly helped in its comeback by the fact that Japanese competitors were fighting with one arm tied behind their backs by not very voluntary quotas. Otherwise Chrysler was largely on its own. Iacocca didn't have to bargain with politicians for further blood transfusions or worry about the political repercussions of his drastic actions—halving the workforce; cutting the salaries by $1.3 billion; closing sixteen plants (not to mention executing horrible foreign investments, like those in Britain).

The combined effect of this ruthless operation was an amazing drop in the breakeven point, down by about half to 1.2 million cars a year. But a lower breakeven is little use unless you can move beyond it, and the key to Chrysler was that favorable verdict of the market. In the first place, had U.S. car buyers turned thumbs down on its price, performance, and perception package, the man in the White House would doubtless have done likewise. Troubled companies, great or small, can come back, but only if the customer says so.

Turn to a crippled giant that didn't walk, the state-controlled BL, and consider one of the few successes it inherited from the past. The Land Rover, one of the most successful models ever to emerge from a British car factory, was also one of the rare examples of a high-quality product (the superior Jeep) good enough and unique enough to create its own market. For decades the Land Rover had that four-wheel, off-road market virtually to itself.

In 1983 it was given its first major revamp in thirty-five years. Why? Because the four-wheel pioneer had been run ragged by competition from Japan, exploiting weaknesses only to be expected from a product launched in 1948. Yet even that isn't the greatest tragedy —to quote the *Financial Times:* "Land Rover has still to tap the potential in North America where, until now, it has not sold any of its products." That's less an opportunity than an indictment.

The British had never mastered the marketing lessons that Iacocca had learned at his first sales boss's knee, and that the pupil-turned-master describes eloquently in his account of the birth of the Mustang in his 1984 book, *Iacocca.* Where the Land Rover had even started in the wrong place, with the product, the Mustang began with the market, according to its father's account:

> Our public relations department was receiving a steady stream of letters from people who wanted us to bring out another two-passenger Thunderbird. . . . At the same time, our market researchers confirmed that the youthful image of the new decade had a firm basis in reality. . . . Not only would there be *more* young people than ever before, but they would also be better educated than previous generations. . . . There were equally interesting changes going on among older car buyers. . . . When we analyzed all this information, the conclusion was inescapable. Whereas the Edsel had been a car in search of a market it never found, *here was a market in search of a car.*

Instead of the usual Detroit procedure, "to build a car and then try to identify its buyers" (the Land Rover routine), the Mustang makers were able to "tailor a new product for a hungry new market." The tailors succeeded by making the market powerfully aware of its hunger and then satisfying that appetite with an abundant supply of a product with three potent selling propositions: "great styling, strong performance, and a low price." For as long as Ford followed the sage advice of Polonius, "to thine own self be true," the Mustang miracle continued. Note, however, what happened when Ford forgot the rules of its own success:

> By 1971, the Mustang had grown eight inches longer, six inches wider, and almost six hundred pounds heavier than the original 1965 model. It was no longer the same car, and our declining sales figures were making the point very clearly. In 1966, we sold 550,000 Mustangs. By 1970, sales had plummeted to 150,000—a disastrous decline. Our customers had abandoned us because we had abandoned their car.

The falling production of Land Rover while the Japanese were stealing half of an expanding market with cheaper, more up-to-date models in better supply made exactly the same point: the market is unforgiving to those who forget it.

4. SECOND-BEST IS WORSE

The fact that it wasn't the quality of the product but the quality of the marketing that let the Land Rover down flies in the face of the new conventional wisdom about quality. For example, a survey by market researchers KAE in 1984 portrayed a great shift in attitudes among surveyed food merchants, who gave their main reasons for the success of the hits and, likewise, the failures of the also-limped. The new champ was "good–excellent product quality," as opposed to the old winner, "consumer demand/satisfaction."

At IBM, which knows whereof it speaks in these matters, quality is actually defined as meeting customer requirements in full. If the argument is that marketing computers, even personal ones, differs from selling packaged foods, that still leaves a big question: What use is a high-quality product for which there is no consumer demand? Clearly quality, though (again) the sine qua non, was not the factor that propelled the top food launches of recent years. The positive marketing value of quality can come into play (and powerful play at that) only when other offerings are perceived as inferior.

In the food trade, that play is far more difficult to achieve than in durable goods. There the problem is often negative quality—poor Lancia in Britain took a long time to dispel the idea that its cars rust in the first rainfall, while Ford in the United States emphasized quality in its ads, not to jump ahead of the Japanese but to stress that it no longer lagged behind. As IBM's former chairman John R. Opel pointed out to his troops, if the quality isn't good enough, customers will buy where it's better.

Yet the KAE quality findings are too conspicuous to be ignored. In 1980 quality got 62 percent in the "main reasons for success" score. It had climbed to 76 percent by 1984, heading toward double the downgraded figure for consumer demand/satisfaction. Perhaps these numbers should be treated with a pinch of packaged salt: Did the surveyed merchants really believe that distinct product advantage, competitive price, and continued advertising support are significantly less important success factors than quality?

If so, they are wrong. The positioning of a product in the market, both in differentiation and price, is what determines success —and you won't get that without strong and continuous advertising, either. This, of course, is a fundamental point. What the surveyed merchants were really doing was catching the spirit of the times; in saturated, highly competitive markets, consumers with large spending power will not be fobbed off with second-best. For new products, which have other steep hills to climb, second-best is the surest route to dying in the cold. But that means second-best not just in quality but in everything else in the mix of marketing.

Second-best marketing misunderstands quality, for starters.

The litany might run something like this: "Quality may be critical in markets such as pacemakers and automobiles, but we have industry standards that have to be met or we don't sell anything. Once we've met those standards, though, customers buy only on price. So we can't afford to invest in quality, because we can't get it back in price." That quote, put in the mouth of a second-best marketer by strategic consultant John Guineven, misses the main point about quality: it is the customer's *perception* of quality that counts, and nothing else.

How does a customer decide whether a particular offering represents good or poor quality, high or low price? asks Guineven —and answers that "He makes that assessment on the basis of comparison; is this offering better or worse than those of competitors? At how much higher or lower a price?" You don't have to look further than IBM and its belated entry into the personal-computer market to see that what tilts the customer toward a product may be simple confidence in the supplier—nothing much to do with R & D and processing power, as the expert notes, but everything to do with perceived relative value.

First-rate marketers make deliberate decisions about where to aim along the quality/value spectrum. Average value, they know, can mean offering comparable quality at a comparable price, good quality at a premium, or inferior quality at a discount. The object is to break out from the average. Relative value can change, notes Guineven, for any one of three reasons: you change what you're doing (you boost quality); customers' needs or preferences change (that's why you need good and frequent market research, to take quick advantage of the changes); or, finally, competitors change what they are doing.

"The notion that quality and value depend on what competitors are doing is alien to most managers. Yet it is the essence of the competitive use of value, and it is an area where businesses frequently get into competitive difficulty." It's also the area where you can find gold. Self-evidently, the most profitable end of the market must be the premium end: that's where you can end up with the highest

103

profitability even if you are offering only average value. But you will do almost as well financially by becoming a high-value business—that is, if the quality is higher but the prices aren't. The consequence is that you will have "a strong tendency to gain" market share.

There you have in a nutshell the Japanese strategy for penetrating Western markets. Suppliers who follow the Japanese line sacrifice price, but "what is lost in price . . . they make up in lower costs" from their larger sales. With any other policy (high price, high quality; average quality, average price; low quality, low price) market share will either rise slightly (the first) or remain static (the other two). So who loses out to the high value business? The low value one, of course, which offers its low quality at a high price.

There couldn't be a clearer demonstration of why second-best is worst. As Guineven, who works for the Strategic Planning Institute, pointed out in *Management Today,* the harder it is to achieve higher perceived quality in a market, the more important it is to strive for that edge. "Because relative value is such a devastating competitive weapon, it is in these markets that relative quality is most potent." Quite simply, best is best.

5. THE SPARK THAT FAILED

All markets are finite, even for the fortunate firm that achieves transcendent superiority in perceived value. Sooner or later dynamic growth comes to an end, replacement sales come to dominate demand, and, depending on the degree of competition, profitability comes under pressure ranging from the excruciating to the infuriating. These days fate may even pass its stern decree with an innovation —maybe especially with one, if Konosuke Matsushita, that greatest of Japanese corporate architects, is to be believed.

In the eighties (his own and the century's), Matsushita said this: "An innovation ought to be good for two or three years:

today, the same day you put a new product on the market, it's out-of-date. We are so over-eager to compete that we spoil a new product by coming out with an even newer one." The truth of that observation raises a cruel paradox for anybody who (rightly) urges Western industry to innovate with new products and processes and to invest in the very latest equipment as the only way to combat the fiendish Orientals and to stay viable in the macho competitive markets that lie ahead.

What's the use, after all, if the result is merely to innovate the product, and maybe the whole company, into obsolescence? The experience of a company called Agemaspark is enough to chill the innovative to the marrow. Agemaspark's light went out even though its baubles—electro-discharge spark eroders—were in the front line of machine shop technology and initially sold well.

The basic trouble with the eroders was erosion of their market. Turnover all but halved in a couple of years, making it small wonder that the loss rose to 56 percent of sales. High technology is not, like virtue, its own reward—and the company's marketing base (let alone its financial one) was simply too narrow to survive recession and also support development.

Obviously innovations, like anything else in marketing, have to pass stiff tests of viability before they justify commitment of funds. The same can be true even of internal innovations, which won't be directly damaged by adverse competition or market conditions—but will be indirectly involved up to the neck. Take the case of the highly automated car plant that once had to make cutbacks in its labor force because of "overproduction"—another word for Agemaspark's problem of underselling.

Emulating the robotic brooms of the Sorcerer's Apprentice, the highly automated line had simply been churning out more cars than the market could take. The single model produced had settled down as a reasonable but not a resounding success—a market share of 6.5 percent compared with the leader's 11 percent—while the new variants on the way were bound to run into even more intense competition. None of this meant that it had been wrong to launch the car or to invest so heavily in automated production. On the contrary, the received view is perfectly justified—without such innovations in product and production, any company's plight would obviously be far more parlous. The tragedy in this case was that the costs of investment had to be spread over too low a mass-market volume because of general erosion of one-time market strengths.

The erosions of Agemaspark, although very different in origin, have a similar explanation. The high-tech niche is the right target for a skilled engineering firm, but the high status of its technology doesn't spare it from the low-down viability tests of low-tech marketing. It has to be the right firm with the right product at the right time —a truism that becomes an insight only because so many companies ignore its self-evident prescriptions.

Agemaspark couldn't adjust to shifts in the market because it had only the one highly specific product; the car company couldn't either, because its line could produce only one highly specific car. Flexibility is the key to adaptability, and the latter is what opens the door to the highest profits in markets that are changing, in tastes and technology, as rapidly as today's. Despite these absolute imperatives of the market, many companies go down for the third time by failing to observe the truths of that tune-calling market—not because the external truths are hard to discover, but because the internal obstacles to truth are too hard to overcome.

6. FIGHTING THE INTERNAL FOE

Most failed firms have one thing in common: they were not defeated by external competition but by the enemy within. Regis McKenna, the public relations guru of Silicon Valley, identifies that internal enemy as the most dangerous competition of all. This formidable foe, he explains in his book *The Regis Touch,* makes its appearance in ten fearsome formats:

1. Change
2. Resistance to change
3. Public knowledge about the product
4. The customer's mind
5. The commodity mentality
6. The bigness mentality
7. Broken chains
8. The product concept
9. Things that go bump in the night
10. Yourself

Why is the first point, change, a self-induced competitor? Because from the moment you enter a market, or launch a product or service, you are building in the need to respond to the inevitable changes that are likely to come thick and fast—or at least thicker and faster than in the supposedly good old days. How do you cope with this competitor?

First, says McKenna, constantly question your assumptions. Ask yourself: (a) What am I assuming about the market? (b) What am I assuming about the competition? (c) What things must happen to make my assumptions valid? (d) Under what conditions are my assumptions no longer valid?

Second, there's only one place to keep your ears: on the ground. "Monitor the market, live with it, work with it . . . work with customers and listen to them . . . meet with dealers and listen to them . . . really listen."

Without question, number 2, resistance to change (spotting it when it occurs, but failing to react), is as damaging as is being oblivious—and even more stupid. Sometimes the explanation for the stupidity is bureaucracy, sometimes just fear of the new, mostly that "people tend to get wedded to ideas. They look towards the past, rather than towards the future." The remedy? Don't let your fixed plant become a source of fixed ideas. Often the "factory becomes the central focus of the company. The company begins to worry more about manufacturing and less about serving the needs of the market."

As for number 3, public knowledge, McKenna points out that "an uninformed customer is easily satisfied. But there aren't many uninformed customers around these days." What you must do is "turn this increasing knowledge . . . from an obstacle into an asset . . . elicit feedback from customers, then adjust products and strategies to meet the market needs." That's basic business sense, and it should not be ignored.

Don't forget, either, the crucial importance of winning the battle for number 4, the customer's mind. "When a customer considers buying a product, the decision-making process is neither simple nor rational. All types of fears, doubts, and other psychological factors come into play." You've got to tackle and defeat "psychological bogeymen."

What might customers be worrying about? Bogeys such as those that bedeviled many ambitious personal computer efforts: (a) Is the company going to be around for a long time? (b) Am I going to be able to get product support after the purchase? (c) Will the supplier be able to supply future generations of products? (d) Will I be technologically behind if I buy this company's products now, rather than waiting for something better from another company?

The questions will vary from business to business. But you still have to look for, find, and use the "comfort factors" that stop a customer from worrying—about you and about what you're selling. That won't be easy if you're stuck with the commodity mentality, number 5 in the list. "By churning out the same product time after time . . . as volume increases, manufacturers move down the so-called learning curve, and their costs drop lower and lower"—which can be deadly in marketing. "Customers usually prefer custom-made, just-for-me products. They want their needs satisfied exactly." The key is to stop looking at your product as a product, and to see it as a problem solver. Then sell it (as great salesmen have always known) on that basis, to solve problems.

The bigness mentality, foe number 6, can afflict quite small companies, which is ridiculous. Ask whether decisions are being made by committees rather than individuals. Is the company splitting up into compartments that don't interrelate? In good small companies, writes McKenna, "people in engineering, marketing and sales talk regularly and exchange ideas. This is vital to creativity and innovation."

Most businesses have never thought about number 7, broken chains. But consider the product-customer chain, which "connects everything in the product development and marketing process. It starts with the design and planning of the product. Other links include product development, manufacturing, marketing, sales, distribution, product support and service. The final link is the customer." Because a chain is only as strong as its weakest link, the lesson is obvious. You must pay attention to every single link in the chain.

The product concept, number 8, can be either broad (right) or, as with Agemaspark, narrow (very wrong). "A company with a narrow product concept will move through the market with blinkers on and is sure to run into trouble." Look around for indirect or future competitors—for instance, TV sets will become competitors for personal computers as TV makers build in computing facilities (easily done).

Number 9, things that go bump in the night, are the unanticipated events that take even the best companies by surprise. All you can do is "stay humble, expect the unexpected and react quickly when the unexpected occurs."

Regis McKenna's final word concerns the tenth enemy, yourself. Three DON'Ts and one DO always apply.

DON'T underestimate your own ideas—or the competition's.
DON'T believe in your omnipotence—or the competition's.
DON'T become unwilling to listen, change, experiment.
DO pay attention to the market, listen and respond to it.

That solitary DO in McKenna's list makes his sermon worth his weight in gold.

109

7. THE TROUBLE IN TOYLAND

When calamity strikes hard and often in the same industry, it's tempting to argue that individual managements can't fairly be blamed. Take toys and games: anybody looking from afar at the awful episodes this industry has suffered worldwide must wonder how the managers themselves could be totally at fault. First Marx, then its British purchasers Dunbee-Combex-Marx, then Mattel, then Atari, then Coleco: the line is alarmingly long. But closer examination shows the catastrophes of each company to be of different orders. The vagaries of the toys and games market were certainly a factor in the downfalls but were by no means the only reason for the mayhem.

Market slumps, anyway, are no excuse. Marketers customarily preen themselves, and expect to be preened by others, when riding a boom. By the same token, they deserve some of the blame when the market turns against them. More often than not, their own policies exacerbate the damage. Riding high (not unnaturally) takes their feet off the ground, and they gallop full tilt into ambitious plans that look splendid in the dazzling light of the boom, but fade rapidly with falling figures. Pride goeth before the falls: the bosses of Dunbee-Combex-Marx used to boast, before their collapse, about the wonders that their English management of Marx had demonstrated to the incompetent U.S. toy industry—but it was their American failure with the ever-luckless Marx business that brought DCM tumbling down.

The wise marketer never forgets that, apart from Japan, the United States is the toughest competitive nut. You crack it this year, only to find that yesterday's triumph is today's disaster. In toys, dominated and doomed by fashion, that's a general truth. In such fickle markets, guessing right consistently is well-nigh impossible. The marketer must take the fashion element out of his product range (no easy task), or diversify away from the fickleness, or maintain an Olympic fleetness of foot.

The strategies aren't easy, but they're not impossible, either. For

110

example, the Quaker Oats subsidiary Fisher-Price, the Lego business (which is Danish), and even Britain's, the little old English toy soldiers firm, have fought through thick trading conditions and thin by creating ranges with secure niches in long-running market segments, making them indispensable to the retailers. By constantly adding new products to the range, often by exemplary innovation, these marathon runners can catch the latest toy trends and win over the short sprints, too. Were they to slip from these exacting standards, though, the result might emulate the rake's progress of Lesney, the Matchbox toy car company.

The record of Lesney's bank indebtedness, rounded off in millions of pounds, over four years was 4, 8, 23, and 46 (against a turnover of 107). If only its customers had been as enthusiastic as its bankers.... With numbers like these, the harsh conclusion is inevitable. Sure, the markets failed the firm, but so did the management. Like Mattel, its arch-rival in die-cast model cars, Lesney had originally been seduced by its own supergrowth, and was then doubly seduced by its triumphant comeback from previous disaster, advancing too boldly from recovery into its final, fatal phase.

The midget motors haven't proved capable of providing the secure, expandable base for successful extension of, say, a Lego. Lesney found itself making a commodity product in a fashion market —a deadly combination. Lesney's efforts to diversify out of this dilemma were less ambitious but in a way even less successful than Mattel's: at least the latter's leap into electronic toys paid off handsomely before video games took the company into the fire of home computers (the very market in which Atari and Coleco got scorched). This violently buffeted market is one in which toy firms are maybe the least likely to succeed. The new market's boundaries hemmed in the company in their turn. Mattel had jumped out of the low-tech frying pan into the high-tech fire.

The variegated failures in toys shared a common explanation that had nothing to do with the fickleness of either fashion or fate. By their nature these markets don't generate giants: the successes grow at best to middling size. Less than gigantic scale doesn't make eventual extinction inevitable, but it does demand especially hard and dedicated application of the basics of marketing success. Again, by its very nature, the toys and games market generates smash hits —such as Coleco's Cabbage Patch Kids. And boom time is precisely the moment when managers are most likely to take their eyes off the ball, the market, and the rules of entrepreneurial success.

8. EIGHT ENTREPRENEURIAL TRUTHS

The failed toymakers were entrepreneurial, all right. But each failed in turn to become an "entrepreneurial corporation"—a company controlled by managers who "know how to anticipate innovation and how to make innovation commercially effective," in the words of Peter Drucker. That's the kind of company whose sales and profits can increase, say, by an average 15 percent compound, doubling its business every seven years, a feat few firms have managed even with the benefit of inflation, let alone without it. Yet 15 percent is the noble standard set by the hundred-odd companies that form the American Business Conference (ABC). Collectively they became the springboard for some blockbuster research into what makes successful companies succeed.

This study concentrated on "mid-size" firms like those in the ABC: mid-size, but far from middling—they weigh in from $125 million to $1 billion worth of sales (the 1971 figure in 1982 dollars). The lessons drawn from this sample by McKinsey men Donald K. Clifford, Jr., and Richard E. Cavanagh in their book, *The Winning Performance* (1985), are universal, and they all revolve around entrepreneurial innovation. That doesn't necessarily mean microchips or anything else highly technical. Indeed, that is the author's Lesson One: Look for innovation in everything—not just in technology.

As they point out, even technological wonders work only if they satisfy real needs—thus Frank Perdue's "ovenstuffer roaster" apparently resulted from the new marvels of mass poultry farming. But that made sense only in the context of turning the commodity chicken into a "value-differentiated product"—that is, people were prepared to pay more for Perdue's poultry because they thought it better. At Lenox China the old idea of the wedding list became a brilliant new marketing tool—no technology there at all.

Lesson Two: Shun bureaucracy and forgive mistakes. The authors found a couple of high-tech firms that deliberately used small teams and individuals to avoid the bureaucratic intrusion of policies, procedures, systems, and structures that gets in the way of innovation. As for mistakes, at the long-distance telephone company MCI, chief executive Bill McGowan has this credo: "Don't forget, we make a lot of mistakes around this place. Have from the beginning. But so long as somebody doesn't keep making the same mistake over and over again, we can live with it and recover." That's the crux. Never forgive the same mistake twice. It will only happen a third time.

Lesson Three: Treat customers and distributors as welcome partners in innovation. Dunkin' Donuts, the smash-hit fast-food chain, has harvested a crop of good new ideas from its franchisees. One in Springfield, Massachusetts, for instance, gave birth to the "munchkin" doughnut hole. That may not rank among the great technological breakthroughs of the late twentieth century but it is certainly true that people out there in the market are likely to be the most valuable source of new ideas. As most companies don't exploit that source, it has still greater added value for those who do.

Lesson Four: Value creativity highly and promote it effectively. The authors say that anybody can develop business creativity. Some of their suggestions are: (a) Think by analogy. Ask yourself what works in other businesses or in any other context that might also work for you. That's how Perdue thought up the idea of guaranteeing his chickens—just like dishwashers. (b) Use contrary or opposite thinking. Since MCI has a huge competitor, the Bell system, everybody in the company was asked to think about things the opposite way to Bell. MCI's boss learned this approach from his days as a turnaround king. His recipe for distressed companies was contrariness: "If the sales force was on commission, McGowan put them on salary; if a clerical process was automated, McGowan made it manual: and *vice versa.*" MCI even made its law department a profit center—and allegedly it pays off. (c) Seek new customers for old products. Drucker has an excellent example: only a fool would sell refrigerators to Eskimos to keep food cold; a genius, though, would sell them fridges to stop food from freezing. (d) Create new markets instead of trying to serve old ones. The possibilities are infinite— Charter Medical has even succeeded in building up a nationwide chain offering psychiatric care.

Lesson Five: Decide what needs to be tightly controlled and what doesn't. Try to control absolutely everything, and you'll end up with an overtight, rigid bureaucracy, which is exactly what you're trying to avoid. Yet with Perdue's key control factor, quality, he sets no less than sixty-seven standards. At the furniture firm of Levitz, daily store stock levels get similarly obsessive attention. The key control factor in every firm should likewise be identified, watched— and obeyed.

Lesson Six: Don't set things up so that one condition makes another impossible. Don't, for example, tell managers to get close to the customer and then impose a freeze on travel budgets; or decentralize into fashionably small business units, each built around its market and each with an accountable boss, without putting in an accounting system that can report on each of the units.

Lesson Seven: The chief executive should follow three key practices: (a) wholehearted commitment to the business, almost (but not quite) to the point of obsession; (b) building on that near-obsession by creating "pervasive corporate values," a company culture that reflects the boss's personal drive; (c) development of perspective— both the spot vision that seizes opportunities and the long-range view that tells, for example, when it's time to change the chief executive's role; like the German genius who built the great engineering group of Mannesmann and deliberately, by developing time-consuming hobbies, reduced his workday to four or five hours. That was a prelude to bowing out entirely in favor of the successors who (Lesson

Eight) had been developed more as their boss's workload grew less.

The true entrepreneurial corporation will survive not just the boom-and-bust cycles that bust the toymakers but the fading of its founding father—and that of his successors. Learning and applying the Eight Entrepreneurial Truths make that survival much more likely. Anything less is toying with the company—and with fate.

9. THE SOFT TOUCH AT BAUSCH & LOMB

Three companies that used the same business tool in three different ways had three different experiences. Two succeeded and one failed. The first, operating from a single plant and investing in automation, computerized design, and expansion of capacity, pushed its market share up from 55 percent in 1980 to 65 percent in 1983. Its gross margins widened 20 to 30 percentage points above those of its competitors.

The second company had mastered an extremely difficult manufacturing process. Because there were material changes in operating characteristics and product quality in scaling up from pilot plants, there was only one way of approaching this market leader's costs— to operate a plant of significant size over several years. But Company Two kept expanding its capacity ahead of demand. Nobody dared to crack its process monopoly.

The third company, fixing prices for a make-or-break new product, assumed that the identical business tool that had worked so well for Companies One and Two would have the typical beneficial (and in this case, vital) effects. It didn't. The resultant losses drove the company into the arms of another.

The three companies and their products are Bausch & Lomb, with soft contact lenses; du Pont, with titanium dioxide made by the ilmenite chloride process; and Douglas Aircraft, now part of McDonnell-Douglas, with the DC-9 airliner. All three examples come from an excellent article in the *Harvard Business Review* by Pankaj Ghamaway about the business tool in question—an economic verity whose workings can make the difference between market loss and market domination: the experience curve.

10. LEARNING FROM CURVES

The magic of the experience curve is described succinctly by Pankaj Ghamaway:

> Use of the experience curve concept began over three decades ago to describe the mathematical relation between the cumulated output of a product and its costs. Literally thousands of studies have shown that production costs usually decline by 10 percent to 30 percent with each doubling of cumulated output. For example, if the thousandth unit of a production costs $100, the two-thousandth unit will normally cost $70 to $90.

This idea sounds wonderfully simple. Get the highest share of an industry's cumulated output and you will also be the low-cost producer, won't you? You may even be advised that your best route to a cost advantage lies through cutting price to buy market share. The increased share of current output is supposed to propel the aggressive business's costs down the experience curve more rapidly than its rivals', thus improving its relative position.

But it isn't that simple, as some companies found when they assumed, as a routine matter, that they had typical experience curves for their products—and advanced into serious financial problems. That's what crippled Douglas Aircraft when it fixed prices for the DC-9 on the basis of an assumed typical experience curve, and the estimated cost reductions failed to materialize.

Big surprises like this happen because experience curve slopes vary widely from product to product. In some industries the slope may be really steep (meaning you gain unusually large benefits with experience); in others there may be no slope at all. Why?

1. Cost reductions are almost never automatic; you must work for them. Incentive programs should reward people for cost-reducing ideas—and you must encourage managers to implement them. Otherwise, costs may stagnate or even increase as time passes.

2. Some products and processes have greater potential for improvement over time than others. For example, manufacturing has steeper experience curves than does raw materials, purchasing, marketing, sales, or distribution.

Watch out for those common situations in which your products are using the same components, production facilities, or delivery systems. Don't ignore their interrelationships, or you may end up with the same dire fate as the British motorcycle industry. Different bike classes share many parts and manufacturing processes, but the sleepy manufacturers didn't realize that achieving and maintaining a viable cost position for one product might require retaining market positions (and experience bases) in others. When threatened by Japanese competition in small bikes, the British therefore just withdrew, boosting short-run profits but destroying most of their remaining motorcycle business in the long run. The Japanese used the cost advantage from their dominance in small bikes to push the British out of larger ones, leaving them with only a small niche in superbikes. The Britons' share of their own home market plunged from 34 percent in 1968 to 3 percent in 1974.

There's another catch. Don't confuse three cost reduction sources: (1) improvements in general technical knowledge and inputs plus feedback from customers; (2) exploiting scale economies; and (3) basic improvements learned from cumulated output (better product design, factory and labor efficiencies). These factors have critically different implications, warns the author.

In businesses in which technical progress is the primary source

117

of cost reduction, "the imperative is to maximize bargaining power with suppliers and buyers. Ways to do this include adroit supplier and buyer selection, threats of vertical integration, and attempts to increase upstream and downstream switching costs." Before the single supplier example of the Japanese brilliantly changed the rules of the game, General Motors and Ford met that imperative by insisting on multiple sources, integrating partially backward into key components, analyzing suppliers' costs in detail, and avoiding long-term contracts.

If it's scale economies that drive costs, though, sustaining competitive advantage obviously requires aggressive pursuit of market share. This strategy won't work, however, unless competitors are unwilling or unable to match investment in large, efficient facilities. Otherwise you won't win competitive advantage—you'll get competitive mayhem as the whole industry becomes mired in overcapacity.

Which of the three possibilities offers the best way of using the experience curve? According to Ghamaway: "Basic improvements learned from cumulative output offer the most sustainable route to a cost advantage." That was the secret of du Pont's triumph with titanium dioxide in the 1970s. The author's overriding moral, however, is that the magic of the experience curve is no substitute for investment—in fact, the one demands the other. Cashing in energetically on the experience curve usually requires measures such as large investments in automation or in *penetration pricing* (going for high share with low prices in the hope of future profits). But "be wary of anything that might make the rainbow's pot of gold disappear." Unexpected surges in demand, for example, can sometimes raise costs—because production systems can't handle surges efficiently.

That sounds more like an inexperience curve. But master the experience curve properly and you might even be a Bausch & Lomb.

11. THE TORMENT IN TIN

Those whom the gods would destroy they first make rig markets. When the London tin market collapsed late in 1985, its members were shown in spectacular manner that the economists are right: price is the mechanism that allocates resources and creates the balance between supply and demand. Remove price, attempt to prevent economic forces from working through, and you build up pressure that, sooner or later, will result in the bursting of the dam—leaving someone owing $600 million on stockpiled tin that can't be sold, a market in utter confusion, and several producers wondering where their next peso or ringgit is coming from.

The sorry fact is that it's all happened before—only in the opposite direction. In the early 1980s the tin industry was foolishly trying to support the price of tin, stockpiling the stuff as a buffer. Back in the early 1960s the copper barons tried to keep their prices not up but *down*. The explanation of this apparent perversity was fear of substitution if the copper price soared, and fear of large losses if it collapsed. The attempt to settle on a golden mean failed because, lacking any price mechanism to warn them, the market-rigging producers were caught hopelessly napping by a surge in demand.

When they nevertheless kept the price at £236 a ton, the irresistible economic force came bursting through in the form of incredible profits for anybody who passed the stuff on, for prices of up to £600. The personal fortunes made on the London Metal Exchange before the cartel collapsed in 1966 were staggering—and should have warned those involved in the tin conspiracy of the 1980s that it was equally bound to come apart at the seams like a badly made tin can.

That humble container is the key to the whole weird imbroglio. The shattering effect of the aluminum alternative, coming at the very time when new production capacity was increasing supply, condemned the buffer operation to a horrible death. Why was production capacity being raised? Because of artificially high prices. Had the price been allowed to reflect fully the 25 percent drop in tin consump-

119

tion, nobody (not even a bullish Brazilian) would have brought new capacity on stream.

This sad and sanguinary story has management implications that extend well beyond the narrow and now devastated world of tin. The temptation to rig markets in what seems to be your favor is ever-present. But the long-term consequences of doing so can easily outweigh the short-term benefits. First, an artificial price must mean, other things being equal, either an artificial demand or artificial profits. Either one encourages artificial—or wrong—decisions. Second, the artificiality of the price prevents it from sending out signals. Instead of responding to the market, suppliers end up trying to make it respond to them. And that's the most slippery slope of all.

12. PRICING BY PROACTION

Price, used in the proper way, is a very powerful tool for improving profitability. Most marketing companies use it poorly, however. For example, how would you react in the following situation? You're an electromechanical components manufacturer, and things are tough. Market share is stagnant and industry prices are edging downward. Your margins are taking a terrible beating, with no relief in sight. To gain share and restore income levels, your right-hand man advises that prices be cut by an average of 7 percent. Do you say yea or nay?

In the real-life case, within three weeks, "the move had provoked severe price cuts from the company's major competitors and set off a full-scale price war. Prices swiftly declined in a kind of death spiral that soon had everyone in the industry doing business at a loss."

That sorry tale is told by Elliot B. Ross, a McKinsey partner, writing in the *Harvard Business Review.* He notes that the unfortunate executive who'd started it all "by failing to anticipate his competitors' reaction to his ill-fated initiative saw his company as the victim of an unprovoked attack. All the information the company had about current price levels in the industry was what it had gleaned from the bids on orders lost to competitors. He was, like most managers most of the time, pricing reactively."

That way, says Ross, you dodge the pitfalls of reckless price leadership. But over time you may also pay a heavy penalty in forgone profits—money left on the table on hundreds or even thousands of orders. So, says the expert, you shouldn't react; you should do the opposite: *proact.*

What does that mean? The following questions provide the starting point.

1. Is your market share constant or declining while prices are falling in real terms?

2. Do you have a nagging suspicion—but no real evidence—that you are regularly bidding too high for contracts?

3. Do your salespeople keep complaining that your prices are several percentage points too high, although your market share is holding steady?

4. Do your contribution margins for the same product vary widely from customer to customer?

5. Are you unsure who is the industry price leader?

6. Do your pricing approval levels seem to be functioning more as a volume discount device than as a control mechanism?

7. Would you have trouble describing your competitors' pricing strategies?

8. Do you find that too many pricing decisions seem aimed at gaining volume—even though they're not supposed to?

9. Are most of your prices set at minimum approval levels?

10. Do your competitors seem to anticipate your pricing actions with ease, although theirs often take you by surprise?

11. Do you have a planned method of communicating price changes to customers and distributors?

12. Do you know how long to wait before following a competitor's price change?

13. Are your prices set to reflect such customer-specific costs as

121

transportation, setup charges, design costs, warranty, sales commissions, and inventory?

14. Do you know how long it takes each of your major competitors to follow one of your price moves?

15. Do you know the economic value of your product to your customers?

16. Do you use the industry's price/volume curve as an analytical aid to price setting?

17. Do you know whether you would be better off making a single large price change or several small changes?

18. Do you know how to go about establishing price leadership in your industry?

19. Are your prices based strictly on your own costs?

20. Do you have a consistent and effective policy for intracompany pricing?

If you answered no to the first ten and yes to the second ten, you are a shrewd pricer. If the results are otherwise, reconsider promptly and thoroughly how you set prices, because it's high time you started to price proactively—that is, to use price to raise profits. Here are some of Ross's tips:

1. Gather all the information you can about how customers buy and how competitors sell. It can give invaluable clues.

2. Never ask "What price will it take to win this order?"

3. Always ask "Do we really want this order, given the price the competition is likely to charge?"

4. Make sure you know your relative prices accurately (relative, that is, to the competition). One firm spotchecked only five of the several dozen orders its salespeople had taken in a month. It found that its prices on average were a full 5 percent below those of the next lowest bidder—far lower than the management thought, or than was necessary to win the business.

5. Check your ideas on price with the reality of the marketplace. For instance, it's a good idea in some cases to lag behind price rises—it helps you win the valuable "low-cost supplier" image. But

in one Ross example, interviewing the customers showed that they were quite happy after only a six-week lag.

6. Keep your pricing arrangements as flexible as you can. One company invariably quoted firm prices for a quarter, with escalation for each following month. It found, though, that a third of its customers made their buying decisions on the basis of the prices offered at the end of the year. Another quarter of them looked at the prices in January and didn't take any notice of escalation clauses. So the firm changed to a fixed inclusive quote for the first group and monthly escalation over the whole year to the second. The results for margins and orders were "dramatic."

7. If new technology will help, use it. Ross quotes a company that uses a personal computer (now quite a cheap piece of equipment) to store information on cost, competitors, and customers.

The most valuable tool of all, though, is the oldest technology: the flesh and blood computer in the skull. Bad pricing decisions stem from poor thinking or (witness the tin market) no thought at all. Thinking comes cheap, but in proactive pricing its results are dear indeed.

To summarize some of the important points I've mentioned in Step Four:

1. The virtues of the product itself sometimes suck in the demand required, but you bet on that at your peril.

2. A rave reception for a new product teaches you nothing, except that it has had a rave reception.

3. One of the greatest mistakes you can make in marketing is to forget the rules of your own success.

4. The harder it is to achieve higher perceived quality in a market, the more important it is to strive for that edge.

5. Sooner or later, in all cases, dynamic growth comes to an end, replacement sales dominate demand, and profitability comes under pressure.

6. Your greatest obstacles to competitive success don't lie out-

side your firm, among its competitors, but inside your own management.

7. Remember that boom time is when managers are most likely to take their eyes off the ball, the market, and the rules of entrepreneurial success.

8. Innovation is the key to entrepreneurship, and the key to innovation is to loosen up the company and its controls.

9. Use marketing tools like the experience curve—they work very well, but they don't work automatically.

10. Maintaining a viable position in one of your superproducts may require retaining market positions in other less wonderful lines.

11. If, instead of responding to the market, you try to make it respond, you're on the slipperiest slope of all.

12. Your pricing is a powerful tool for improving profitability, but only if you use it with planned dynamism.

Step Five: Maximizing the Competitive Thrust

1. THE MAN WITH TWO LIFES

It's possible to crack markets that are dominated by giants, given one condition: that you're better than they are. That probably means being different as well, like Mark Weinberg, the man who created both Abbey Life and Hambro Life. The first Life is currently worth some $900 million, and the second sold in 1985 for a billion. Not many men can build one significant business, let alone two—even if the markets are the same. (Weinberg's different, differentiated product was the sale of life insurance linked to mutual funds, a business since broadened into a wider concept of financial services.)

When Weinberg first investigated insurance, one look at the sales material gathered from a saunter around the existing giant companies told him all he needed to know about the competition:

"Nobody tried to sell—which was enormously encouraging." Many years after his start, when Abbey Life was the aging wunderkind of the industry, Weinberg used to pull out examples of the collected leaflets. He would then reveal that they had been picked up not a decade before but that very day.

Weinberg's approach became the fastest-rising general product group in insurance. But after he left his own creation, Abbey Life, to the mercies of ITT, Weinberg's first child reacted (or didn't react) in the classic manner when its creator started up against it with Hambro Life. Had Abbey thrown a mere $400,000 of advertising into the market, it's said, Weinberg Mark II might have been stopped in its tracks. True or false, it may seem surprising that there was room for so large and determined a new runner.

But the market dominated by a large and established company may be the one to attack, on much the same principle that dictates opening a competitor to McDonald's right next door. Identifying a market that doesn't exist is far trickier than spotting one that is already large and flourishing, however strongly occupied. Thus, a couple of Frenchmen named Gault and Millau decided to attack the gastronomic guide area, in which Michelin was not only established but had become a household name, the sacred tablet of restaurateurs and gourmets. By providing much more descriptive information than Michelin and taking a more positive approach to restaurant evaluation and promotion, the pair built what is now a large, rich and very well fed business. Equally, a whole trio of Japanese companies weren't put off by the size and strength of Xerox. They saw the giant's sheer scale in copiers as their opportunity.

Weinberg by that second time around had plenty of business confidence behind him. That wasn't true when he first launched Abbey in the face of a disbelieving City of London. But the successful entrepreneur never takes somebody else's no for an answer. Many of the world's greatest money-spinning operations have been laughed out of court by people and companies who have been laughing out of the other side of their faces ever since: xerography is the most famous example. All you need to turn negatives into resounding positives is an excellent, differentiated product and a market in which you have an excellent, distinct opportunity to achieve a large profitable share—if, that is, you sincerely want to be rich.

2. CRACKING SEWN-UP MARKETS

If you sincerely want to be poor, enter a product that hasn't a chance in a market where you haven't a hope. To achieve this nonachievement, managers need only form a wholly erroneous set of views about their product, their competitors, their market, and their talents. To raise the art to its highest pitch, however, the project must also involve such awesome costs that failure would bankrupt the company.

This makes aerospace companies prime candidates for nonsuccess with no-hope projects. Their expenditure is so gigantic, their economics so finely balanced, and the market so furiously competitive that nobody in full possession of their natural senses, it seems, would ever seek to break in from scratch. Lockheed did so with the Tri Star, whose shutdown in 1981 cost the company a $400 million writeoff—and this was only part of the pain inflicted by this ill-starred attempt of a military contractor to break into civil aviation. Since 1972 the plane had cost $1 billion; it hadn't even covered its start-up costs in all that time. Worse, this was Lockheed's second disastrous bite at the civil cherry; it had earlier lost a fortune on the Electra turboprop in much the same way.

Just why Lockheed failed to learn its Electra lesson illustrates the dangers of too much corporate strategy. Dependence on any one market, or any one customer, naturally worries a company; if customer and market are the same (the U.S. military, in Lockheed's case), the perfect strategy surely demands a major diversified market somewhere else. Equally, sound strategy uses a company's existing strong suits, and Lockheed was brilliant at designing and building military aircraft. It wasn't, judging by the Electra, much good at marketing civil ones, but nobody's perfect.

If not perfect, Douglas is highly proficient at marketing airliners, and it clobbered Lockheed heavily with the DC-10. Thus Lockheed did not repeat its Marketing Error One (coming in much too late—the Electra arrived just in time to be comprehensively leapfrogged by the pure jet). Instead, it committed Marketing Error Two: plunging into a two-horse race with prizes enough for only one; and where the winner will not, by any stretch of the imagination, be you.

It's rare that a critical writer on such affairs can deny the charge of hindsight. But long, long ago, before the traumas of the Rolls-Royce bankruptcy and allied RB-211 troubles, long before TriStar drove Lockheed itself to the financial brink, I observed that this second attempt to crack the civil market was gravely overstretching Lockheed's finances, was overreliant on a financially unreliable engine supplier, and was dependent on selling at least 300 planes—a total nowhere in sight, certainly not within an economic timespan. Actually, Lockheed never made the magic 300. As the blade of the guillotine fell, some 230 to 240 TriStars were in service or on order with airlines—after a decade of hard work (not to mention the odd enormous bribe).

It's ironic to recall how Rolls-Royce busted itself, metaphorically speaking, to get the order for TriStar engines, and then really did bust itself in the effort to supply them. The orders added up to some 750 engines, which sounds great until one fact is called to mind. As the *Financial Times* delicately put it, "It is thought unlikely that much if any of the RB-211 work for the TriStar program has been carried out at substantial profits." The TriStar was a born loser for everybody involved, except those lucky subcontractors who were paid at profitable prices for their contribution to an unprofitable certainty.

It would have been a miracle if the TriStar had succeeded. Sometimes miracles do happen—or, rather, they appear to. In fact, the impossible has been wrongly defined. Medieval man would have thought heavier-than-air flight, computers, or television beyond all bounds of possibility, though he believed with ease in miraculous healings, apparitions, and visitations. The great entrepreneur achieves the impossible by refusing to accept its wrongly defined existence.

That doesn't mean, however, that nothing is impossible: many things are—including, in the Lockheed case, the cracking of a high-risk market, in which it had no presence, in competition against one determined, solidly based opponent and allied with that financially dodgy engine supplier. In contrast, Mark Weinberg, the man with the double Life, made his miracle by breaking into a fragmented market, full of sleeping giants, with a differentiated product and a dynamic sales technique. "Miracles" never defy the laws of marketing economics. They obey them—and that's how they happen.

3. THE BETTER BUSINESS OF BALL

"A manager has got to know an industry intimately; to know and adjust to its mentality—it is amazing the variety of mentalities in different industries. You can't come in from the outside and hope to get that last 5 percent." The percentage to which the speaker, Richard M. Ringoen, was referring in *Management Today* is what results when you squeeze the last ounce of profit from the humdrum activities on which his company, Ball Corporation, thrives.

Even Ringoen was "just amazed at how well we do in some of the mundane businesses we're in. Because of this, we find the managers don't want to leave and go somewhere else in the company. They have their customers. They know the technology. What they want is to stick with it forever." The mundane businesses are in dreary, sometimes disaster areas such as metal and glass containers, and zinc and plastic fabrication—in most of which Ball doesn't even have significant market shares. In 1983 it did get up to 15 percent in glass jars for food; but in the two-piece beer and beverage can market, the figure was only 8 to 9 percent. So how does Ball succeed?

First, its market-imbued managers concentrate on carefully selected niches; second, they are obsessed with achieving the lowest possible costs by the highest possible technology. In commodity markets like Ball's, as one analyst remarks, "Manufacturers can't control prices. So they must control costs. The low-cost producer is the king of this business." These two principles carried Ball through recession and industrial shake-ups with far more success than its competitors who have sought to diversify heavily away from packaging and containers: American Can into financial services, Continental into gas and oil, Owens-Illinois into hospital management. "When you talk with most corporate managements, the conventional wisdom you hear is that a company should have a balanced portfolio of investments with countervailing cyclicalities," said Thomas B. Clark, director of corporate planning. But Ball "found that it just wasn't true. The probability of being able to do this is minimal."

In other words, Ball managed what was actually a fair degree of diversity by *not* acting like managers of diversity—another paradox, which Ringoen explained. He treated all the business lines with an even, strategic hand, because "I hate to see companies that allocate priorities and express preferences about their different lines of business and say, 'This one is a cash cow, and that one a star.' Theoretically, we could squeeze all the cash out of the glass business and then plough it into high-technology defense areas—meanwhile telling the different management teams different things. [But] you don't get the best results that way. It could be devastating for the motivation of young guys in glass. We want to treat them all alike, and expect each to do his best."

What does the center at such a company do? It searches constantly for ways in which the individual businesses can better serve their markets and run themselves. In 1978, for instance, Ball bought a plastic injection molding plant that was far more profitable than its own troubled business. Why? "We got the founders, who were two brothers, to sit down and define their principles of operation,

130

something they'd never done." Among the principles they wrote down were a high level of automation, operating-room cleanliness, no secondary operations, and small productive units. That opened Ringoen's eyes to a principle of his own: make divisional bosses work out their own principles, and stick to them. In beverage containers, for instance, Ball's principles said it would make only nine- and sixteen-ounce cans, two sizes that together have 80 percent of the U.S. beverage can market. "Every month, somewhere in the country somebody comes to our people with an idea for making a different size can—say, a seven-ounce can for the wine market—but they know to tell them no," according to Ringoen. "If the divisions manage within those self-imposed constraints they'll be left pretty much alone," Clark told writer John Thackray.

Following that kind of approach makes managing and marketing, even with businesses that vary far more widely than Ball's, far easier and far more effective. The logic of diversification is ultimately the same as that of concentration. Bad businesses obey Gresham's Law and drive out good ones. The multiform firm really needs to be managed like a product portfolio—in which no product is allowed ascendancy in the top managerial mind, but every product, as at Ball, gets the concentrated attention of the managements who have it in their ever-loving care.

4. LOW-RETURN LEADERSHIP

To be fair, sometimes market forces do drive managements into projects that, left peacefully to themselves, they would have shunned. The chemical giants, for instance, have often faced the dilemma of knowing that too much capacity by far is being installed, but knowing also that unless they add to the excess themselves, they will inevitably lose market share and maybe their whole market. The correct solution, of course, is to accept that unpleasant consequence

131

rather than be dragged down (like the aforesaid giants) into permanent overcapacity and price depression. The solution is very difficult to accept, but if it's refused, the difficulties will be far greater.

In any case, as Ball's example shows, the pursuit or defense of market share can be a snare and a delusion. An article in the *Harvard Business Review* agrees. Its findings go right against the entrepreneurial grain, for every entrepreneur loves the thought of cornering the largest share of the market, and with it (naturally) the most in profits, prestige, and price. Well, nature doesn't necessarily imitate art. To take one example, in rental cars, Hertz has constantly suffered from intense price and nonprice competition offered by the also-rans. From 1978 to 1982, Budget (ranking fourth) pushed up earnings by 27 percent, while Hertz's profits declined by a total of $110 million.

Ball's giant former rival, American Can, and Georgia Pacific and Goodyear have all produced lower returns than smaller competitors. As the article comments: "Despite the usually strong correlation between market share and profitability, clearly the benefits of dominance are not universally enjoyed." Does the explanation lie in rotten management or in rotten markets?

The article's author, Carolyn Y. Woo, has studied 112 examples of market leaders with low returns and has found reasons for them. Such companies tend to operate in regional or fragmented markets (where there are more than twenty competitors). A regional basis, she says, may not yield many cost advantages over competitors. In fragmented markets, too, the many competitors indicate that there are low entry barriers—as well as product and process characteristics that favor a range of skills and sizes, rather than one monolithic supplier.

Unstable market environments are also unpromising—meaning those in which businesses have more frequent product and technological changes, but the frequent changes don't boost demand. The chopping and changing merely intensify the competition for existing volume. Watch out also for markets in which conditions are deteriorating; for example, more firms are quitting than joining the market.

Businesses with low value-added are vulnerable to suppliers' cost increases, but have less chance of passing them on to customers. In markets where customer service and professional support are very important, the expenses of leadership can be especially severe, and in markets for capital goods and (less often) those connected with materials and components, it can be unprofitable to lead.

In fact, though, the key to feeble performance turns out to be weaknesses of the companies rather than their markets. Woo notes that the low-return leaders tended to have a worse reputation for quality (defined as the difference between the percentage of products judged superior to competitors' and the percentage of products judged inferior). The quality levels for low- and high-return market leaders were 31 percent and 48 percent, respectively. Low-return leaders tended to charge higher prices and also shouldered heavier costs than their competitors; while spending on their product R & D wasn't much greater (in percentage terms), on process R & D it was actually lower. They made less active selling and advertising effort, too. "Overall, the findings reinforce the conclusion that the competitive posture of the low-return market leaders was inconsistent and did not match their market and product characteristics well"—that is, they were badly managed.

There's one final, very significant point. The low-return leaders tended to share more marketing resources around different parts of the business. Some 51 percent of the low-return group shared more than four-fifths of the marketing programs with other lines of business, compared with only 39 percent of the high-return leaders. And 66 percent of the low-return group shared more than one-fourth of the marketing channels, as against 58 percent for the high returns.

Successful marketing companies these days give carefully defined separate businesses their own distinct marketing resources—meaning the resources they need to sell effectively. It's the unsuccessful business that muddles up the marketing. In other words, the no-way, no-hope, no-win condition isn't generally inescapable or irreparable for the low-return leaders. They can win, if they want to. It isn't as if, for example, they were shelling out millions for something they didn't understand, with a wholly unpredictable future, and which didn't exist elsewhere in any profitable shape or form. Would anybody? They certainly would—witness the three-dimensional disaster of a company named Nimslo.

5. THE NEMESIS AT NIMSLO

If capitalism, as its opponents like to allege, is on its last legs, it's certainly been showing some amazing turns of speed. There was a time when products actually had to reach the market before their proud possessors could make a mint—and even then, years of waiting were generally required. Now the shrewd cookie can rake in negotiable cash before a single member of the paying public has laid hands on the product.

That was merely one twist in the extraordinary Nimslo 3-D saga. By selling all his own shares before a London public offer that had attempted to value the company (whose 3-D camera hadn't yet earned a penny) at $340 million, inventor Jerry Nims cleared, according to report, at least $6 million. Here beginneth the mystery— not about why anyone in his right mind would pay that kind of money for several million birds in the bush but why Nims tried to jump off the bandwagon so soon (as an investor, that is—he still took a $150,000 salary as chief executive).

Nimslo's forecasts had been going up by leaps and bounds. By year four of actual trading (1985), sales were supposed to hit $735 million and profits, $156 million. Believe it or not (and anybody could be forgiven for not believing), that was *half* the current sales of Polaroid, which was much nearer year forty than year four. As chief executive, Nims must obviously have authored the forecasts. Translated into share price terms, his $6 million bird in the hand began to look like a distinctly bedraggled canary.

Indeed, the history of great marketing entrepreneurs, including

Polaroid's Dr. Edwin Land, has been marked mostly by their reluctance to part with even a tithe of their estate, beside which Custer's Last Stand, Horatio's resistance on the Tiber bridge, and the Trojans' hold on Helen were but feeble gestures. The true marketing genius, convinced that, say, 3-D cameras will sweep the world, identifies with the wonder so totally that he can't bear the thought of any separation—especially if the part being separated is his wallet. Indeed, that identification is one of his sustaining and driving forces, and persistence and drive are the crucial ingredients of marketing success.

No doubt it was the fact that some such dark thoughts were running through investors' minds that then persuaded Nims to reinvest in his company. It can't have been an improvement in the trading position, because the truth was beginning to dawn that the Nimslo camera was overpriced, very hard to market, and moving very slowly—even at the sharply cut price that had been forced on the management. To achieve stunning triumph, Nimslo had to do only a quarter as well at selling cameras as in selling equity to the City of London, but that was a terribly tall order. Sure enough, in 1983, Nimslo brilliantly succeeded in losing $10.6 million *more* than its $26.2 million turnover.

But terribly tall stories have become much easier to believe in an age of technological miracles. Unfamiliar, technically mysterious products actually do make magical millions for unknown entrepreneurs. Such miracles only happen, however, when the businesses are based on solid markets. The existence of these everyday miracles makes it more, not less, important to ask the economic questions and do the economic homework. It may still be necessary to take a leap in the dark. But wise marketers first do all in their power in the daytime to check where the obstacles are placed—and the exact location of the door marked "Exit."

6. COUNTING THE COSTS

Later on in Nimslo's saga it tried further savage cuts in prices in a forlorn attempt to stimulate demand, while also cutting back output. This introduced a new twist into one of the oldest marketing games of all: determining how much sales will rise if the price is cut, and whether the additional turnover thus achieved will yield more profit. In Nimslo's case, the rate of sales at the original, excessive price was so low that the question never had to be asked: no price cut, no sales.

In companies in a happier position, the equation turns partly on the extent to which higher volume generates lower unit costs. One of Henry Ford's most brilliant business breakthroughs was his exploitation of a key fact. Not only do lower prices greatly expand volume (so that, other things being equal, profits will be higher by the amount of the extra sales) but other things are not equal. As volume rises, so unit costs, both fixed and variable, decline by more than cuts in price.

That's why entrepreneurs down the ages have generally sought to maximize volume rather than price. Occasionally the policy has led to disaster, for example, at Texas Instruments, where what worked wonders in semiconductors flopped in watches and also in home computers. In TI's base of microelectronics, the decline in prices as volume increased wasn't optional—it was an inevitable consequence of the technology and the market. In the consumer areas where TI tried its luck, a low-price policy merely took the company away from the zone of premium quality and technological superiority that was its natural positioning.

In other misled companies, the great marketing myth is that the rate of production determines not so much their profit as their level of sales. That is, the only determinant of turnover is the amount they are able to produce. Now, there are indeed companies whose policy is always to expand supply by rather less than the rise in demand: Waterford Glass and Mercedes-Benz are examples from very different fields. It's a difficult feat of balance, that is never demanded of the mass producers.

You wouldn't think so to hear them talk, however. To a car company, output lost through a strike equates with lost turnover—although in nearly all cases the "loss" in sales is made up after the resumption of output. The same fallacy leads producers to say, when in possession of unfilled orders, "We could have sold more, if only we could have made more." Maybe they could and maybe they couldn't. The market, and only the market, determines true sales potential, and that can be tested only in conditions of full supply.

That's rarely the case at that most hysterical of marketing moments: the launch. Often (it happened with the De Lorean car) early rapturous reports of huge orders and divine public reception are followed (after ominous delay) by disappointing sales figures and dreary cutbacks. The awkward balance between too little and too much demand underlies the story of one costly auto plant that closed in 1981 after a mere five years of money-eating life. One account of its unavailing struggle called the works "the showpiece plant that never stood a chance." Output had never crawled up to much above half capacity, despite the same account's observation that "the old factory had always sold more cars than they could make." That clever trick goes to the core of the problem. It is, of course, impossible to sell what cannot be produced. The writer meant that the company had never contrived to satisfy the latent demand.

At launchtime that's deeply debilitating. The task is to phase out the old and phase in the new, in plant and marketplace, without causing undue problems in either location. Excessive overhangs of the previous model can murder the economics, and so can shortage of supply. In this particular car plant, output never rose above a quarter of the breakeven level for a full year. By the time reasonable output had been won, the fuel crisis had torpedoed sales of the larger cars to which the plant was devoted—though *devoted* may be the wrong word: the product's equally shaky quality and reliability spoke ill of the degree of dedication.

Achieving high stocks and a rapid buildup to planned output levels in a launch period is critical. But it mustn't be confused with the creation and satisfaction of long-term demand. Probably every successful launch runs into supply shortages—the syndrome profoundly afflicted IBM's runaway personal computer. But the car plant problem was one of inefficiency rather than insufficiency; the bungled production buildup was further hampered by late prepro-duction changes in the detail design; the further models needed to build on the original launch and take up spare capacity weren't there; limitations in the body plant and lack of overseas sales were crip-pling, though (completing the vicious circle) the shortage of supplies would have been fatal to the absent export drive.

Does this justify the observation about selling "more cars than they could make"? Preconditions to selling anything at all include getting adequate stock into the outlets and the backup areas. With-out that supply, the question of being able to sell doesn't arise. Ultimately, demand creates supply; but supply has a prime function in ensuring that demand can exist at all.

Supply and demand determine the possibilities for the third factor in the equation: costs. Basic management performance hinges on *LIMO:* least input for most output. If relative LIMO performance lags, then either management is deteriorating or (which comes to the same thing) other companies' managers have been getting better faster. As with price and value in the classic marketing equation, the position relative to competition is what counts.

Companies can improve greatly in the four *M*s—models, mar-keting, management, and manufacture—and get nowhere if competi-tors have likewise improved their 4M performance. The situation is much worse if rival gains in efficiency are being applied to far greater volumes. One major manufacturer of light bulbs with a proud brand name found its basic manufacturing cost being undercut by a full third from overseas sources, meaning a foreign company half-owned by itself. The obvious solution, as the company had access to the foreign machines and methods, was to exert might and main to make its domestic costs competitive. Only it couldn't.

Why not? Because years of poor marketing had eroded market share to the point where sales volume couldn't support three-shift operation of the machines, without which costs couldn't be cut. Much the same factor has decimated American production of many

138

consumer durables. Greater Far Eastern efficiencies have been applied to ever-increasing shares of the world market, which is partly why, for example, the once-great manufacturer RCA now merely assembles TV sets supplied from Taiwan and Mexico and gets its videocassette recorders straight from Hitachi.

The cost-output-sales balance can go grievously wrong in either direction. Plants that produce more than they can sell may be in even more dire straits than those "selling" products they can't make—and the latter phenomenon easily leads to the former. Oversold factories, complacently regarded as evidence of successful marketing, get treated with large, lethal doses of underinvestment—like the Detroit car plants over the long and critical years during which their domestic and world market shares slumped in the face of competitors whose 4M progress wasn't offset, as it should have been, by determined American advance.

The same debilitating process can occur for what seem like entirely virtuous reasons, for instance, when sharp financial management sets stiff ROI targets for a business. The targets are missed, so investment gets withheld. The business promptly becomes less competitive, and ROI sags further. Reversing that process—the dreaded inward spiral—can be achieved by better application of basics, but it also requires courage, imagination, creativity, plus some unique strength on which to build. And that may have been sucked away in the spiral. It's infinitely better never to let the spiral start to swirl; by keeping the costs low, the output high—and the sales just right.

7. THE PILEUP IN THE PITS

The experience of Britain's National Coal Board clearly demonstrates that, although the link between productivity and marketing isn't one of the best explored aspects of management, it is decisive. The NCB had been compelled to grasp the marketing reality that there's no point in pressing people to buy your wonder product if you simply can't deliver the goods. The pay carrots dangled in front of its workers to make them mine more coal and the hard marketing sell presented to industrial users to make them buy that coal were two sides of the same coin. Popping the coin in the slot, however, landed the NCB with two crises at once: the biggest stocks and strikes in the board's history and the longest, most bitter strike in all of Britain—although the protested pit closures were made inevitable by the coal mountain, whatever the strike leaders thought.

Criticism of the board for conjuring up its own calamity is unfair in one respect. In coal, as in many other industries, production planning is essentially very long term, while the recession that crunched energy consumption was essentially short term (although on the long side of short, alas). But the common reaction in companies, high and low, to equate production shortfalls with lost sales, when the two phenomena are quite plainly not the same thing at all, could hardly be disproved more dramatically.

There are only three possible solutions (which are not mutually exclusive) to a coal-style mountain: (1) slash prices until the mountain moves; (2) keep on piling; (3) cut production and/or capacity to bring supply and demand into balance.

The first is no good if you go bankrupt. The second, whoever finances it, prolongs the bad times at the expense of the good. The third, cutting capacity, is what the NCB was seeking to do. The strikers urging it to retain the old uneconomic pits didn't seem to understand that their survival could only be won at the expense of the new, highly economic and enormously costly facilities which were the industry's rightful pride and joy. Sacrificing the new to the old always has predictably dreadful results.

There is, of course, a fourth alternative: to stimulate demand so that it soaks up the superabundant supply. But the Coal Board had no means this side of heaven of achieving that result. Nor did the chemical companies that found themselves in so severe a plight in the 1970s that, as one executive complained at the time, "the only way I can affect the level of business is to insult one of my customers."

The sovereign power of the market is something that even the firm that could genuinely sell more than it can make must watch and respect at all times. The market has a nasty habit of reasserting itself when least expected—and what makes Mercedes-Benz so strong is its faithful, unremitting observation and service of the market that it always *slightly* undersupplies. That's the key: if *slightly* becomes *severely,* the seller's market will one day vanish—and not so softly and silently, either.

8. OVERSUPPLY AND UNDERMARKETING

What happens, though, when a market is grossly oversupplied not just for the products of one unhappy firm but for everybody's offerings? In some cases, the surplus is endemic. Too much fixed capacity has been put in place (for instance, in man-made fibers and some key petrochemicals in Europe), and demand will not, in the foreseeable future, rise to the level of potential supply. In such circumstances, though, nobody is likely to aggravate the problem by adding brand-new capacity. The situation is awful, but at least it is stable.

Nothing destabilizes a market more effectively than a Hagler-Hearns contest—two giants of an industry squaring off for a fight to the finish. In marketing, as opposed to boxing, there is rarely a clean, cold knockout. The above-mentioned chemical surpluses are the aftermath of a misbegotten battle for market supremacy between American and European giants, who now, all passion spent, are licking their various wounds. When giants fight for leadership in this way, the only possible result is the undermining of all profits, maybe forever.

When a General Motors, a Ford, a Fiat, and a Volkswagen scrap for top position in European cars, with Renault and Peugeot equally interested in the outcome, the financial results are entirely predictable. GM is the late starter in this race. Thanks mainly to a

141

famous surge in Britain, it doubled its market share from 8.4 percent —but only at the price of losing $519 million in two years. The damage to Ford in the UK was more severe. Instead of making $1.2 billion (as in 1979), it managed only $147 million in 1984, breathing hard. The head-on meeting of the mastodons has been set against one of the worst possible backgrounds. Western Europe emerged from recession with ungovernable overcapacity in cars. Against actual 1985 sales of around 9 million vehicles, potential output numbered 13 million; sales growth, anyway, was plodding; and competition would have been fragmented even without the interference of the Japanese.

Despite the Japanese intrusion in the United States, the situation there was almost the exact opposite: three-quarters of a booming market (up from 8 million cars to just under 10.5 million since 1982) was in the hands of the Big Three: GM, Ford, and Chrysler. The trio carved up $9.8 billion of profit among them in 1984—so the Big Two (Chrysler having retired from the European fray during its financial holocaust) had in reality been underwriting their European slugfest from their American bonanza. This made an interesting change from the recent time when Ford had been kept afloat only by European profits, but it still left European companies such as VW (not to mention the rump of the once-great British car industry) holding the fuzzy end of the lollipop.

By interesting arithmetical coincidence, VW suffered two years of loss that totaled almost exactly the same as GM's: 515 million, but (Gott sei Dank) in deutsche marks rather than dollars. Aided by the sensational success of its second-generation Golf (Polo in the United States), VW has begun to make inroads into that deutsche-mark mountain. But as for generating the fortunes that Ford deems necessary to make Europe competitive ($70 billion, according to *Business Week*), the Europeans looked in no position to fund even $40 billion.

The less competitive the factory, the less the power to resist the Japanese challenge, hence lower sales and returns; the lower the profits, the greater the shortfall of sorely needed development capital and thus of spending; the lower the investment, the less competitive the factory . . . and so on, to the crack of doom. Is there any way out of the labyrinth? The positive answer from consultants DRI Europe contains some highly negative items: cuts in employment of 250,000 workers, a 15 to 20 percent slash in capacity, and 850,000 cars a year shipped in from the low-cost East. That might work in economic terms, but politically the formula is certainly unacceptable —at the level of both the international firm and the nation-state.

There is a less pessimistic view. One researcher holds that, as markets segment and new technology lowers the cost of competing, Europe can cash in on the design strengths that, for main examples, have left Mercedes-Benz and BMW as shining standouts. On this argument, the strength that leviathans such as GM, Toyota, and Ford derive from operational scale can be offset by smaller-scale production of more desirable cars. The argument is attractive, but it ignores two points. First, the benefits of scale leave the U.S. giants with a cash flow beside which those of the Europeans are as a trout stream to the Mississippi. Second, if the Americans need European design skills, they can always buy them—as GM demonstrated in picking up Lotus Car, and Chrysler by mooching on Maserati.

Yet there is something in both: the thesis of excess capacity and that of specialization. To answer the initial question—What to do when a market is grossly oversupplied?—action to reduce capacity is always inevitable. Without that, the market can't stabilize. But even in stable markets the lesser players in a great game can never match the billions of the giants. The same conclusion follows down the scale, into the millions of sales, the hundreds of thousands, and the thousands. The smaller businesses must find a better (that is, cheaper) way to compete.

The difficulty of combining low-cost production with the best niche marketing, though, is extreme for firms that don't have the benefit of scale. That isn't because scale benefits are automatic, or even easily attained. It's simply that the very technological developments that leave Europe with a chance are the same that enable Japan to achieve its world advantage in production costs. Neither does it follow that the smaller Western producer can always exploit

143

a niche more successfully than the Japanese leviathan—or even the American one.

The reality is that all the major European manufacturers lost their way while continuing to add capacity. VW took far too long to replace the Golf; Renault had too many models, too many of them uncompetitive; Peugeot was stuck (or stuck itself) with an outmoded product line, outdated in its engineering; Ford lost sales in the mid-priced market by a less than successful model change, while also losing out on sales of larger executive cars; GM left its European upsurge too late for its financial comfort; Fiat failed to break out from its long-standing inadequacy in the middle and upper price brackets.

In other words, the bane of oversupply comes about largely because of undermarketing. It's not entirely true that if you look after the marketing, the markets will look after themselves. But the element of truth within that statement is enough to make the difference between a Mercedes-Benz and a loss-making mishmash; or between a miracle and a might-have-been.

9. THE CATERPILLAR CRAWL

One supreme fact tells more about the market position of a product, service, or company than any other: price, or, to be exact, relative price. Not only does price determine one crucial dimension of profit, it also usually marks out the leader from the pack and (which the leader may well not realize) establishes the degree of the leader's vulnerability. That hidden weakness was laid hideously bare in recession when, one by one, the lordly names of the American market fell from grace—sometimes after decades of uninterrupted financial beauty. Even Eastman Kodak slid down the hill that took heroes like Caterpillar with its excavators into heavy loss. Kodak's 48 percent fall in 1983 earnings, in terms of its own past record, was near disaster.

The causes were partly outside its control: the rise in the price of an essential raw material, silver, the soaring dollar, and the lingering impact of recession on Kodak's nonphotographic sales. But beyond these transient factors lies the same long-term problem that reduced Caterpillar to a financial crawl and that has made dominant price leadership a thing of many pasts. The markets from which both companies gleaned such a rich harvest through the decades have become very mature. Even though Kodak's innovative thrust puts many another giant (including Caterpillar) to shame, its excellent new products (the disc camera and superfast color film) are likely, at best, to defend its share of that overripe (that is, slow-growing) market.

The difficulty is inevitable when you have as much as 85 percent of the market at home, and half of all sales abroad. These were Kodak's figures for film, and from such dominant shares there's usually no way upward—Caterpillar was no different. Even IBM, before the advent of its personal computer, had dropped from 60 percent of the total computer market to 40 percent. In the past, the few film competitors, like Caterpillar's rivals in construction plant, had been too feeble in their technology and marketing to capitalize on Kodak's strength, so to speak. But the Japanese are anything but feeble; Fuji has used the tried-and-true national recipe of making an equally good product at lower costs, which enables the market outsider to undercut a high-margin champion. In Caterpillar's markets, the same strategy has worked wonders for Komatsu.

Like Caterpillar, Kodak has always exploited its market strength to get the greatest prices and the most glorious margins (16.2 percent back in 1973), and has been slow to move into new segments that are a long way from maturity. It does have a promising new business in consumer batteries, a fast-growing one in copiers, true; the latter market, however, is now showing signs of congestion, and its leaders are moving as fast as their feet, and their feats, can carry them into the office of the future.

But the virulent new phenomenon is that even the future's front line offers no protection. One widespread and unforeseen side effect of the microelectronics revolution has been to create so great a product proliferation as to destroy price levels, make competition a nightmare, and utterly confuse the consumer. Since using the personal computer itself can be bewildering for the purchaser, the result is one of the strangest boom markets in history. All over the world, people have been buying sophisticated machines in very large quantities and often at quite stiff prices; and then using no more than a portion of their potential.

Because of the attractive potential of the market and the ease of design, manufacture, and entry created by the chip, this curious bazaar became almost anybody's game—or was, before IBM's success changed the rules. So sweeping a spate of introductions and innovations simply gave the consumer too much choice. The consequences are inevitable. The price wars that forced down Sinclair's bottom-of-the-range machine to $15 in the United States will become endemic in many other product markets. The office of the future is likely to be hit by price wars even before that future has become reality. The pace will plainly become too hot for many companies— and none is immune from the dangers, not even IBM. This has been dramatically shown by the impact of the Far Eastern "clones" that have undermined the strategy—and the prices—for its market-making PC.

Truth has become as strange as fiction in this process. In 1967, when Ivor Williams began his *Management Today* series on a fictional company called Minipute, he thought up an obviously mythical product: the expendable computer. At $15, his myth has become reality. The only trouble is that it probably means expendable companies. The moral of these extraordinary goings-on will apply to many other sectors where the same technology-led market forces are at work. Prices will be stable for only a short time. Then the tumbling will begin—and, as IBM now knows in PCs, the market leader won't be able to resist by virtue of his perceived preeminence. The leader will have to win through at the other end of the economic spectrum—cost and all-around efficiency of supply.

146

10. HIGH MARGINS AND LOW COSTS

The cost-push argument was dramatized by General Motors when it tried in early 1982 to push through a deal cutting both its wages and its prices at a single stroke—to the great joy, no doubt, of its then recession-hit salespeople, whose prime article of faith, from the highest to lowest, is that price is the prime selling weapon, and the lower the better. Give salespeople an inch in price, and they'll take a mile, which is why generations of marketers have fought uphill to put across the (true) concept that profit or contribution, not volume, is the name of the game.

Of course, the twain are indissolubly linked, especially in a business like GM's, in which a low volume of output has horrifying effects on huge manufacturing plants, especially if they have recently absorbed billions in capital spending. The catch, as many a marketing company has found in recession, is that a cut in prices unsupported by reductions in cost seldom generates enough volume to pay for the price damage. Hence GM's desire to persuade its car workers that $20 an hour, or $8 more than their beloved Japanese friends (or enemies) receive, was too high a reward.

It's the reverse of what old Henry Ford did in a famous foray into economic theory. He *raised* pay to an unheard-of $5 an hour, reasoning that the higher level of worker prosperity would raise car sales, which would increase volume, which would lower unit costs —despite the five bucks. It worked because labor costs as a proportion of added value (a concept unknown in Ford's time, but which existed all the same) were much lower in those days. In the 1980s, at GM and many other companies, this vital ratio has risen so high that price cuts can't be accommodated without destroying added value altogether.

The lesson is to pursue efficiencies in operations that will relentlessly reduce costs, so that, whether prices are under external or voluntary pressure, the company can take price cuts without profit destruction. That's why IBM has been automating what were

147

already highly efficient, modern plants: price leadership in turbulent conditions must be backed by, indeed must go hand in hand with, cost leadership. Production and marketing have always been two sides of the same coin. High margins obtained by low costs are highly defensible. High margins obtained by high prices are highly dangerous.

The recent history of the airlines demonstrates the point. In truth, if an airline doesn't use price as a weapon, there's precious little else at its disposal. Apart from price, convenience of schedule is by far the most important factor in choosing an airline. Thus, on the Scottish routes, British Midland Airways, operating from Gatwick, beat the BA Shuttle, operating from the more convenient Heathrow, by the simple device of offering appreciably more for significantly less. In contrast, what shattered the transatlantic air trade and its profits was the advent of competitors offering a little less for tremendously less. The eventual ruinous free-for-all was proof that sensible managers should always seek the middle ground between extreme A, charging so much that they stifle the growth of traffic (as on the European routes), and extreme Z, charging so little that they fill the planes at little profit or even large loss (no small feat on a jumbo).

On the gamut from A to Z lie endless permutations and combinations of fares and services. But the major airlines, when threatened by the Freddie Laker onslaught, didn't attempt sophisticated or even smart solutions. They licked Laker by pouring resources into defending market share, even unto the destruction of their own profits. The way to large airline profits is by intensive employment of a carefully selected fleet, as demonstrated by Cathay Pacific. Cathay will fly 747s even on routes that look lopsided for such huge planes; "misusing aircraft intelligently" is what a Cathay boss called it. In translation, this means minimizing overall system costs. Combined with maximizing overall system revenue (not, be it noted, *prices*) that means not only surviving the inevitable price wars but thriving through them.

11. THE $640 TOILET SEAT

There is an alternative to minimizing costs as a means of achieving miraculous profits, and that is to maximize prices. It has been the dream (often fulfilled) of mercenary businessmen ever since commerce began. But the trick has become harder to pull off, even at times like the launch of a new and wholly original product, when the supplier has the market to himself—and at his mercy. The catch here is that pricing the original at a superpremium will defeat the more important purpose of building up a market. This is why, when a new wonder like the laser audio disc appears on the scene, wise shoppers wait for the inevitable price fall as the manufacturers seek to widen the market and as new, cut-price suppliers, attracted by the high prices, join the feast.

Also, too rich overpricing has too rich results. For example, when a senator revealed that Lockheed's plastic and fiberglass toilet seats were costing the U.S. Navy $640 a throw, the great defense contractor was forced into undignified retreat, first to a mere $554.78 and then to a measly hundred bucks. Lockheed had been under fire for its pricing for some time, but whether or not the defense put up by its president, L. O. Kitchen, had been long in preparation, it was a model of its kind.

"Existing cost and pricing practices," declared Kitchen, "even though proper, inevitably result in prices being charged which appear disproportionately high when compared to the intrinsic value of the particular part." He can say that again—and, given the peculiar pricing practices of much of world industry, he'll probably have to.

12. DYNAMICS OF PRICING

The fact that combining minimum costs with optimum prices creates maximum profits is obvious. Yet there are, in this day and age, a few companies that think pricing policies are not important in their marketing, and, much more serious, there are plenty—in one survey, 34 percent of firms selling capital goods, 18 percent of those making components, and 21 percent of those supplying materials—that think pricing is only "fairly important." Only a minority of these firms surveyed seemed to agree that price is vital (as it is; utterly and undeniably so): the figures were 12 percent in capital goods, 20 percent in components, and 18 percent in materials.

Considering that price provides the only common feature for all kinds of goods, is one of the major factors influencing the customer's mind, and is a key determinant of profit, that's truly a strange approach to the market. Any good business thinks about its prices all the time. Yet "too many companies try and run their businesses on the basis of keeping prices stable. This is particularly true of small companies—it might even be one reason why they stay small. Prices need to be constantly examined: not changed all the time, but examined. Price is too important an issue to be left alone for long."

So writes marketing expert John Winkler. But what sort of examination do prices require? The research quoted (from an industrial market research survey titled *How Industry Prices*) also shows that an unbelievable 81 percent of these companies fixed their prices not after examination of any meaningful kind but by "cost-related systems," either adding a fixed percentage to cost or taking a fixed margin off selling price. What's more, two-thirds of the companies only "sometimes" or "rarely" modified this cost-based approach by "non-cost-related factors."

Winkler rightly calls this "an appalling situation." "A very substantial proportion of industrial companies are still living in the dark ages of the industrial revolution when all you had to do was produce the product and the world would demand it." The attitude is especially hard to understand given Winkler's example: a $10

150

million business with direct costs (material, labor, and production) adding up to $6 million; fixed costs (overheads, distribution, and sales) coming to $3.5 million; leaving $500,000 in profit. Increasing the sales by 25 percent and holding fixed costs steady, would double the profits. Holding sales steady and lowering $4 million of material costs by 12.5 percent while keeping fixed costs steady would also double profits. But *you can achieve exactly the same effect by better pricing.* "Increase your average prices by 5 percent (through a different product sales mix), holding sales volume level and all costs level," and the million-dollar trick is done. Which is easier—raising sales by a quarter, cutting material costs by 12.5 percent, or getting an average 5 percent more out of your prices? The answer is as obvious as the results of increasing sales by 25 percent while cutting material costs by 12.5 percent and getting that 5 percent price uplift on top. The company gets a profit of $2.6 million—a miracle result of over five times what it used to achieve.

Those companies that do use non-cost-related factors to set prices refer to competitors' prices more than they conduct market studies when trying to determine how much they can or should charge. That's an improvement—but doing the market studies would obviously be better still. For one thing, the company might be in an industry where everybody is charging less than the traffic will bear.

Beyond that, Winkler writes in his book *Pricing for Results* (1984), all Supermarketers

> calculate their costs, but they do not let them rule their decision. If the costs come out too high to enable them to make a profit, then they either find a way of reducing their costs or they do not go ahead with the product. Consulting the sales force is a sure way to drive your selling prices towards the floor. Unless it is handled with great skill and the sales force is objective, then it will be the worst method of all.

Pricing is never a cut-and-dried affair, however. Far from it. The aim is "flexibility, surprise and economy of effort." In other words, pricing in the dynamic company is a dynamic process. But note that the companies in the survey were asked another highly relevant question. Did they ever try to find out how acceptable their prices were to customers before making the final decision on price? Two-thirds replied that they didn't. That has to be the greatest pricing error of them all.

To summarize some of the important points I've mentioned in Step Five:

1. You can crack markets dominated by giants, but only if you are better than they are.

2. Identifying a market that doesn't exist is far trickier than spotting one that is already large and flourishing.

3. However numerous your products, the company won't succeed unless each of them is treated with concentrated care.

4. Successful marketing companies give carefully defined businesses their own distinct marketing resources.

5. Don't believe the marketing myth that the only thing that determines turnover is the level of production capacity.

6. Supply and demand combined decide the possibilities for the third factor in the vital marketing equation: costs.

7. If you suffer from oversupply, it has generally been caused by undermarketing.

8. Niche marketing offers no escape if you can't serve the niche at competitive costs.

9. In many markets, even the leaders won't be able to sustain profits by virtue of perceived preeminence: unless they are also preeminent in keeping down costs.

10. If you combine minimum overall costs with maximum overall revenue, you can survive price wars—and thrive.

11. Maximizing prices looks like an alternative to minimizing costs, but it has become increasingly difficult to achieve.

12. The greatest pricing error you can make is the simplest one: failing to find out what the traffic will bear.

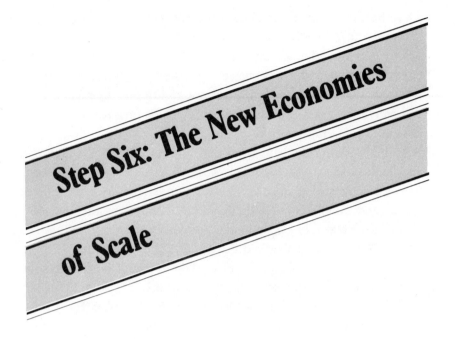

Step Six: The New Economies of Scale

1. THE LONG LEGACY OF ITT

Late in 1985, the large electronics company STC startled the cogno-
scenti by appointing Peat Marwick's experts to peel away at the
corporate apple and find its core businesses. Why the surprise? After
all, the world of management is as quick off the mark as pop culture
at pursuing new trends and turning them into old clichés—and
managements the world over have recently been pontificating about
core businesses (those from which the company earns its basic bread)
as though that were some revelation. The concept of core businesses
has always been fundamental to modern marketing strategy—but
not at STC; hence the surprise.

Until relatively recently, STC rejoiced in being a wholly owned
subsidiary of ITT. How could a company in so sophisticated a busi-

153

ness as telecommunications, reared, what's more, in the allegedly white-hot management crucible created by Harold S. Geneen, be in ignorance of so central a matter as its own core? Hubris is one answer. As the company entered 1984, its chairman, Sir Kenneth Corfield, the man who was ousted in the following year, was "confident that our stewardship will continue to bring prosperity to your company." Said stewards had, indeed, doubled turnover and tripled post-tax profits in four heady years.

It's by no means baffling to find, in the context of a high rise and high conceit, that cash flows too freely on everything from business entertaining and chauffeurs to supreme salaries and annual management conferences at luxury hotels—simply because they are drops in the ocean of a $3 billion turnover and (before the slump to $85 million that cost Corfield his job) $225 million profit. But the lush executive life certainly can't explain apparent innocence over that basic question, What business are we in?

The poser was put famously long ago by Professor Ted Levitt, in an essay titled "Marketing Myopia," which was widely and permanently misunderstood. The shortsightedness referred to failure to anticipate technological changes that would radically affect (what wasn't yet christened) the core business. But STC had recently purchased its own computer company; that had surely been farsighted. All agree that methods of transmitting and handling data, from tiny telephone handsets to mighty mainframe computers, are converging. The purchase of computer capability, in theory, smartly solidified STC's new core as an all-purpose data-processing business. The tough reality, though, is that convergence is in the future, whereas sales and profits are made (or not) in the present. There, STC was busily engaged in hybrid circuits and electrical wholesaling, TV rental and airport services, submarine cables and baggage X rays, radio pagers and interior lighting, and so on ad infinitum. If the group's vaulting ambitions hadn't been brought to earth by its fall from grace, would the buying ever have stopped?

The echo of ITT itself is unmistakable. STC's former parent, which still owned a strategic quarter of the equity and maintained vital technological links with its offspring, had also diversified far and wide from its core business of telecommunications. In the process, its core neglect had become so pernicious that up to two billion hard-to-find dollars were required for a catch-up effort of uncertain outcome. ITT had been forced to sell some of the very treasures whose acquisition had taken management's eyes, and hands, off the telecommunications core.

Similarly, while all STC's apples, big and little, were being juggled, the company's position in the same core business was slipping just like its management controls. Consultants also had to peer into cash management—and into the components business, a fifth of the entire company. Innovation, too, had suffered from severe corporate arthritis. The company had become locked into a marketing relationship with a conservative single buyer (the British telephone monopoly). Custom, conservatism, and caution (bred by a strongly top-down management climate) had combined to stop the company from even thinking properly about exploiting its scale, let alone acting properly to achieve that sine qua non.

2. FINDING THE REAL CUSTOMER

It's the old, old lesson. Taking care of the future always starts with the here and now. But there's another moral. You can set a company free from the titular ownership of Big Daddy, as STC was freed from the control of ITT; but shaking free of the large paternal culture is another matter altogether—especially if the Daddy was represented by so pervasively powerful a persona as Harold S. Geneen. A *comptocracy* is the word writer Nancy Foy used in describing the ITT regime. In her time at STC, "it was said that the company had 700 people in the comptroller's function. . . . It was a company that ran by the book, and the book was a five-foot shelf of manuals."

The comptocrats were kept happy as STC was managed by

Geneen's magic numbers. But the company lacked the "smaller, more accountable, more motivated, more manageable units" that have come to be recognized as the keys to entrepreneurial marketing. Stories abound of important businesses placed in a straitjacket by self-important managers of both overseas and domestic proprietors. For instance, subsidiaries are commonly held responsible for events that are totally outside their control, like the exchange rate. As one U.S.-owned manager in such a fix bitterly complained, he was expected to make up any shortfall if the local currency fell, but when it rose he wasn't credited with the equally artificial gain.

Heads he lost, in other words, and tails he didn't win. Yet the underlying performance of the business plainly hadn't altered one iota, no matter whether the profits were expressed in dollars, yen, or baht. Underlying performance should be Big Daddy's only concern, and parents should take great care at all times to ensure that no condition they impose impedes the child from producing the best possible performance.

Combine lack of interest in true performance with the setting of any number of restrictions on its achievement and you get the characteristic situation, and generally awful results, when Big Daddy is the state. Government doesn't even have to own an industry to bedevil its results. This was one of the main arguments for deregulation in the United States: the artificial restraints imposed by the regulators prevented efficient working by the market and the regulated companies. But governments as a rule find such hard truths hard to swallow—even Mrs. Thatcher's in Britain. Her renowned belief in market forces was more passionate than that of most marketers—except when she disliked the results.

Take the drug industry: as fine, full, and flowing an example of capitalist competition as you could hope to see. Spurred by the prospect of golden profits, the umpteen likes of Glaxo, Hoffmann-La Roche, ICI, SmithKline, Beecham, and Eli Lilly have always striven furiously to be first with winners, weighed in with "me-toos" when they've lost, and at all times bombarded their market with messages and massages.

Their only sin, in many governments' eyes, is that they succeed too well. Not that tax authorities agonize over having to collect their take from those abundant profits. (In 1984 Glaxo made $370 million before tax, $240 million after.) The rub is that governments resent their own contribution to the bounty, via nationalized health services. That's why the Thatcher government limited the companies' marketing activity (they were allowed to spend only 9 percent of turnover on promotion); tried to limit what could be marketed (by restricting the drugs doctors could prescribe); and limited the return on capital that companies could earn to between 17 percent and 18 percent after tax. This all took place at a time when one U.S. multinational (not in drugs) wouldn't even look at any British investment yielding under 45 percent; and when a British one (in drugs) had 30 percent as its aim.

Whenever governments interfere in private industry, the results are usually the same—harmful at worst, unhelpful at best. That truth can still be seen even in cases that fall far short of disaster, such as the computer company ICL, one of the very few mainframe makers to have a significant share of an IBM market—Britain.

At all times, the Big Daddy of the state has been in the background of most European competitors to IBM. Nowhere has government intervention been more evident than with ICL: providing money on some occasions, favored orders on many others. All marketing involves structuring a company or a product line to meet the freely arising demands of the customers whose business is truly profitable. If you introduce nonmarket factors, like Big Daddy, that essential marketing structure, and with it the essential marketing success, may never fall into place.

Indeed, some American research seems to prove that when Big Daddy—whether the state or some stupidly proud corporate parent—keeps an unviable operation alive only by massive infusions of money, the fractious child never comes to good. Time and again, no matter how many millions are lost or how many captains are press-ganged to man the sinking ship, sink it continues to do.

With no Big Daddy around, drastic private solutions may, or

157

must, follow. But Papa's presence puts off that vital day of facing the
market realities: in ICL's case, that meant the point of recognizing
that a customer base weighted too heavily in the UK can't support
across-the-board competition with IBM, and that ICL's across-the-
board philosophy helped make its marketing image fuzzy compared
with the diamond-blue hardness of an IBM.

Marketing, not technology, is the ultimate key to winning scale.
ICL has been squeezed between IBM's general market strength on
one side, and the powerful specialized positions occupied in areas like
small computers or banking or retailing by other U.S. competitors.
The new regime that took over in 1981 acted bravely to counter this
situation by linkups designed to fill the yawning gaps in its range
while striving to establish the clear, coherent identity—inside and
outside the company—which is and should be forced on firms that
must survive in markets on their merits and can never count on any
Big Daddy's noncommercial blessing. To prove the point, merely
compare these figures. Company A in four successive years made
£153 million, £161 million, £225 million, and £255 million. Company B earned £25 million, lost £50 million, earned £24 million, then
earned £46 million. The first is IBM (UK), the second ICL. Small
wonder that ICL was finally swallowed by a somewhat smaller Big
Daddy—none other than the aforementioned STC, then heading
straight for its own disaster.

3. THE MAN WHO SHAVED REMINGTON

IBM goes to elaborate pains to ensure that all its operations have the
freedom and the ability to build the essential component of marketing success: a strong share in an attractive, well-defined niche or
sector. It's the exploitation of such positions that explains the embarrassing examples of companies that, when pried loose from Big
Daddy, proceed to perform wonders of growth.

That's what came to pass when Victor Kiam liked his Remington razor so much that he bought the company, lifting it from the giant Sperry conglomerate which had lost $30 million on the subsidiary in the previous four years. Kiam proceeded to double both Remington's U.S. market share and its total sales, which shot up to $150 million with pretax profits of $12 million. What did Kiam have that Big Daddy didn't?

One unique thing he had, for certain, was independence: the purchaser was rich enough to put up a million of his own (vastly outweighed by bank indebtedness of $24 million—paid back, though, in twelve months) to buy the company. The second asset was speed of execution and decision—an immediate cost-cutting program that cost seventy executives their jobs and was linked to swift measures to improve quality. But the third asset was the most decisive: the marketing smarts that Kiam had learned from his career with Lever Brothers.

Three marketing decisions were crucial. First, Kiam spoke to the retailers and found out why they wouldn't carry stocks: because of rapid product replacement by new versions. Kiam promptly slowed down the new product program, thus also saving money. Second, he broadened the range by adding a new model aimed at a carefully chosen price point: $19.95. This was half the price of any other shaver on the market and reaped a rich harvest from the gift customers. In the first year 500,000 units were sold. Third, Kiam kept up the advertising pressure in a highly intensive mode, even sacrificing profits to maintain a very heavy spend. All these actions had been available to Sperry. Its failure to take advantage of them resulted from its orientation toward investment, as opposed to the all-marketing slant that Kiam brought to his task (and to his vast personal profit). There's the vital difference. Little Daddy brings concentrated marketing smarts to bear. Big Daddy tries to make the investment pay off without understanding the market, and often ends up sending good millions after bad.

4. VIABLE SHARES OF VIABLE MARKETS

Companies are worth backing only if they have, or can develop, viable shares in viable markets. The larger their losses, the greater their inability to finance themselves, the less likely it is that they'll have viability either in present or future markets. The more competitive the world scene, the more vital it is that a company be built around its viable markets—and viability can never be achieved by producing an object that is not covering its true costs in the market; that can only mean that part of the cost is being carried by somebody outside the marketplace.

Moreover, as the fundamental deficiency lies in the overall marketing stance, it cannot be cured unless those financing the cure are deeply involved in the market. Bankers and bureaucrats never are. In the excitement of the chase after jobs for workers or contracts for companies or a foothold in new technology, eyes are never on the goal—building a profitable, long-term enterprise around its markets. Hence the chain of Pyrrhic victories in state-aided competition. The eventually catastrophic Rolls-Royce contract for the Lockheed Tri-Star engines, for which the British government lobbied so hard, and the crash of the De Lorean Dream (attracted to Belfast after vigorous competition between public authorities), are among the saddest examples.

With equal certainty, the lapsed will produce countless excuses. The Reagan recession, and the loss of confidence caused by financial uncertainty when UK government backers finally took fright, have been thrust forward in De Lorean's self-defense. The jury will ignore these claims—and rightly. The whole Belfast project was predicated on sales that far exceeded any likely share of the U.S. car market. That was a far greater weakness than trying to establish a greenfield mass-manufacturing operation in Northern Ireland.

You can indeed start from scratch, with no labor force, no manufacturing tradition, no markets, and no products—and win— even in the green fields of Ireland. Waterford Glass did so long ago.

But its founders built slowly, learned the hard way (by observed experience), became ambitious with success (not before it), and didn't have a Big Daddy government in the wings, pouring out millions.

It's also true that they didn't have John Z. De Lorean. But neither did innumerable other companies that, without benefit of charismatic charmers, still plunged into situations where viability was unlikely ever to be achieved—when all concerned, including the plungers, know that viability is harder to find than Holy Grails, Golden Fleeces, or crocks of gold at the end of the rainbow.

No market event has been more widely or long expected than the shakeout in small computers. Yet the new contestants piled in: in Britain alone 80 to 90 micromakers were competing for a mere 15 percent of the market left by IBM and a couple of others. Overcrowding on that scale is bound to result in underselling. The consequent crashes have nothing to do with high technology, everything to do with low levels of marketing shrewdness and basic common sense.

In all boom markets those inside, and still more those outside yearning to get in, believe in the inexhaustible boom. But doubling every year (as European personal computer sales used to do) evidently can't be maintained forever. And in conditions in which all players are doubling their bets, a 30 percent growth rate (to which the PC sales dropped) has the devastating impact of an all-out slump.

Like the battered mainframe makers of a previous boom and bust, the legion of competitors based their loose ambitions not on genuinely unique selling propositions (that is, a market appeal all their own) but on the vague assumption that strength in their own markets would slosh over into personal computers. L. M. Ericsson, which had a miraculous 10 percent or so of the global market for telephone switching, was one of the PC seekers, but in 1985 it sold only 3,000 PCs in the United States. According to *Business Week,* that was an embarrassing 12,000 short of its tiny goal. Ericsson then made its first intelligent move: it became an early American PC dropout.

161

As noted in Step Three, section 6, Apricot's ambitions in the United States were minuscule, too; in that it sought a share so infinitesimal (1 percent) that Princess IBM would never have noticed the pea under her mattress. But quite apart from the fact that IBM (like the princess in the fairy story) seems to notice every last pea, the Apricot/Ericsson approach contravenes the big bang theory of market entry: backed by convincing research, this holds that starting small pays off far less than the major push aiming for major penetration.

There is an obvious catch-22. From the moment IBM entered the market, scattering all before it, hardly anybody—except IBM clones—had a realistic chance of capturing a significant share. The universal marketing moral applies: if a significant share simply isn't available, forget it. That problem is compounded in the computer market, of course, by the ineluctable fact that IBM created an industry standard. As Apricot (and Apple) found out the hardest way, either your software is compatible with IBM, or you're dead. Get such market basics wrong, and all the astute, cautious, financially oriented, technically ingenious management in the world won't win you that viable long-term share in that viable market. And if somebody else *is* setting the standard, viable for all other runners means at best second place. Few other places are worth having.

5. THE JUMP AT JAGUAR

One of the most powerful forces stripping the naked market bare is loss of the security that used to lie in economies of scale. This isn't because its components have disappeared; as ever, the learning curve still reduces production costs with each cumulative doubling of output; as ever, the costs of marginal output diminish as production rises. But fast-changing technology is shortening product life and thus that of the learning curve, while technology, too, is making it possible to produce shorter runs at far lower cost.

162

Add to these phenomena the segmentation of markets and the movement upward in price and quality within these segments, and you have today's and tomorrow's strengthening of the smaller, more specialized producer at the expense of the mass-market mass producer: the BMW coining deutsche marks while VW in its off years wobbles into losses. But how much smaller is small? In that same car industry, firms can survive on minute output, as do Aston Martin and Lotus, both of which have so far always been able to find new hopefuls to share in their often perilous fortunes.

But the price tag for Aston Martin in January 1981 ($2 million on the installment plan) contrasted tellingly with a price announced the very same month by the equally double-barreled Daimler-Benz. That very different car aristocrat planned to spend a further $45 million, or the price of two dozen Astons (the company, not the cars), on strengthening its hold just on the UK market.

Throughout the decline of its mass car production, Britain has maintained a clutch of minority marques, often (like Astons) of enormous expense, always made in diminutive quantity (prepurchase, Aston once managed eight a week). German manufacturers also know full well how to charge for conspicuous motoring, but Germany's expensive motors are numbered in the thousands, whereas British makers slay their hundreds.

A national ethos has played a part in the British gravitation toward high-class luxury products with excessively limited markets —a trend clearly visible in the evolution of the Jaguar. Once it stood on the threshold of Mercedes-Benz scale. (In 1960, their sales were actually equal.) It became a strictly exclusive car, with only 6,532 sold in its home market in 1980. This was the inevitable outcome of a journey governed by what can be called the Rolls-Royce Syndrome: the British preference for making the best, or what the maker fondly believes is the best, often without regard to economics, while volume sales and volume profits are left to lesser breeds.

When a new chief executive, John Egan, saw that there was no future in making Jaguar cars in tiny quantity and infamously bad quality, dramatic results followed. Output expanded sharply; quality improved out of all belief; sales rose strongly all around, especially

163

in the United States; and profits leaped ahead, enabling Jaguar to finance things like a $75 million investment program centered on robotics to improve its production still more. The result was a net profit in 1985 of $84 million, giving Jaguar a 37 percent return on stockholders' equity, and exceeding by two-thirds the latest returns from Vickers, the group that incorporates Rolls-Royce Motors.

The Rolls-Royce Syndrome puts product before production, and such a policy has been disastrous in market after market. Successful competitors have shown that high prices can go hand in hand with high output—and even with higher quality. That's because, with modern techniques, efficient production has much more effective quality control built-in. And these days, without quality, the marketing task is all but impossible for firms of any size and any economy of scale.

6. WHEN SHARE EQUALS PROFITS

But is larger scale, in any case, redundant when it comes to the vital matter of making profits? One British commentator was overjoyed by a *Harvard Business Review* study that suggested that "businesses with a small market share can be just as profitable as ones with a large market share." Hallelujah, indeed: Since Britain's market share in all too many world markets is small to infinitesimal, that would have been the best UK business news since Arkwright invented the textile industry. True, conventional wisdom which, in this case, holds that large share equals large profits, often makes better sense stood on its head. But not this time, alas.

The study, by two Purdue University professors, found only 40 low-share, high-return businesses out of a total of 649. All 649, moreover, were part of larger parent companies, and thus had a less hostile environment than an own-two-feet firm as they followed essentially conservative policies: standardized products, rare product

changes, little sales support, frequently purchased industrial products, and high value-added areas. They didn't (for which you might
as well read "couldn't") compete across the board. Even if they
couldn't win on quality (which they tried to do), they generally
charged low prices.

On the study's own findings, this is a minority strategy that
works only in a minority of cases. As an attack on the Big Is Beautiful school, it makes little dent. The BIB theory, as it happens, has
far more serious defects. In an age of fragmentation of technology
and markets, having the largest share of, say, European polyethylene
sales may be more incubus than asset. Specialization is being forced
even on giants because of the inroads made by smaller, concentrated
companies with (apparently) small market shares.

But an elementary question in marketing is, How do you define
the market? Daimler-Benz and BMW have been cited by one struggling undersize car maker as "examples of successful medium-size
companies," and Chrysler as a disaster, despite its "relatively large
share of the market." The latter made a stirring comeback *despite*
what was actually a relatively small share of U.S. sales. But if you
define the great German firms' bailiwick as the expensive executive
saloon market (as you must), they are dominant in Europe and have
been for years. Unlike the forty low-share winners in the *Harvard
Business Review* study, these German firms are innovative, high-
priced consumer marketers.

There is, however, a catch. What if the specialized, concentrated
firm finds itself locked into a segment from which the growth and
the glory have fled? A very early exponent of specialization was a
company called BSR, which at one point had 50 percent of the world
record turntable market. Unfortunately, this share was all at the
low-priced end. BSR depended on economies of scale to give it
unbeatable costs and become the sacrificial victim when recession
decimated the low-priced record-player business—and much of what
was left moved decisively up-market.

As it all but collapsed, BSR had the rare experience, in these
inflationary times, of a sharp fall in turnover—which in 1981

dropped all the way back to the 1977 level. But then, under the leadership of two entrepreneurs from Hong Kong, BSR changed the whole nature of its business. Its once huge base in turntables had shrunk too much to support a major company: from 48 percent of turnover in 1980 to a mere 25 percent. Hence the big and quite impressive push into growth markets in computer electronics (almost all of the nonconsumer variety and mainly served from the Far East). This made BSR once again a stock-market star and virtually created a new company, a Phoenix rising from the ashes of the old.

Not that growth markets provide a place where small companies may safely hide, as BSR discovered when it lost over $9 million in the great computer slump of 1985. The afflictions of lesser players in computers and allied fields have often been peculiarly grim. Just like BSR in its turntable prime, they tend to lose control of their base markets precisely when they badly need profits to finance the disproportionate investment which alone offers any hope of salvation, let alone sustained growth. As the crash of high-flying Osborne proved in portable computers, a fat portion of a thin market is no substitute for a major piece of the overall action.

Lesser companies with the largest shares of circumscribed sectors are especially prone to the mindless extrapolation of past supergrowth into the future—without the realization, which has overtaken every overtrading store on Main Street, that growing pains can be the most acute. Fast growth, grand profits, and high and mighty stock-market prices, apart from anything else, act as honey to bears. As too many optimistic competitors crowd into the small wondermarket, its wonders will become less marvelous.

"What goes up must come down" is one of the oldest, strongest laws in economics. Yet investors and managers alike find the law desperately hard to obey, especially when the market atmosphere, as in the electronic booms, is ecstatic. Surely firms in the thick of the fastest action in town should maintain lavishly profitable growth? Tell that to investors in Data General, Wang, Control Data, and all the other companies that have achieved stock-market poverty in the midst of prime-market plenty. The reasons lie partly in the variable competence of managements. But the ultimate explanation, for big and small share companies alike, lies in the variable, capricious nature of markets themselves.

7. INTEL'S BUST AND BOOM

Marketers in nonglamour industries must have gloated more than somewhat over the 1985 travails of Silicon Valley. The glamour managers with their glamorous profits and glib talk about new management modes were suddenly humbled by collapsing demand and falling prices. But gloaters would be better occupied looking for lessons from the microcircuit massacre. It followed the compression, into a short time span and a concentrated sector, of cycles and sorrows that in an age of ferocious competition could well affect (and are actually affecting) markets into which no whiz kid would ever wander.

The basic problem, the investment cycle, is as old as time. Scarcity breeds surplus because the high prices, profits, and growth rates in times of shortage encourage both old and new players to invest in extra capacity (to the microtune of $6 billion in 1984). The growth rate (like the prices and profits) is artificially inflated as customers down the line jockey and jostle for scarce supplies. Supply and demand come into balance only precariously, because customers have by definition overordered. Hence the boom-and-bust syndrome.

In microelectronics, the pain is intensified by the mountainously rising cost of chips (in both senses) in the great capital game. According to Andy Grove, the president of Intel (quoted in *Management Today*), "The cost of building a state-of-the-art wafer fabrication facility, in 1973 $10 million and now $100 million, will by the later 1980s have reached $200 million." So far, so good—if the yield and the pricing are right. Then you can wallow happily in sales of $900 million a year and gross margins of 50 percent. With the wrong yield and pricing you'll have $300 million of sales at a 20 percent negative margin.

But how can you get prices right in boom-and-bust conditions? In July 1985 the 256K dynamic random-access memory cost $2.50; eight months before, the price had been 620 percent higher. It's hard to believe that any marketer in the Valley (or anywhere else) had built this possibility into his equations. Prices were supposed to drop by only 90 percent in a whole decade, on the industry's rule of thumb. Adding to the misery, development costs had tripled between 1978 and 1983; by 1998 they will have tripled again to as much as $140 million. Silicon Valley's only consolation was that the bust was bound to unwind the same way as the boom, only in reverse— investment in the game is slashed, the number of players dwindles, and, with underlying demand continuing to advance, shortages rebuild.

Clearly, nobody would want to replay the 1985 catastrophe. So what are the lessons to be learned for micro and macro markets alike? One is for customers: get some in-house capacity, or the equivalent, to cushion you from the boom-time rush. Another is for suppliers: take into account not only your own expansion but that of competitors. Third, lower greedy expectations of market share. Fourth, have only a proportion of your eggs in any basket of the products that might become commodities—that way, in any market, misfortune lies.

8. COMPETING AGAINST GIANTS

No precaution a prudent small company can take will ever eliminate its vulnerability to competition from giants. In a business world being reshaped by megamergers, that places a higher premium than ever on superior management—especially after the Reagan years made the antitrust authorities unlikely to intervene to protect the vulnerable. Nobody faces the problem in more acute form than companies competing with an unleashed IBM. The survive-and-prosper kit in their cases has to become the model for all comers.

The first essential, evidently, is to maintain product superiority. That's why the people at Compaq Computer Corp. breathed a sigh of relief when IBM announced its portable computer in February 1984. The machine reached the market fifteen months after Compaq's, had fewer features, and weighed two pounds more. "IBM gave the portable its best throw," claimed venture-capitalist Ben Rosen, Compaq's chairman, "and still got it wrong." IBM, however, has a habit of righting its wrongs. What other strengths could the portable upstart throw into the fight?

The first rule is that, in this kind of competition, life is real and life is earnest. Simon Caulkin, writing in *Management Today,* noted: "No drop-outs in denims, Compaq's senior managers wear dark suits and ties. They share long and hard engineering and management experience, often in the tough profit and loss environment of Texas Instruments or the sales and marketing side of IBM." According to one of its co-founders, they "make decisions on logic, stripped of emotion." That's as good a place to start as any. Emotion-free logic certainly explains the key decision to make the portable compatible .with the IBM standard. Failure to accept the reality of IBM's market dominance has frustrated the efforts of many of its rivals, including Apple, which was finally forced to swallow some of its pride and go compatible in early 1986.

The second rule of giant competition is that you don't fight on battlefields where you cannot hope to win. You pick the point where the giant is weakest, not the point where its strength is hardest to overcome. And then you attack with the same weapons used by the mighty competitor.

To put it another way, you walk tall from the start, like Compaq president Rod Canion, whose attitude has always been that "we're a large company in the formative stages," according to his chief financial officer. Hence the then-record $30 million initial funding of the Compaq venture; hence, too, its early construction of a high-class financial control and forecasting system, which was operating well before the start of production. The common error of smaller companies is to install professional management and effective systems only when burgeoning growth has drawn pained attention to their absence. That delay can be afforded only if competitors are suffering from the same deficiency. Giants are unlikely to be defective in these respects, however weak they might be in entrepreneurial zing.

Without that infrastructure, the astonishing pace of Compaq's early growth might well have broken its back. Sales went from a first-year record of $111 million to $329 million, and profits from a net $4.7 million to $12.8 million. That sizzling financial growth looked pedestrian against the physical realities of the production buildup: from 100 people in January 1983 to 600 in December, as output rose from 200 machines to 9,000. Without that dynamic pace, though, Compaq would have missed its market chances. Rule Three: strike while the iron is hot; build up significant market presence before the giant notices your existence.

"If you're growing slowly, problems can sidle up on you almost unnoticed," argues Canion. "With high growth, if you don't get out of the way first, they knock you down flat." But Compaq's biggest problem was and is another concomitant of high growth: its riches are noticed and coveted by the giant. Even after seeing off the first challenge from IBM, or the second, or the third, Compaq can never be sure that the next blow won't strike home.

For Davids facing Goliaths, product superiority alone is an inadequate shield. They need heavy reinforcement by equal strength in distribution, which is no easy trick. The mightiest force in the market must by definition dominate the existing distribution system. Frontal assault is therefore impossible; the challenger must find a way around. The Compaq outflankers were recruited in the obvious place—two heroes of IBM's own fabled PC launch were poached—and they identified the Achilles heel of their former employer: its own powerful sales force competed with the dealers.

Very well: Compaq would promise never to do likewise. The promise was backed by generous margins, salable machine features, and the vital compatibility with the IBM PCs that the courted dealers already carried. The courtship paid off. Compaq got into two-thirds of the computer specialty stores, within range of IBM's 80 percent-plus. But the shield, even with good distribution added to product superiority, was still inadequate. Another former IBM Supermarketer, having generated the Charlie Chaplin ads for the PC and run the campaigns for half the giant's product line, told his new Compaq colleagues after only a few months that a third defense was essential: massive advertising.

For 1984, advertising and promotion spending was magnified sevenfold to $20 million, a full one-fifth of revenues. Market research had clinched the case by showing that, without the creation of public confidence in Compaq, its runaway word-of-mouth sales boom couldn't be sustained. The argument is rammed home, too, by the impetus that IBM's own sales have received from the meticulously crafted image of the corporation. Other runners in the personal computer rat race have ignored the power of persuasion, or reacted too late to its necessity. Delay is fatal for Davids—and not just in marketing.

That's why, when Compaq went up against IBM with the desktop Deskpro, "We decided to do it on 5 January. On 28 June, we shipped the first product from a brand-new factory." The leader of this forced march adds that "I wouldn't want to do it that way every time. But we forced it to come right in the end." As Caulkin notes, "In truth, Compaq *had* to get it right. It couldn't afford an error like Lisa, the Apple III or the PC jr." With the Deskpro, the Telecompaq (a combined computer and telephone), and the portables, the company has the final defense against Goliath: the product portfolio recommended in Step One.

Having made the *Fortune* 500 in the record time of four years, with $504 million of 1985 sales and $26.6 million of net income, David might seem to have won his fight. But as venture-capitalist Rosen warns, the PC business "has become a very unforgiving industry," in which, on most expert reckoning, Compaq still needed another couple of star products for final safety. Rosen, though, gives his protégé a pass mark on the six vital attributes of success (he likens them to an electronic N-gate: "there's no output unless all six signals are positive going in"). The six are:

1. Good people
2. Good products
3. A marketing strategy
4. Financial resources
5. A world presence (on which Compaq embarked in its second year of life)
6. Excellent execution.

Without the six success factors, there's only one possible word of advice for those thinking of competing with giants: *don't.*

9. THE WATCHWORDS OF WACHOVIA

"The bigger they are, the harder they fall" has been a depressingly true axiom for some American businesses, including banking. Not only did Continental Illinois, the nation's eighth largest bank, suffer a technical knockout, but the largest of all, the Bank of America, slid spectacularly downhill only a few years after reigning as champion over the East Coast money-center banks. It doesn't follow, though, that the smaller they are, the faster they rise. Which makes the achievement of Wachovia Corp. of North Carolina, the fourth most profitable U.S. bank, all the more remarkable.

In 1984, its return on assets was more than double Citicorp's. Its loan-loss ratio was among the lowest in the United States—yet its lending had been vigorous enough to fuel an 18.6 percent annual growth rate over five years. Given that record, it wasn't surprising to find the bank, only thirty-seventh largest as measured by its $8.7 billion in assets, ranking thirteenth by market value among the country's banks. Obviously, being in the right place (the tobacco capital of Winston-Salem) at the right time helped. But Wachovia also outperformed the local talent—and its chief executive, John Medlin, had a simple formula to explain why.

"The secret of our success," he told *Management Today*, "is articulating some simple standards and not deviating from them." The standards include maintaining an unusually large capital base and refusing loans that fail to match up to relatively strict criteria. Wachovia adds to this fundamental caution an adventurous approach to new cost-cutting technology. Among the first banks to install computers, Wachovia has developed them to provide a distinct marketing edge: corporate cash management and pension fund supervision, along with personal banking for all 500,000 depositors, were among the goodies the computers made possible.

This small-is-very-beautiful picture changed radically in June 1985, when Wachovia announced a size-doubling merger with First Atlanta Corporation of Georgia, in pursuit of true national bank status. "Weak banks will fall by the wayside and excellence will be rewarded," explained Medlin, "that's why we've decided to expand now." That policy was debatable. But there's another watchword of Wachovia that isn't arguable at all: "It's the way you manage, not the size you are, that counts."

10. SIX POINTS FOR SMALL SUCCESS

However you look at it, the lesson is the same: to win the benefits of smallness, naked marketers must be as good as, or better than, the large—and that is by no means so easy as it has sometimes been made to sound. To return to the *Harvard Business Review* study of successful low-share companies mentioned earlier, the smaller you are, the more you may have to avoid what seem like the most desirable markets: those with high growth, innovation, differentiation, and so

173

on. Instead, the smaller business is better advised to seek a low profile.

The two Purdue professors who wrote the study (Carolyn Y. Woo and Arnold C. Cooper) argue that high-growth markets are turbulent arenas, meaning that all competitors try to grab share leadership and competition gets intense. With rapid product and process changes, the uncertainty gets worse; the inevitable shakeout follows, with weak competitors forced to the wall. When the market stops growing and goes into retreat, the turbulence starts all over again. Mature, though nondeclining, markets with low real growth seem to provide a more stable environment, one in which there is less elbowing to gain share.

As for frequent product changes, everybody in an industry may have to spend heavily on launching products as well as on research and development—and that's difficult for smaller businesses, with less revenue available. The faster the change, too, the earlier you have to scrap production tools and dies—maybe before their useful lives run out. The professors were surprised to find, too, that 72.5 percent of successful low-share performers "competed in markets characterized by standard products." That kind of market lets you focus your strategies, so that you don't run into the costs of providing custom-built products or special services.

Then why do industrial components and supplies dominate, representing 70 to 80 percent of successful low-share performers in the sample? It's because "purchase decisions for industrial products are based largely on performance, service and cost." So expensive advertising is usually less important, while, in addition, the purchasers of industrial products frequently like to operate on contracts. With a guaranteed market, the seller is better placed to project sales volume, capital spending—and costs. The more often products are bought, too, the less important market share appears to be. Also, the faster a product turns over, the less working capital is likely to be needed.

With a small share, though, a company needs high added value, because that means margins wide enough to absorb cost increases from suppliers or to carry price declines when markets weaken. Also, when value-added is high, there are plenty of opportunities for giving a product different characteristics to mark it out from the herd. It also needs focus—don't try to do everything, but select carefully what you *are* going to do. It must go for quality—special performance and reliability are the only real safeguards. It must compete on price—medium-to-low relative prices usually go hand in hand with the kind of market position described. It must keep costs low —that should be relatively easy when concentrating on a narrow line of standardized products and spending less on product R & D, advertising, promotion, sales force support, and new product introduction.

It's no easy matter, however, to combine a low market share (meaning less than a fifth of the combined output of the three largest competitors) with high profitability. There's a general rule, so other studies suggest, that "a difference of ten percentage points in market share is accompanied by a difference of about five points in pretax return on investment." A company can buck the rule, but that will be hard work and, in some circumstances (say, on the advent of new, well-financed competition), dangerous work at that. But look at these necessities again: high added value, differentiation, close focus, quality, competitive pricing, low costs. That is a six-point plan for marketing success on any scale, in any business.

As the Woo-Cooper research suggests, though, making small beautiful is even tougher in consumer marketing. The proudest possession in such markets, a fine old brand name, can be rapidly devalued. The product may practically bring tears to the eyes of people whose families have consumed the stuff for generations. But although nostalgia makes for moving TV commercials, consumer franchises need continuous updating. Otherwise, the fine old firm will inevitably bury its fine old customers.

Even when the product doesn't need rejuvenation, or has received it in goodly measure, the writing may still be on the wall. The more successful the brand, the greater its attraction to wealthier groups wishing to get richer still. In the current theory of management, size no longer has many friends—but it does on Wall Street. Small may not only lack economic beauty and adequate defense against predators; it may be hopelessly weak against competitors and customers and thus in no position to sniff at the offer that, in any case, it can't refuse.

It's no coincidence that the pitiful array of so-called new products that win space and sales in the supermarkets come almost exclusively from big companies. Small-business fans have good reason to fear that bad large-company money (and muscle) will drive out small good firms. That leaves managements in the lower echelons with little option: either they develop the business to the stage where it can be sold as a thriving concern for much fine gold, or they build their own well-spread, broad-based group. But companies centered on fine old brands—or fine new technology, for that matter—don't often generate the talent required for the second option, creating a multiproduct, multimarket (let alone multinational) success.

Anyway, the second option can only rest firmly on the first: maximum exploitation of the base market. The more money and skills the company achieves in this manner, the higher the chances that, having made an optimal success of one market segment, it will have the management capacity (in both senses) to build a similar success in another. That strategy came to the rescue of Nippon Kogaku when hit in mid-1983 by an 11 percent fall in Nikon camera sales, partly because of worldwide conditions, partly because it was underusing its innovative and technological strengths—a common syndrome in smaller companies, and often a fatal one.

But in better days, Nikon had diversified on the back of its optical skills. In its hour of need, the camera company could fall back on doubled sales in equipment for making semiconductors, and an advance by a third in optical measuring instruments. Other Japanese camera manufacturers have shown the same fine strategic appreciation and smart operational results: Asahi Optical, unable to conjure any growth out of the Pentax, pushed up sales in computer-aided design and manufacture (CAD/CAM) by half.

The seventh factor in small success—getting some tasty eggs out of the single basket—can only follow from the effective application of the first six points in the base market. Then, as Nikon showed a couple of years later by storming back with radical improvements in its camera range, for the first time throwing competitive pricing into the mix, the six-point plan has to be applied all over again—in all the markets of the firm.

11. THE SHARP BROTHERS

"Planning for a thousand years": so ran the headline over a corporate ad for Hitachi in which one of the dominant father-figures of Japanese business, president Katsushige Mita, gave forth his wisdom. He was actually quoting Hitachi's founder, who had observed that "a man lives for less than one hundred years, but he must plan for a thousand." What that means in terms of competition in today's markets can be gleaned from another Japanese quote: "The consumer electronic markets where we do excel were reaching the stage of consumer satisfaction or saturation; we are looking for new worlds to conquer."

The speaker was Akira Saeki, president of Sharp Corporation of Osaka. The first world Osaka ever conquered was that of the propelling pencil: its founder invented the Ever-Sharp in 1915. Half a century later, the company came up with the first all transistor-diode electronic desktop calculator. In its progress from pencils to advanced electronics (including the complex business of voice synthesis), Sharp has followed a straightforward marketing strategy, as described by a writer in *Management Today:* "It has chosen the right field to be in at the right time—in the recent past, the burgeoning business of consumer electronic products—and built on that choice a worldwide sales network and reputation."

Put that way, it sounds simple. So does the way Brother Industries, which started in the 1930s making industrial and domestic

177

sewing machines, advanced under the guidance of the Yasui brothers into knitting machines, microwave ovens, washing machines, machine tools, pianos, organs, and office equipment—including electronic typewriters. According to a Brother director, "it all got going from a manual Smith Corona. My chief, Masayoshi Yasui, brought it home from his second trip to the United States in the early 1950s. He almost dropped it on my desk and simply said—that is always the way with him—'let's make typewriters.' "

It took three years of research and development before Brother could ship its first machine, in 1961. A quarter of a century later, Brother was one of the world's leading producers of electronic typewriters, living up to its slogan that "he who makes good products makes good friends": SCM, from which that inspirational typewriter had come, had succumbed to a bid from a British company, Hanson Trust, that had but recently been a fraction of SCM's size. It's no surprise that in markets like audio, machine tools, copiers, microwaves, and many electronic sectors (all Japanese-dominated), the Japanese regard only each other as competitors.

Because many Western firms don't share the Japanese obsession with seeking higher market share as a strategic objective, they are easy prey for those that do. Nobody can claim that this pursuit of market penetration and new worlds to conquer has anything to do with the celebrated cultural distinctions between the West and Japan —not unless the capacity to mark, learn, and inwardly digest has fled from the Western cultural heritage.

Japanese businessmen such as the brothers Yasui, Sharp's Saeki, and Hitachi's Mita (the fifth engineer to run the firm) are acutely aware that the next thousand years, or months, depend on the quality of thought and action now; and that knowledge is the key to market power. Of course, the point can be fairly made that comparisons with what are by definition Japan's best-managed and most aggressive groups must do some injustice to the whole motley Western crew. But the question must be asked. Is it because the Japanese are so good? Or is it that so many of their ostensible competitors are so bad?

12. SIMPLE SECRETS FROM JAPAN

The Japanese have succeeded abroad by brilliant use of the concept of *strategic windows*—meaning the opportunities created by new market segments, changes in technology, or new distribution channels. Managers who don't know about that are in good (or bad) company. Fifteen substantial local firms, competing head-on in a European market with fifteen locally established Japanese firms, mostly didn't. In fact, two-thirds of the non-Japanese (compared with only one-third of the Japanese) didn't believe they were any good at sales and marketing; and on that the non-Japanese were obviously right.

For instance, two-thirds of the local companies gave defensive reasons for entering a new market, such as "we had to in order to survive." Several admitted that they "had never really thought it out." The Japanese? Over 70 percent said that their moves were "part of a planned global expansion" or related to the "potential of the market." Some 87 percent of the Japanese gave "aggressive growth" or "market domination" as their goal, which is no surprise. Neither is the fact that only 20 percent of the rivals did likewise.

Lesson 1. Maintenance of the status quo or prevention of decline is not a viable objective. You must have a positive aim if you want to achieve positive results.

Obviously, any marketing effort has to aim at profit. But what kind? Short-term profit was much more important to the local companies (93 percent) than to the Japanese (40 percent). Are you willing to allow your market position to be eroded in order to bolster short-term profitability? The Japanese aren't. They had the same choice as the locals—improving profitability by raising volume or by cutting costs and improving productivity—but the Japanese overwhelmingly chose volume: 73 percent were out to stimulate primary demand (against 47 percent of the locals); 67 percent thought that "entering newly emerging market segments" was a good description of what they were up to (versus 27 percent); and 87 percent aimed to build

179

up market share by getting customers away from their competitors (against 53 percent).

Lesson 2. Since a lower market share usually results in a higher unit cost of manufacture (and marketing), cost cutting and market building must go hand in hand; they aren't alternatives but complements.

Can you divide up your market into relatively uniform groups of customers, so you can target your offerings at the groups with the greatest potential? The survey by Doyle, Saunders, and Wong found that 47 percent of the non-Japanese companies (13 percent of Japanese) were unclear about their principal categories of customers and their special needs: "We have not broken the customers down. We have always held the opinion that the market is wide . . . and the product has wide appeal, therefore why break the market down at all? We do not see the market as being made up of specific segments. Our market is made up of the whole industry."

Lesson 3. Divide and conquer is the essential approach to modern markets: competing blindly across the board wastes both money and opportunities.

As everybody knows, the Japanese have achieved marketing marvels in becoming identified with quality and status. In fact, 40 percent of the Japanese firms reckoned their customers were up-market—but only 13 percent of the locals did. The Japanese like to position themselves in the quality, high added-value sector of the market. Only suckers allow themselves to be positioned by their competitors—at the price-sensitive commodity end.

Lesson 4. The bottom end of the market produces the worst bottom line. If you want profits to go up, go up.

Given those up-market aims, it's not surprising that 87 percent of the Japanese cited "superior quality and reliability" as a key characteristic; only 47 percent of their rivals made the same claim. Twice as many Japanese as local companies thought, too, that they enjoyed a real competitive advantage in the area of customer service. What advantage did the nationals think they had? Most frequently mentioned were low prices, a "traditional brand name," and simply being nationals.

Lesson 5. No customer benefit is worth more than quality, reliability, and service, and without them there is no benefit.

The non-Japanese companies considered themselves weaker at R & D, design, volume manufacturing, production engineering, and the ability to cost accurately. The Japanese also tended to spend more on promotions, in contrast to their rivals, who spent more on personal selling (which was actually more efficient for their smaller numbers of customers). The Japanese also gave a much higher rating to dealer support. In other words, the locals simply weren't geared up to make the best or most of their businesses.

Lesson 6. A business is only as good as the sum of its parts, which means you can't afford to have weak parts.

Virtually all the non-Japanese companies had traditional, functional structures, but two-thirds of the Japanese were organized along product-division lines. Does it matter? With a functional approach, say the authors, few managers feel totally dedicated to the performance of key products. Appoint a sales or marketing director to supervise sales of a whole portfolio of products, and you won't have somebody with the knowledge, incentive, or time to champion an individual line.

Anyway, the non-Japanese companies for the most part didn't have budgeting or information systems that showed up performance at the market or product-line level. Systems designed to show results by factory, and not by product or market, are no help at all to a company that's serious about its marketing.

Lesson 7. Use your organization and systems as bureaucracies, and you'll get bureaucratic results. Use them as dynamic means of separating out and stimulating market performance, and you'll get dynamic profits.

A final quote commented that the non-Japanese companies were "too often finance and production oriented; they were focused on the short term; and their strategies generally failed to reflect the dynamics of markets. Perhaps most importantly, many of them failed to

181

realize that, in order to win today, companies need to be highly professional, committed and aggressive."

That's marketing Lesson 8.

To summarize some of the important points I've mentioned in Step Six:

1. Taking care of the future always starts with the here and now.

2. You can't market properly unless you're free to structure a product line to meet the freely arising demands of customers whose business is truly profitable.

3. Don't go into anything unless you can clearly foresee winning a viable share of a viable market.

4. Never assume that because a market is booming, it will boom forever, or for you.

5. These days, you're unlikely to accomplish the marketing task, whatever the size of the firm, without one thing: quality.

6. A small-share business can match the profits of a firm with a large market share, but the odds are against it.

7. As a customer, get in-house capacity, or the equivalent, to cushion you from boom-time rushes; as a supplier, take into account everybody's expansion, not just your own.

8. To compete in the big leagues, get yourself good people, good products, a marketing strategy, financial resources, a world presence—and do everything well. That's all!

9. Go for strong, simple standards, and don't deviate from them, and you can outdo anybody, no matter what your size.

10. If you're relatively small, the six essentials of marketing success matter more than ever: high added value, differentiation, close focus, quality, competitive pricing, and low costs.

11. If you want to flourish for the next one thousand days, plan for the next one thousand years.

12. If you're highly professional, committed, and aggressive, you don't have to worry about the Japanese: you'll be just like them.

Step Seven: Making Promotion and Publicity Pay

1. THE TWO HIGH ROLLERS

Marketing men indulge in exaggeration (or outright lies) more cheerfully, it seems, than anybody else in management. Often there's no apparent point to their inventions about their market shares, their product's charms, their profits—but apparently nobody minds. The issue is not the same as truth in advertising, something on which everybody is insistent but which—in all truth—is among the more boring of management issues. Truth in marketing actually matters far more, because the foundation of a product's success is its credibility. Whether it is possible to tell the truth, the whole truth, and nothing but the truth is beside the point. Unless the public believes the message conveyed by the product and its promotion, the marketing game is lost.

In some conspicuous cases, though, the promotion stars the producer more than the product, a strategy never illustrated more mordantly than when Sir Freddie Laker spent some of his last hours in command of his doomed airline starring in a TV commercial. Laker had been Britain's most visible exponent of this form of star marketing in which the businessman himself both provides and promotes the product. Another practitioner of this art form was John Z. De Lorean, whose brief but florid fame expired as described in Step Two, section 7.

What did the two have in common, apart from a penchant for getting into the euphemistic hole known as "financial difficulties"? They both exhibited a large size in egos, which makes it difficult to decide whether the marketing method was truly chosen for its supposed efficacy alone. Even if it wasn't, even if the man really revels in seeing his name in lights, the technique could nonetheless be effective. But it has obvious limitations: the rich man's image is purely promotional; it can of itself contribute to the image of the mass-market product; it can't contribute anything if the product won't wash.

This criticism doesn't apply to Victor Kiam (see Step Six, section 3), whose selling pitch in Remington ads was not his then far-from-famous self but a great line: the razor was so good that he bought the whole darned company. What undermined Laker in the marketplace was a credibility weakened by the confusion of its (or his) image as other airlines muscled in on the cheap fares act. "Standby," not "Laker," became the synonym for flying overseas cheap, to be followed by People Express, which at least didn't repeat that particular mistake. Its image stayed sharp. It's a sign of Laker's own confusion that its final, forlorn marketing ploy was a first-class service lumbered with the name of Regency.

Maybe analysis would show that people never fully believe the owner's pitch for his product. But there's little doubt that he himself does: the same ego that contributes to those personal displays can blind its owner to the unpleasant realities of his business. In marketing, blindness is invariably deadly and entirely inexcusable. Vision can always be miraculously restored, by common or garden research.

2. SHIFTING THE CONSUMER PREFERENCE

In advertising, as in the rest of marketing's mix, it's always right to research. Many marketers don't. Indeed, why marketing companies so often misuse or mistrust research is one of those mysteries, like vanishing ships in the Bermuda Triangle, that are impossible to solve. One common excuse—implicit or explicit—is precisely that research can't measure the imponderables, especially in "creative" areas like advertising. This view is poppycock, and there's the word of a creative genius to prove it. Writing in the *Harvard Business Review* with an agency colleague named Joel Raphaelson, the great David Ogilvy, founder of Ogilvy and Mather, discusses research to profound effect.

Only by research can you find out, for example, whether it's a good business idea to build an advertising campaign around a celebrity, like one of the high rollers. It sounds like an excellent notion, and there's a long history of such campaigns, ranging from soap endorsements by prewar society beauties to those Laker Skytrain ads. But research shows that although the celebrity ads score 22 percent *above* average recall, they change consumer brand preference 21 percent *less* than the average of advertisements studied.

The reason for the discrepancy is less important than the conclusion. (In fact, what happens is that attention gets focused on the celebrity instead of the product.) The attitude of the consuming public to the advertising isn't the point—it's how they react at the point of sale. The shift in brand preference is the truly vital measure, and even more significant than may at first appear.

According to Raphaelson and Ogilvy, the research found that viewers who changed brands bought the product concerned 3.3 times more often than nonchangers. O. and R. of O. and M. cite these Magnificent Seven shifters:

1. Problem solution
2. Humor ("when the humor is pertinent to the selling proposition")
3. Relevant characters ("personalities, developed by the advertising, who become associated with a brand")
4. Slice-of-life ("enactments in which a doubter is converted")
5. News ("new products, new ideas, new information")
6. Candid camera testimonials
7. Demonstrations.

Thus the reason heiress and society figure Gloria Vanderbilt proved so brilliant a choice to promote (and name) designer jeans: she was a "relevant character" who became much more famous by being associated with the advertising and the brand. The brilliance, moreover, lay partly in the fact that "Vanderbilt" is something of a brand in itself, immediately suggestive of the smartness and wealth that she embodied.

The Magnificent Seven are a concise and clear guide to preference-shifting ads, and what O. and R. have to say is none the worse for its lack of earth-shattering information. In fact, the rules of successful advertising, like those for all successful business, are simplicity itself. If you want your ads to work, use cartoons and animation to reach children—not grown-ups. Avoid many short scenes and changes of situation. Words on the screen ("supers") are super but only if they reinforce the main point. Show the package, and always end with the brand name. Start with the key idea.

The same simplicity applies to the rules for print ads: for instance, as in TV, press ads with "news" score above average; it pays to show the product in use and the end result of having used it. "Copywriters who believe they can tease readers into reading an advertisement are throwing money away." Yet you need only glance at a TV or magazine to see flagrant breaches of these self-evident rules.

The truth is that too many managers think themselves wiser than any research finding and more knowledgeable than any advertising agent when it comes to promoting their product. They thus encourage the very split between "pure" advertising and the impure world of the naked market that produces schizophrenia about what is and isn't effective. The truth to remember at all times is that advertising which isn't *commercially* effective is a waste of money; and such effectiveness must be measured only where it counts—in the marketplace.

The key to that effectiveness is understanding that advertising invariably conveys a promise—and the promise must be kept. The techniques recommended by Ogilvy and Raphaelson, if closely examined, clearly support giving authentic promises in an authentic manner. The good marketer offers a real solution to a genuine problem, and does so with pertinent humor, using only relevant characters in authentic "slice-of-life" situations, stressing news of new properties, using believable testimonials, and demonstrating how the product works. True, these strategies lead to the endless series of housewives being shown how to remove stains from clothes and sinks —the very mind-numbing commercials to which advertising's critics object.

But the marketers who run soap companies don't run these ads entirely because they are unable to think of anything else but because of the proven past effectiveness of this particular sales approach. The effectiveness, as with bank or gasoline advertising, though, gets diluted if all soap companies take the same tack. A glittering prize is offered to the innovative marketer who can break the industry mold. That is most unlikely to happen, however, if the rules of truly effective advertising are broken—and it'll never happen unless the claims and the reality match.

3. THE BAD ADS OF BANKS

It may be that no advertising can be very effective in a particular market. Take banking as an example. Choice of bank may be influenced predominantly by quite extraneous factors like where Father banked, or even location—which brings to mind an oil company study made long ago that demonstrated fairly conclusively that, in anything but the short term, for all the intensive hullaballoo of the marketers, the dominant force determining share of market was simply the siting of service stations. The same phenomenon almost certainly takes place in banking. All those friendly advertising campaigns probably cancel each other out to a considerable extent. While it then becomes imperative for each bank to maintain its "share of voice," the total vocalization doesn't add a penny to the total of deposits or profits.

Any research that confirms these probabilities would doubtless share the fate of the oil study mentioned above. Nobody would take the blindest bit of notice, especially if the whole industry were engaged in a bout of highly visible competition. The banks have been conspicuous among institutions once innocent of marketing in their subsequent wholesale conversion (at least in principle) to the religion. Whether the new disciplines or diversions have made much difference to the competitive battle is hard to determine. Among the prime objects of marketers are to win more (profitable) customers and to win more (profitable) business from them, partly by introducing more (profitable) products. To the extent that new banking products have swayed the struggle, advertising has certainly been indispensable. No better method exists of blazoning forth and explaining the virtues of an innovation, and there have, of course, been highly significant innovations in this market.

The most notable is certainly the bank credit card, pioneered by the then high-riding Bank of America in California, and picked up in Britain by the relatively agile Barclays. Because both are the biggest in their own markets, this proves that the race doesn't have to go to the small and swift. But financial products have one great defect: they are far too easily imitated. One banker's innovation rapidly becomes another's imitation. When every competitor can afford to match the competition on every point, none can hope to gain a lasting advantage from a new product, any more than from a new advertising campaign.

In such circumstances, the use of advertising is fundamentally strategic. The spender should lay out the least money necessary to reinforce positive emotions among existing and potential customers —feelings that can be measured by intelligent research. The research can also show how the bank, or any other organization, ranks against its competitors. But the banks' most powerful marketing weapon is probably the oldest one of all—high standards of customer service. And they can't be advertised effectively unless they actually exist. In most cases, alas, they don't.

4. WHY MARS NEEDED ADVERTISING

Does the lesson of the banks—that advertising occupies a position of secondary importance—apply to consumer markets? One thing's for sure: most managers wouldn't dare try to find out. The penalties for being wrong would be unthinkable. But one excellent thing about having a business of your own is that you're free to experiment. You can try different approaches to the business, which are fine if they work and, if they don't, you've learned a valuable lesson for the future. That's what you *can* do, but most proprietors don't.

In reality, the owner of a business is usually at least as cautious, and as averse to risky experiment, as the hired corporate manager. Both hate to lose money to find out that they were wrong. But one great entrepreneur was always an exception: Forrest Mars. Though American, he made his reputation, and created the base for one of the world's largest private fortunes, in Britain. Mars would do such

189

costly things as adopt a totally different policy on promotion or marketing in one region to test whether what he was doing elsewhere made sense. The bravery paid off in both candy and pet food. At one point, more cans of Kit-E-Kat were sold every day than cans of baked beans or tomato soup—making the Mars product the bestselling canned pet food in Britain.

The advertising was handled by a genius named Jack Wynne-Williams, builder of what was the biggest local agency, Masius Wynne-Williams, before upstarts like the Saatchis (and the feebler efforts of his own agency's lesser successors) pushed it down the leagues. Mars should have been delighted by the results of the cat food campaigns. But according to Elizabeth Francke, who worked for Masius, Mars began to wonder whether the $3 million a year he spent on ads was really necessary:

"Kit-E-Kat seemed unassailable, and the mountainous stacks of cans piled upon miles of supermarket shelves as permanent as rock. So Forrest Mars made one of those daring executive decisions that mark the born leader. . . . 'Stop the advertising,' he ordered. The only person who could challenge Mars was somebody who didn't work for him, Wynne-Williams—and argue he did. The pair locked horns, but the outcome was inevitable. Forrest Mars, though no more determined than his opponent, had the unarguable power to sign, or not sign, the checks."

So the advertising ceased. And, in no time at all, so did the sales of the beloved cat food. According to Francke, sales slid "faster and faster: down past baked beans; past tomato soup, past the next bestselling pet foods, down into the limbo of also-rans. This dizzy slide towards commercial oblivion took much less than a year." The point is that brand preference among cats, their owners, and the supermarket operators didn't result from any greater nutritional value, as stressed in the Wynne-Williams ads; it resulted from having a good product placed constantly before the eyes and ears of the buying public—and thus before the whiskers of the consumers.

As soon as Forrest Mars realized what awful damage he had done, he countermanded his ludicrous order. Showing the essential magnanimity of a great businessman, he gave the task of rescuing the product to Wynne-Williams, who "since the cost of climbing back is always higher than the cost of defending a strong market position . . . in the end probably made money out of the near-demise." The lesson drawn by Francke, writing in *Better Business,* is that "in the assurance of his gigantic market share he did not appreciate the intensity of the non-stop competitive pressures that assailed his brand." That's a telling point. It's when you're riding at your highest that you must ask why you're doing well and look for the Achilles heel you certainly have.

One of Mars's weaknesses was that nobody could say him nay. If you are able to force through an idiotic policy it proves you are a powerful leader, but that's no way to run a good business. A second point is that economizing is an excellent way of boosting short-term profits. But you must always analyze carefully the impact on the medium- and long-term market stature (and thus profitability) of the brand. On that, Wynne-Williams had not only the last but the best word. As he argued futilely with Mars in a favorite phrase, "you've got to spend money to defend money."

Those eight words are golden.

5. THE SUBLIMATION OF THE SAATCHIS

In 1971 two young brothers, one an ace copywriter, the other a magazine business manager, took a full-page advertisement in the London *Sunday Times* to announce that "a new type of advertising agency has been born." Probably nobody believed it except the Saatchi brothers. Admen are notoriously given to exaggeration: new agencies were not rare species even in 1970 (although new *types* of agency were rarer than the white buffalo), and the odds against an agency born in Britain cracking the mold were overwhelming anyway.

191

The ad market was dominated by powerful, rich, U.S. multinational agencies, living high off the hog provided by the massive billings of U.S. multinational and national clients. One by one the bigger, established London agencies were being taken over by Madison Avenue firms. A brand-new agency like Saatchi & Saatchi, even though it started with a respectable million pounds in billings, surely didn't stand a chance of joining the mega-agencies then in the process of formation, whose full strength unfurled in the 1980s.

By then, astoundingly, the infant agency of 1970 was right up among them. In 1985, billings were two thousand times that first-year level while revenues were $440 million on a $3 billion total, producing profits 360 times those of that first bumptious year. Acquiring companies on both sides of the Atlantic—not only in advertising but in management consultancy, marketing services, public relations, and so forth—Saatchi & Saatchi, if not a new type, was certainly a new force, or rather an embodiment of new forces.

Charles and Maurice Saatchi had followed the golden rule of large-scale expansion: sail before the wind. They arrived at a time when rising American domination had been accompanied by a pervasive blandness and repetition in the actual creative work of advertising. It gave British agencies, mostly new, the chance to become the Greeks to the Romans of Madison Avenue. A rolling tide of brilliant British advertising reset the standard and the style. The Saatchis shared in this flood. The difference was that their ambitions were Roman in scope. They wanted an empire.

Marketing managements aided and abetted the new creative emphasis for a simple reason. In the saturated, slow-growth, affluent markets of the 1970s and 1980s, intense competition for market share has become obligatory. Basically similar products must be sharply differentiated to win this competitive war, and no weapon works better than sharply differentiated advertising. It cuts down the enemy, not only in fast-moving consumer goods but in arenas like politics, where the Saatchis, doing highly effective work for Mrs. Thatcher's Tories, became a household name—which helped greatly in winning fat accounts for household goods.

As the brothers consolidated their empire—7,000 employees in 150 wholly owned offices in 28 countries in 1985, before the purchase of Ted Bates made them the world's biggest—they purported to have discovered a novel principle. The multiform communications conglomerate was only one aspect of the change they blazoned forth (again in large ads on their own behalf). The prophet to whom they turned was Theodore Levitt, who had become famous through his earlier work on "marketing myopia," in which he posed the seminal question: "What business are you in?"

As Levitt has engagingly confessed, that innocent question led to all manner of corporate catastrophe as managements overstretched both the Levittian definition of their businesses and/or their own managerial talents. Levitt's new and equally pregnant phrase is "the global corporation," which "operates as if the entire world (or major regions of it) were a single entity; it sells the same things in the same way everywhere."

This definition comes complete with an awful warning: "Corporations geared to this new reality can decimate competitors that still live in the disabling grip of old assumptions about how the world works." The message was taken up with evident glee by Saatchi & Saatchi. A global advertising agency obviously sees great attractions in having global customers. That means exclusive possession of the biggest accounts in the business—and there are indeed some great companies that operate as Levitt describes, often by the very nature of their industries. Coca-Cola, oil companies, and international airlines such as British Airways (for which Saatchi's has already done some definitively global work) are prime examples.

So were the Saatchis as right in 1985 as they had been in 1970? By the fall of 1986, the Saatchi arguments no longer looked so convincing, not because of intellectual weakness but because the apparently overhasty purchase of the Ted Bates agency, followed by an exodus of accounts and executives, had marred the brothers' reputation for infallibility. It was a high price to pay for staying number one. But on the globalization issue, this time the brothers weren't alone in believing their own publicity. And if they were right, then advertising was a whole new world.

6. GLOBAL IS AS GLOBAL DOES

Whatever happened to the multinational corporation? Instead of the top 300 MNCs dominating the world, to quote again that awed prediction of the 1960s, some have been forced to retreat into Fortress America; some were defeated in competition by local, national rivals; some were taken over; and all, in varying degrees, were affected by the prolonged recession and the prodigious Japanese. Attention has turned to the more successful of the giants, above all, IBM. The multibillionaire of mainframe and personal computers represents a further evolution of the MNC into the transnational corporation, which differs from the MNC by doing more than joining different national subsidiaries together: the TNC transcends them. Just as the Saatchis say, it's global.

There is a real difference, though, between a company that sells a single commodity (a bottle of Coke, an airline seat, a barrel of oil) around the world and a corporation like IBM, which sells a complex line of products to a wide variety of markets. In fact, only product development is global at IBM: production is regional; marketing is national. Despite that important reservation, IBM is truly global in many striking ways. Its culture is homogeneous.

All its national marketers conform to the same governing principles, just as all its plants perform at the same standards. As the products are identical, anything less would be economically absurd. Economics, in fact, explains the global trend. In markets where the costs of research, development, tooling, and product launches have become enormous (as in computers), corporations must seek to maximize turnover and minimize variations.

That iron law of economics, and not any newfound love of

194

international ideals, drove Ford Motor to develop cars for trans-European sale, despite marked differences in national tastes in cars at the time. Coming late into the act, General Motors went one stage further, and for exactly the same economic reason produced the first world cars. The number of industries to which this logic applies is restricted, but they include such vast and powerful companies that the influence and example of the global corporations is far greater than their number.

For a start, they have a decisive impact on their supplier of goods and services. Professor Ted Levitt believes that "as more and more of the world's activities fall into this global pattern, the result is greater interdependence between client and service company; more international relationships; and more long-term relationships." He goes on to argue that "the organization of a global product is too complicated and individual repeat negotiations country by country are too much of a hassle, and too costly. Marriage is both more convenient and more necessary."

The case is certainly overstated. IBM, for instance, makes a point (for political as well as economic reasons) of drawing its supplies as far as possible from national sources. But the incentive for an IBM supplier, or for one of Ford's or GM's, to seek the widest possible share of the giant's business could hardly be bigger.

The frontiers of world competition have shrunk as goods have imitated people in taking advantage of the new freedom and low cost of travel, and herein lies the reality of the global corporation. The present competition for market share, the most intense the world has ever seen, is international. Consequently, the pacesetting companies are international as well, those that use the networks and the airlines most intensively as they seek outlets and opportunities in any territory where potential sales are sufficiently large.

The main arenas for this competitive struggle are obvious—the United States, Europe, and Japan; what McKinsey's Kenichi Ohmae calls "the Triad," a marketplace containing 600 million consumers "with converging needs and preferences." In his book *Triad Power*, Ohmae argues that increasing capital intensity and soaring R & D costs (already mentioned in the context of the car giants and IBM), plus converging worldwide consumer tastes, and intensifying protectionism make it essential to establish a presence in all three Triad areas. His warning is blunt: "Quite simply, global enterprises organized for doing business in the 1960s are out of date."

The message is the same as Levitt's and equally visionary. The vision is that old, unrealized dream of the first multinationals. Like that vision, the global one contains its fair share of exaggeration, as Levitt has cheerfully admitted. His confession, given to Christopher Lorenz of the *Financial Times,* covers three main examples: that "the world's needs and desires have been irrevocably homogenized" (they actually haven't); that "everything gets more and more like everything else" (it actually doesn't); that national and multinational companies that do not "go global" have little chance of survival (they may actually have a greater chance, though they will have to be nimblefooted). You don't have to look beyond the United States to see the force of these objections. The persistence of marked differences between regional markets in the States has been developed by expert marketing companies into a powerful tool for winning share (see Step Twelve). Not only do national markets differ, in other words, but so do markets within nations. This is a fact of the global marketplace, although it may be changing.

But the strong survival of regional and national markets in the era of global competition is something that will change only over a long time. Step by step, however, efforts are being made to match the global marketplace with global marketing. Playtex, for instance, cut down from a situation in which forty-three different ads were running worldwide to a point where it used only one agency, Grey Advertising, and produced a single campaign for its new bra, *Wow.* The difficulties are obvious, though, from the three ads for Britain, West Germany, and Spain. *Wow* doesn't translate exactly. So the German uplift came under the title *Traumbügel* (which apparently means "dream wire"), and the Spanish version was called *Alas,* which looked as sad as those particular ads. In fact the adaptation of a single campaign to so many markets was so complicated that it must have eaten into the savings in production costs—a very small part of the total campaign expense for a mass-market product.

Business Week quotes Professor Philip Kotler to that effect: "What efficiencies there are," he adds, "hardly offset Playtex's risk in assuming that one campaign will be equally effective everywhere." Note, moreover, that the mono-campaign involved Grey executives in global travel to an extent that the traditional separate campaigns would never have done. (One vice president, armed with 150 bras, even got accused of smuggling at Sydney Airport.) In the global marketplace there's a long way to go—literally, because business travel makes the world go round, and metaphorically, because the realities of the marketplace restrict its globalism.

Yet a great historical trend is surely under way and will not be stopped. A businessman traveling from Kennedy to Heathrow uses a global airline flying the same plane bought and operated by other airlines all over the world. During the flight he drinks spirits, reads magazines, watches films, listens to music recordings, all of which are marketed globally. His portable computer is likewise a global product. He may be picked up at the airport by a car broadly similar to others sold worldwide, which takes him to a hotel that is part of a global chain in which every unit is managed on the same pattern and to the same standards.

For all that, the old days have gone, days when a great corporation could develop a product in its home market and then introduce it a few years later into overseas markets where the managements were either its own nationals or local stooges. As Ohmae says, "Today, they don't have time to leisurely market new and probably much more expensive technological developments; many competitors possess comparable technological skills, making it almost impossible to sustain a technological monopoly; and the global diffusion of new technology has become a matter of months, not years." So the Saatchi brothers *are* right. The global product and the truly global management *have* taken over the running. Where they are running to is not yet clear, but marketers had better be aware that the race is on.

197

7. THE CLASS OF '82

What do the following brands have in common: Chrysler, Miller
Lite, ActiVision, Burger King, Maybelline, General Electric, Pru-
dential, Jack Daniel's, Del Monte, Commodore, Tylenol, 7-Up,
Marlboro, Hilton, Maidenform? It obviously isn't any particular
business activity. The gamut runs from personal computers to eye
shadow, insurance to soft drinks, bras to hotels. Nor is it the advent
of troubled times, although Miller Lite has lost its impetus, GE has
sold its appliance business, Philip Morris has had its fill of 7-Up,
Tylenol has suffered two cyanide disasters, and Commodore has
plunged into the red since 1982—the year when the above were the
fifteen top brands in the United States.

Do they have anything else in common, some highest factor that
would explain their preeminence and provide a clue for would-be
kings of the market? Age has something to do with it. Nine of the
fifteen have been as familiar and American as the Stars and Stripes
for decades; another (Marlboro) was converted long ago from a
ladies' smoke to the exact, macho male, opposite; but the remaining
five are relative newcomers. Even for the golden oldies, underlying
change has been so great that only one, Jack Daniel's, can claim
continuity as the secret of its success.

The predominance of senior citizens, however, means that innovative R & D doesn't loom large; it is a factor in only half a dozen
of the Fabulous Fifteen. *Market segmentation,* the buzzword of mid-
1980s markets, didn't hum that much in 1982: seven out of fifteen,
the same score as that for quality, another factor that developed
currency and power later on. Positioning was significantly more
important than either. Two-thirds of the bunch owed their success
in part to the careful marriage of the product and the brand to
selected and profitable customer profiles. Only ActiVision, Maybelline, GE, Jack Daniel's, and Commodore do not rank as masters of
the positioning arts.

So what was the Highest Common Factor? Far and away the
winner is investment in advertising. In only three cases—Maybelline,

Commodore, Jack Daniel's—was advertising a lesser contributor to major brand success. In Commodore's case, that may have been a grave error. When the market changed dramatically and home computers no longer sold themselves, the strong image that only advertising can create might have spared the company at least some of its traumas. Old or new, eight times out of ten, advertising is the most important name in the marketing game—in any year.

8. HOW ADS GINGER UP SALES

The experience of the Fabulous Fifteen proves conclusively (as if proof were needed) that advertising pays. But there's obviously no point in just spending massively. What should you spend on? How? Why? These are the basic questions on which success hinges.

There's a fascinating case study about the answers that comes from a relatively small ad agency named Dexter Brent and Paterson. In this case, the client was Stone's Original Green Ginger Wine, an unpromising mouthful in name and taste, you might think. The stuff has been produced in London since 1740, and hasn't changed much in all that time. Not surprisingly, after 240 years the drink was losing popularity. But its owners didn't take the usual line of least resistance and let it slowly die (often a product's life cycle is purely, stupidly voluntary—managements kill products that still have plenty of life in them).

Ginger wine had plenty of sales, too. Stone's had two-thirds of a retail market worth $20 million or so. As press ads and posters had done nothing to stop the slide, television seemed the only possible answer. The strategy was obvious. Stone's had to appeal more to the twenty-five-to-forty-four age group (men and women), to sell more outside the Christmas/New Year's season, and to widen the whole ginger wine market without making more sales for the competition than for itself.

That's Principle One. The advertiser must form a clear, sensible strategy, based on thorough knowledge of the market, so that the company can play to its strengths and seek to eliminate its weaknesses. The broad aims, though, must be broken down into specific objectives and decisions, the first being the choice of media. Television was the logical choice because the client needed (a) to reach a mass audience; (b) to hit a target audience within the mass; (c) to cover the areas of Stone's own geographical strength (which covered 60 percent of sales); (d) to demonstrate the versatility of the product; and (e) to encourage the trade (it's often important, in any business, to use TV for exactly this latter purpose).

Principle Two is thus to make the media fit the message. Use whatever most effectively meets your aims at the lowest cost. With the medium chosen, on those grounds, Stone's and the agency had to set down the precise marketing objectives. This may sound banal and hardly worth doing. But statements of the obvious are essential —especially because, time and time again, missing the obvious is what causes failure.

Principle Three is to put everything you're trying to do down on paper. Stone's listed five aims:

1. To halt the sales decline of recent years.
2. To continue to promote the product in both bars and retail stores.
3. To concentrate the promotional activity in the areas of strength.
4. To increase the number of outlets stocking the product.
5. To improve its positioning in all outlets.

The next stage is to write down some more statements of the obvious but essential, those needed to guide the agency's creative work, advertising objectives, and strategy. In this case, they ran as follows:

1. To promote Stone's Ginger Wine as a winter drink, unrelated to the short festive season.

2. To project Stone's to adults across all socioeconomic groups.

3. To encourage the under-forty-fives to try Stone's Ginger Wine—on its own, with Scotch (as a "Whisky Mac"), or as a mixer with any other drink—without alienating existing loyal drinkers.

4. To appeal equally to men and women.

5. To increase sales through all outlets.

Principle Four is that you won't, except by sheer good fortune, get an effective creative campaign from an agency unless you've done the kind of homework described here. For Stone's, the agency's creative people duly did their stuff, coming up with an animated film, combined with live action, using the theme "It's what winter was invented for" (previously used in the press and on posters). The film didn't cost much to produce, and was also economical in another sense: it was used for a second season in the effort to repeat the success of the previous year's November-to-March drip-feed campaign.

But the most important question of all is, Did it work? "Spontaneous recall" of the wine among the vital twenty-five-to-forty-four age group increased significantly. An interesting fact, but it must be translated into sales. The same can be said about recall of advertising, which moved significantly upward.

The sales numbers echoed the recall figures, with four clear proofs of success: (1) a marked increase in the number of the target audience claiming to have bought the product within the last three months; (2) volume sales in total for January–June increased by 10.1 percent over the same period the previous year; (3) during the prime selling/buying period (October–December) the sales decline appeared to have been turned into a modest increase; (4) sales during and after the TV campaign were considerably higher than a year before. The sales increases, what's more, were achieved profitably and without price cutting. In fact, the product maintained its price premium against the competition.

The cost of the campaign, including some press advertising, was a bargain $450,000. But note (Principle Five) that you only know whether you have a bargain, or a bust, by following up closely to ensure that the company has received what it is paying for: more and more profitable sales. Large brands with large shares and sales, like those of the Fabulous Fifteen, won't get away with bargain spending because of their scale. Neither can massive investment in advertising pay commensurate returns unless you follow (as the Supermarketeers always do) the Five Principles that gingered up the sales of a 240-year-old, very nonvintage wine.

9. THE DIRECT APPROACH OF MONTREUX

It's a wise marketer who has full information on all the following: interactive/videotex, inbound telephone marketing, marriage mail, personalization, deduplication, response-activated wrappers, laser-compatible labels, and pop-up. There's even a round of applause for any marketer who can promptly name the thread that binds all these mysteries together. It's direct marketing, a field in which the United States leads the world. Direct-mail campaigns in America are five times as numerous per capita as those in Europe.

Some of the U.S. recipients no doubt feel that, even at a fifth of the inundation, they would still be getting too much junk mail. But the mail gap is really evidence of the lag in Europe behind the best business and marketing practice, at least as advocated (to nobody's surprise) by participants at the annual Montreux Direct Marketing Symposium. After all, if your life is spent in telebroking, affinity groups, and lead generation, you're not about to deny their validity.

The case for the offense is well put by direct expert Peter Rosenwald, who attacked Britain as the "listless society" back in the 1970s and found no reason to change his language in 1985. Inability to gather lists of names of target groups may not be the gravest economic failing of a society. But at a time when markets are fragmenting and indirect marketing costs have been soaring, listlessness is at best a heavy drawback.

Direct marketing's many gurus are understandably fond of quoting examples of obscene indirect wastage, like that of Hertz and Avis who are major national advertisers even though only 6 percent of the TV audience they reach so expensively will ever hire a car. This statistic comes from Lester Wunderman, the wonderman of Young and Rubicam, purported to earn more in a month than some chief executives garner in an entire year. That, too, is a revealing statistic—direct marketing has made big money for its ace practitioners because it is making much bigger money for its users, and they are an infinitely varied bunch.

Insurance companies; electronic games; Huggies disposable diapers; computer hardware and software; *The New Yorker* magazine; Ronald Reagan—these are all among the parties who have presumably been persuaded, to quote one expert, that "dollar for dollar direct mail returns more than any other medium." Every business has some significant aspect, if not the whole caboodle, for which direct marketing can pay dividends now—and will pay more in the future. Those marketers who know neither the medium nor its lore (for example, only 25 percent of people read beyond the headlines) have every reason to start learning fast.

But that is only a part—though a very valuable one—of a much wider lesson. Successful marketing communications isn't only or even mainly about advertising and sales spiels. The available armory is far larger. And the biggest weapon of all is the corporation itself: the sum of all its channels of communication, all its external aspects, and all the perceptions of the company and its products that these tools, direct and indirect, can create.

10. MANAGING BY DESIGN

Direct marketing is by no means the only form of direct contact a company can have with its customers. As the Supermarketers of IBM have long known and practiced, the impact of the corporation on its customers is achieved through many routes, and it's no good concentrating on just one, or even two. Consider what happened to Chrysler after it decided, in 1964, to enter Europe in style. It bought Rootes in Britain (a sick company), Barreiros in Spain (a raw new truck maker), and Simca in France (a Ford discard, but the best of the bunch). For a while, Chrysler persevered with the plethora of brands, good, bad, and indifferent, that it had acquired. Then it decided to call everything Chrysler.

As design expert Wally Olins describes it, "There were advertisements for Chrysler cars. Showrooms redesigned in the Chrysler idiom, complete with Pentastar, replaced Simca showrooms in the Champs Elysées and Rootes showrooms in Piccadilly. And in these showrooms sat Chrysler cars. Or were they?" The nameplates were changed, sometimes at front and rear, sometimes only at the front. But the product policy contrasted oddly with the efforts in what Olins calls the other "crucial points" in a design policy: environments and communications.

> Chrysler, he points out, had a communications policy that "was very carefully thought through. It had a graphic design program commissioned from a skillful, experienced American consultancy. The program was applied with rigor and care throughout Chrysler's operations and in environmental design. There was also a policy, associated with, if not linked to, the communications policy. It was progressively applied to showrooms, factories and so on. In product design, however, there was either no policy, or there were three policies. In any event, it didn't work. And, much more important, there was no overall design management and no overall design coordination."

You can't level that criticism against IBM or Olivetti, Kodak or the Le Creuset cookware people, BMW or Porsche, Benetton or McDonald's. It's not just management of design that's at issue but managing *by* design—making sure that the same message rings through loud and clear at all points where the purchasing public comes into contact with the company. As Olins says, concluding his indictment of the pre-Iacocca shambles in Europe, "the design of the products should have been associated with the design of environments and of communications. But it wasn't. Consequently, Chrysler's message was hollow. The Chrysler idea did not exist. Customers did not know what a Chrysler car was. That's why they didn't buy the products."

Most companies are no better than those out-of-their-depth Chrysler hands at coordinating all the corporate elements to put over the desired idea of the company, and mostly for the same reason: they have no idea in mind. But existing customers (the most important marketing resource) do have an idea of the company, one that managements can easily discover, if they so choose. The answer may be deeply unwelcome, in which case it's highly unlikely that potential customers—the second most important marketing resource—will be converted into paying ones, no matter what expedients the company's marketers adopt.

The first necessity is thus to settle on the right message with the right results—that is, an outcome that is in line with the company's strategic objectives and that achieves its specific tactical aims. At Apple Computer, in its tearaway start, the inspired choice of the half-eaten, highly colored apple logo to link with the name successfully rammed home the idea of an approachable, lively, total newcomer in a business dominated by overly technical, user-hostile giants.

Because Apple didn't take similar care over product development and its image among big-business users, though, it was another victim of the same all-not-in-one-piece syndrome that struck down Chrysler: the managed-by-design strength of IBM proved decisive in the marketplace.

Similarly, Kodak's design policy remained exemplary, and its products (like the disc pocket camera and the new fast films) models of good development. But somewhere along the line Kodak lost sight of the Grand Design, of the idea, once strongly entrenched in the consumer mind, that Kodak was the be-all and end-all of photography. Being scooped by Dr. Edwin Land was excusable—great inventors and inventions are a law unto themselves, and Kodak never (as its court defeat in 1986 showed at such great cost) managed to outinvent Polaroid. But to allow the Japanese to steal so much of still camera sales, gradually working their way into Kodak's own mass-market territory—that was unforgivable.

Kodak's management had become frozen in the belief that the photography market was its own stamping ground, never to operate except in the way that best suited Kodak. In that delusion, they reversed the old King C. Gillette formula. Where he had sold razors cheap so he could sell blades dear, Kodak ended up selling film cheap (because of Japanese competition) to fit into the cameras (Japanese-made) that others were selling dear. In the process, its designers and designs were heading down a blind alley, as Kodak itself recognized in 1986 by returning, desperately late in the day, to a 35-mm camera market it should never have left—but selling, of course, Japanese cameras.

The Grand Design of a corporation demands coherence. No longer can any of the features that create its identity in the marketplace be produced in total independence. Yet in most cases today packaging is independent of advertising; advertising is independent of letterheads, brochures, and other corporate print; print is independent of building interiors and exteriors; architecture is independent of products. People who are involved in any of these activities are directly concerned with the direct marketing of the business—and their work, as Olins pointed out in *Management Today,* is just as close to the total performance of the company, and just as essential a uniform component, binding together all functions, as financial control itself.

His recipe for achieving coherence differs very little from that for effective control of the company's money.

1. The top management must be committed to the policy.
2. One of top management's members must be the design champion.
3. There has to be a centrally located management function, with opposite numbers in each of the operating companies.
4. Relevant task forces are required in purchasing, marketing, production engineering, advertising, whichever department controls premises, and so on.
5. A manual must lay down the design guidelines.
6. In total analogy with financial control, it is essential to have a system "for monitoring and checking what is done, when it is done, how it is done, and at what cost."

It sounds like a lot of trouble. But far more trouble can result from taking less care. Taking trouble over essentials not only marks out the company that manages by design from the rest; it also separates the IBMs from the also-rans and the nonstarters.

11. THE MESSAGE IN THE PACKAGE

Marketing, defined as the effort to relate everything the business does to the customer and to serving customer needs, pays off in a thousand ways. But most companies use only a few of this multitude of methods. Take, for example, packaging. Hardly anybody takes packages seriously enough. Yet they are decisively important marketing tools. That's made clear by a piece in *Viewpoint,* a magazine put out by the Ogilvy and Mather advertising agency, in which O and M's own Michael Ball says, "Packaging as a medium of persuasion is an island of neglect."

One recent study, however, found that 66 percent of all purchases are unplanned. That's why, says Ball, for the large marketer, "a message on the package is important. For the smaller national brand that can't afford a massive advertising budget, the need for a message is utterly compelling; packaging may well be the smaller marketer's main medium for persuasion."

Doubts that a package can communicate, or that shoppers take the time to read what the package says, are founded on simple ignorance. Research shows that labels are read by 86 percent of women shopping for beauty preparations, 92 percent of women shopping for health items; and 95 percent of women shopping for food products do likewise. Eighty-one percent usually look for the amount of goods contained in the package, another 81 percent look for the price, 57 percent for the name of the manufacturer (which shows the importance of corporate reputations), 53 percent for the ingredients, and 47 percent for instructions for use. Moreover, a third of shoppers presold by an advertising campaign change their minds and switch to another brand when they get inside the supermarket. Why? "One all too common reason is that the package doesn't live up to the advertisements." The rules are simple for companies that want to avoid that trap:

1. The package is an advertisement.
2. The principles of producing a package should be the same as those for producing an ad. It must deliver its promise loud and clear.
3. The package must be researched and tested in the same way as any ad.
4. Be sure that the package says the same things as the statements in other media.
5. Ensure that designer, researcher, and marketer work hand-in-hand in the production of the package.
6. Ensure that the advertising has content. If the campaign lacks a big idea, you can't design a good package to go with it, and that's for sure.

12. TRADING ON TRADE SUPPORT

Trade support, like packaging, is Cinderella. It isn't normally associated with direct marketing, that extremely effective marketing tool. But what does a marketer do when the direct marketing rug is suddenly pulled out from under his feet? Twenty-five years ago a government ruling stopped direct-response commercials on TV, and, along with many others, a man named Alvin Eicoff lost a big chunk of his business. In that emergency he made a great discovery about where trade-support advertising works.

His discovery is effective for two purposes in particular—introducing a new product and reviving a dormant one, both keys to brilliant increases in profitability. He can produce examples of effectiveness from products as far apart as exercise bicycles, car polish, gardening equipment, and building materials. And the principle, like those of profitable packaging, is simplicity itself.

The canny trade supporter puts a carefully worked-out quantity of goods into the stores, giving them the right to return anything that's unsold. Since the merchants don't bear the cost of carrying the stock, they should be happy to oblige. Get them to accept a lower margin—30 percent instead of the usual 40 to 50 percent—and there's a very good reason, apart from the inventory savings, why they should play ball.

According to Eicoff, writing in O and M's *Viewpoint,* customers who enter the shop to buy the advertised product spend a lot more on other purchases: $14.70 on average. "Promotions," writes Eicoff, "usually involved excellent positioning on the shelves, room for large, eye-catching display, and an inventory tally at least every two weeks." Of course, that's little different from the standard promotions in any supermarket. The difference lies in the advertising, which is geared to the direct-response principle. "The commercial had to motivate the viewer to act. We couldn't afford pure awareness-building commercials. They had to be jammed with specific benefits; those benefits had to be clearly demonstrated; action had to be called for."

That's as excellent a guide to good advertising as could be wished for. If you can't answer the following three implicit questions with a loud and ringing yes, your ads are likely to prove ineffective: (1) Does the ad offer specific benefits? (2) Are the benefits clearly demonstrated? (3) Does the ad call for action?

Eicoff adds one further crucial point: "There had to be advertising accountability: we had to know precisely how the advertising affected sales in each outlet." That's the very essence of the direct-response approach; any such campaign is judged by how much business it produces via the response—that's the toughest of all schools of advertising, and that's the principle of using trade support.

It's the same whether using TV or radio or press. Eicoff claims that the method is particularly cost-effective—much cheaper than test marketing, for example. You can get by, he says, with no more than three weeks of advertising in no more than two markets, and companies "have gone from a handful of markets to national distribution in less than six months as a result of their success on the trade support front."

Nothing in life or business, of course, is perfect; there are no panaceas. But trade support is plainly much too promising to be ignored. The only condition is that you must be prepared to follow the Eicoff credo all the way:

1. Begin with a product that is unique and demonstrable and has wide appeal.

2. The markup must be high enough to supply enough money for adequate advertising.

3. You determine the advertising budget by calculating how much you can spend and still earn a profit immediately, starting with the first ads. No investment spending is allowed.

4. You put the product into distribution. The stores receive a less-than-normal share of the markup; in return, you give them semi-exclusive rights to carry the product, and you let them send back any goods they can't sell.

5. You place enough merchandise in the stores to meet the

demand you hope your three-week advertising campaign will stimulate. Running out of stock will destroy your measurements of success or failure.

6. At the end of three weeks, you should get a record of sales from every outlet. If profit targets are being reached, supply more of the product and reschedule advertising for another three weeks. If not, don't give up. Leave the unsold merchandise on the shelves and continue to get sales records. But schedule no more advertising until you see whether or not you eventually reach your target. If sales come tantalizingly close to the target, reexamine the advertising and choice of media. Changes may make all the difference. If you can't reach your target, ask the chains to return the unsold merchandise for credit.

7. If the first markets you try prove profitable for several months of advertising, select five to ten additional markets and repeat all the steps.

The first two principles, like the three rules for effective trade-support advertising, apply universally. Unique products with wide appeal and high enough markups to finance fully adequate advertising are the only kind that interest Supermarketers. As for the other five principles, they collectively enshrine one of the foundations of Supermarketing, which applies with great force in advertising and promotion: if at first you *do* succeed, try, try, again. That has an important corollary: if at first you *don't* succeed, you also try, try again. But not for too long.

To summarize some of the important points I've mentioned in Step Seven:

1. If the public doesn't believe the message conveyed by your product and its promotion, the marketing game is lost.
2. Whether people remember your ads doesn't count; what does is whether the ads make people buy.

211

3. If you can't offer a meaningful advantage to differentiate your offering, you can't sustain an edge through advertising.

4. You've got to spend money to defend money—and don't you ever forget it.

5. The fact that the globe is shrinking means that your marketing horizons have got to expand—globally.

6. Don't go global or follow any marketing fashion for its own sake; do it because it pays, and only then.

7. You can create a great consumer business in many ways, but advertising will almost certainly have to be among them.

8. The more care you take over your advertising, before, during, and *after* the campaign, the more effective it will be.

9. If you know nothing about direct marketing, start learning fast—you may well need it.

10. Your most powerful means of communication is the business itself, with all its external aspects and perceptions.

11. The rules for good packages are much the same as those for good ads: that's what a package should be—your best ad.

12. If your promotion does at first succeed, try, try again; if at first it doesn't succeed, you also try, try again. But not for too long.

Step Eight: The Rewards of Marketing Ethics

1. THE POITIERS PLOY

At least one thing is sure about advertising: it is supposed to be true, honest, and fair and, if it isn't, due opprobrium will be heaped on the perpetrator's head. But what about the rest of marketing? In a perfect world—or market—only the true, honest, and fair would prevail. But in the real, imperfect world, marketing is rife with tricks, dirty and otherwise, by which companies seek to achieve a decidedly unfair advantage over others.

Nor are governments in much of a position to cluck tongues and hand out demerits—for they are sometimes the dirtiest tricksters of all, none more so than the French. Even by Gallic standards, the Poitiers Ploy of 1983 was a remarkable piece of untrue, unfair, and unjust interference with the free market, in this case, that for videocassette recorders. Confronted with an unwelcome influx of VCRs, the French authorities decided that from then on, all import controls on the offending objects would be carried out by the customs post at the commercially obscure town of Poitiers.

In no way, *bien sûr,* did this contravene the rules of GATT (the General Agreement on Trade and Tariffs), the principles of fair play, or the ideals of free trade. With only four officials and no computer, of course, Poitiers would take forever to clear VCR shipments. Otherwise Sony, JVC, and the other competitors were left at perfect liberty to flood the French market with their products—which, incidentally, the French didn't then make at all.

It would be a mistake to assume that marketers in other lands were steaming with righteous indignation over the Poitiers principle, as opposed to its practice. That includes the sinned-against Japanese; when it comes to excluding unwanted machines (or anything else), they are dyed in the deepest villainy. As for British marketers, they are less likely to complain about the perfidious French than about the mad British who don't do likewise. Fools that they are, Brits play by the rules, while the French (and the Japanese) make up the rules as they go along. Thus when the French once decreed that quality labels for wools had to receive prior government approval, it turned out that the Gallic definition of quality included *(naturellement)* "Made in France."

Before concluding that other governments should undergo a crash course in cheating, it's sensible to ask what benefits arise from protectionism, covert or overt. The answer depends on whether the protected industry is internationally competitive or is moving in that direction. If not (on either or both counts), a protectionist policy gets you nowhere; it merely forces the local consumer to pay more for worse goods. If the industry is competitive or is making genuine progress in that direction, protecting it is superfluous in the first case and dangerous in the second—dangerous because the protection will reduce the competitive stimulus. France is an excellent proof of the argument. For all its protectionism, in which world car markets are French imports the leaders? And how was it that the French electronics industry was so battered and backward that it wasn't making VCRs at all?

Those who retort by pointing to the Japanese juggernaut are misled. There's no evidence that the Japanese would have fared any less well in cameras, motorcycles, stereos, cars, TV, and so on if they hadn't played the Poitiers Ploy on so grand—and silly—a scale. As economist Henry George wrote, "What protectionism teaches us is to do to ourselves in time of peace what enemies do to us in time of war." All the same, it requires virtue and fortitude beyond human nature to suffer the protectionist blows of others without striking back. Few firms, anyway, can resist the temptation of getting from government what they can't get from the marketplace. But are they right to do so?

2. OFFERS THEY CAN REFUSE

In the end, all the tricks a company plays by itself (like, ultimately, tricks played by government) will fail in the face of the more fundamental forces of markets—although that won't stop either countries or companies from playing the tricks. In 1983 one of the most remarkable endeavors of this kind was staged by Ford in Europe. As the sales battle raged between the Asconas and Cavaliers of General Motors and the rounded Sierras of Ford, the latter resorted, on a larger scale than anybody could recall, to hype, with huge financial inducements offered to force sales through the trade.

The effect of this, and no doubt the object of the exercise, was to boost Ford's apparent market share and thus keep it at the top of the heap. But no degree of hype could offset the fact that the Sierra's sales performance had not matched that of its Cortina predecessor. Even if the odious comparison really reflects the decline of the entire segment, the underlying market situation was worse than Ford had known for years. It had been the unquestioned master of the market:

first to produce an integrated model range, first to find the right mid-range formula, first to produce and succeed with a pan-European model policy. Its marketing had been equally surefooted, with carefully researched product design supported by strong promotion which both reinforced and was reinforced by a Ford brand that was pushed steadily up the quality ladder as the cars were upgraded.

What Ford couldn't control was the inaction or reaction of General Motors. The fight against the giant was tougher than any Ford has fought before, because it stems from the worldwide counterattack of the vastly richer GM, whose integrated range was designed to make Ford the European underdog. The hyping up of Ford's sales figures reflected, no doubt, the vital importance of maintaining the company as number one against a rapidly growing rival, one that can match Ford almost dollar for dollar in advertising and take the consequent excessive costs on the chin, despite its smaller share of the market.

The suspicion is that Ford's whole tactical plan in the Sierra's first year was directed internally as well as externally—including an advertising slogan, "Man and machine in perfect harmony," that, while lacking in meaning to anybody else, may have helped convince the management that its controversial Sierra concept was correct. Maybe that's part of the function of much marketing by Muscle and Machination: to hide from the management concerned the reality that its hold over the true marketplace has weakened.

The Japanese, being nothing but realistic, will go to any lengths, not to hide their weaknesses but to repair them. Hence the California Caper, the attempt to steal IBM secrets, which raised the possibility that some of Japan's brilliance in world markets rested not on quality circles, or better strategies, or the spirit of Zen, but on simple theft of Western technology. Even more than other examples, the behavior of Hitachi in this respect offends against the principles of truth, justice, and fairness. In naked markets these principles are usually honored as much in the breach as the observance. But note that dishonesty and dirty tricks always carry a cost—even if it's less than

216

the $300 million Hitachi allegedly had to pay IBM. Serve it right.

Much reaction in the West to the methods of the East—fair, not so fair, and plain foul—has, however, been uninformed and fundamentally defeatist. The battle against the Japanese (or Son of World War II) has moved into a new and disturbing phase: if you can't beat 'em, stop 'em. Faced with better, or matching, products selling for prices at which Western firms take a loss, the losers seized on the Poitiers Ploy—the hope that lobbying would win where management and marketing have failed—and they may, alas, be right. The EEC's imposition in 1986 of a 35 percent antidumping levy on Japanese electronic typewriters looked like the thin end of a very thick wedge.

The Japanese are, of course, absolutely to blame in one respect —their insistence on being too competitive for their own good (or that of their competitors). The flavor of that insistence can be gleaned from an embarrassingly leaked internal memo in which Hitachi ordered its salesmen to undercut the U.S. competition by 10 percent. "If they requote, go 10 percent again . . . don't quit until you win!" The *Financial Times* calls this "predatory pricing," the very phrase that Virgin Atlantic's Richard Branson, following Sir Freddie Laker's lead, applied to retaliatory price cutting by British Airways, Pan Am, and other airlines. But there is a world of difference between a cartel ganging up on price cutters and the latter using, like Branson, Laker, and Hitachi, the price sledgehammer to crack a market.

More properly, the latter is *penetration pricing,* which is predatory only when you are at the receiving end. In their home markets, the Japanese loathe price competition, which is one reason why, to the disgust of the EEC, home prices for things like typewriters and copiers (also the subject of an EEC dumping action) are higher than prices in Europe. There price levels are often established by the kind of asinine you-cut-my-throat, I'll-cut-yours wheeling and dealing that was bankrupting the mass car makers at one point in the mid-1980s. Unless the Japanese compete on price when they enter markets of this Hitachi-like nature, they don't compete—and that goes against their nature.

THE SUPERMARKETERS

The paradox is that the powerful forces that cry "dumping" from the rooftops include firms such as Olivetti and Xerox, which are actually importing typewriters and copiers from Japan to sell under their own labels. Now, their suppliers would hardly be so insane as to sell to such customers (and rivals) below cost. Thus Canon, Brother, and so on must equally be obtaining their own supplies at a price that includes a profit. If so, where's the dump? Like predatory pricing, dumping is subjective—one person's dumping is another's low-margin export.

What happens if and when the antidumpers stop 'em? Prices may rise temporarily. But the Japanese will raise output from local plants, which will again outgun the protectionists. The copier and typewriter firms' last state (U.S. car producers very definitely face a similar threat) could thus be worse than their first. Serve *them* right.

3. THE NO WONDER OF WOOLWORTH

The power of advertising as a marketing tool has never been doubted by either its defenders or its critics. The latter believe that ads can actually persuade people, by some form of mass hypnosis, to act against their own interests, to buy what they don't want, watch what they don't wish to see, even vote for candidates they don't really prefer. If only it were that easy. . . .

The marketer knows that, for all its power, advertising is like patriotism—not enough. That isn't only because alternative means of promotion can be just as effective. Indeed, one of the world's most elegant brand leaders, the Moët et Chandon champagne house, performs beautifully sans advertising, relying solely on heavy spending on other forms of promotion. The problem is rather that even effective advertising can be frustrated by bad performance anywhere: from poor product to dire distribution.

What does *effective* mean in this context, though? Some of the criteria used to answer that crucial question don't really pass effective muster themselves. This is a thought that should be troubling the managerial memory at the fairly mighty retail chain of F. W. Woolworth. Its 1985 sales came to an imposing $6 billion; they would have been mightier yet but for the miserable performance, over many years, of its important British offshoot. What should have been the jewel in the American crown became the thorn in its side—finally torn out and thrown away, for peanuts, to a local consortium.

The last effort to make sense, and money, from the ailing chain was backed by a massive advertising campaign. It succeeded marvelously, if you believe the agency responsible, Allen, Brady & Marsh. The "Wonder of Woolworth" ads, which first appeared on British TV in 1975. Before ABM took over the advertising, spontaneous recall by viewers asked if they had seen the store chain's advertisements had run at a microscopic 1 percent. Only a year after the campaign began, the recall sprang to 75 percent and six years later the figure had apparently reached still more Himalayan heights—86 percent.

Did this spectacular increase in impact improve Woolworth's business to match? From 1975 to 1982 sales indeed grew by 128 percent, to $1.5 billion (against, however, 228 percent for Marks & Spencer). But margins, 10.4 percent in 1973–74, were only 7.1 percent in the first Wonder Year. They bumbled along in the sevens until 1980–81, and then nosedived: 5.4 percent, 3.6 percent—and a loss in the first quarter of 1982. Either the campaign prevented the fall from being still more fearful, or it wasn't effective advertising in the sense that it didn't successfully encourage consumers to buy the right, higher-margin, goods from the stores, or the fault lay with the way Woolworth's itself was managed.

The three alternatives are not mutually exclusive. The clue may lie in the agency's view, expressed in a panegyric to its own wonders, that "the real truth about Woolworth, the truth to be *advertised,* was that Woolworth was a wonderland of variety, an Aladdin's Cave, a cornucopia." Well, it wasn't: the product belied the promise. Woolworth's High Street stores resembled Aladdin's Cave about as closely as the Politburo does Snow White and the Seven Dwarfs. Woolworth

219

was stuck with self-evident problems of merchandise, display, and service of the kind that can't be washed away by all the advertising money can buy.

The aftermath of the profit collapse was that, after the chain's American parents sold their stake in the British Woolworths, dropping $1.6 billion of sales in the process, new and tougher owners took over the reins; then, among other changes, ABM lost the account, Wonder of Woolworth and all. Unfair though this must have seemed to the agency, it was an understandable reaction to the lack of success in the marketplace. Even highly "effective" advertising, judged by the criterion of recall, cannot, whatever advertising's critics may think, take customers to water—let alone make them drink.

4. *TRUE* WAYS TO RETAIL RICHES

In the age of the naked market, it has become commonplace that some are more naked than others—the better-clothed being the great and increasingly dominant retailers. Their huge strength at the sharp end is wielded through both the national brands (which cannot live without the big retailers' distribution) and the stores' own-brand strength: the combined weight has radically altered the balance of power in a marketplace that will never be the same again.

But the top retailers haven't succeeded by the natural, unaided working of economic forces. The successful store chains have won their increased power deservedly; likewise, the unsuccessful have lost out on their demerits. The failure of Woolworth in Britain to replace an increasingly obsolete and uneconomic marketing image was paralleled in the States by the long decline of the once-legendary A&P. In both cases, and in many others, the roots of trouble had been sown during the triumphant expansion of much earlier days. Fighting the legacy of too many shops, too many of them the wrong size and in the wrong places, selling the wrong goods in the wrong ways, while also facing the challenge of a highly competitive present, would have defeated abler marketers than those who were actually running Woolworth and A&P.

The winners were, as it happens, far abler. But as the subsequent turnabouts at both afflicted giants prove, supernatural feats of Supermarketing are not required. Good retailing demands much expertise and many essential techniques but none of baffling complexity. For instance, it is axiomatic that, unless shopkeepers know what is selling where (sales analysis), they can't make the intelligent decisions that will maximize turnover and profits. Woolworth conducted no such analysis; it was as far behind the times in retailing techniques as in choice of merchandise.

But technique alone didn't create the retailing successes of the 1980s. A chain of shops is a brand. Its strength depends on how the brand is perceived—on what makes the shopper enter one store rather than another and keep on coming back, as the ultimate repeat purchaser. The best store chains have built the best markets, those that last longest and pay most, by being TRUE: Trustworthy, Recognized, Unique, and Efficient. These champions of the primary marketplace are recognized as different in identity (the essential of branding), but the same in one key respect. They are trusted to sell top-quality items at top-value prices that will never, in any particular, depart from what is expected of a product sold by that company.

These principles of retail stardom are not confined to chains that number their outlets in the hundreds and their values in the billions. You couldn't improve on the exposition of the meaning of modern retailing given by Gerry Taylor, a toy retailer who began in the late 1950s with one exurban store and built up to a total of ten, with a turnover of some $8 million. He concentrates on what he calls the "cut-and-thrust side" of the business—that is, the prime site store located as close to the big chains as rents allow, and aiming for a high turnover with a low profit margin. That is his clear answer to the first crucial question: *What kind of business are you running—or do you want to run?*

Having made up his mind on that point, as above, Taylor con-

221

siders what to carry. As he says, "If you're aiming for a large turn-over, you *must* stock certain of the ranges. If you don't, people will be entitled to ask 'What kind of a [toy] shop do *they* think they are?!' " Those ranges must form the solid basis of stock (and sales), which is the answer to question two: *What do you* have *to do, like it or not, to retain a strong position in the marketplace?*

The matter can't be left at that. There are always alternatives —in Taylor's case, whether or not to stock the *whole* range. He comes down heavily on *not.* He notes that you can obtain as much volume and profit by selecting from a range as by taking all of it: "Some of the major retailers, in fact, run on very limited selections from ranges, trying to avoid padding out with items of slow turn-over." Lying somewhere midway between them and the specialist, Taylor can't afford to do that. So he runs through the whole range and then counts "the number of lines I've selected. If that turns out more than I wanted, I cut back by eliminating what I believe will be slower sellers." That is his answer to question three: *Are you applying selectivity to the business—deliberately choosing what you will offer and what you won't?*

The retailer who does not apply selectivity is almost certainly wasting resources and not getting the optimum bang per buck. Taylor is eager to deny that he's playing safe: "Quite the reverse. I believe in taking risks. If you've never lost money on a risk, then you're not buying properly. After all, the riskier items almost always carry a bigger profit margin." His point is, though, that rewards should be commensurate with risks. The successes will then compensate for the inevitable failures. Question four asks: *Are you taking reasoned risks that, if they come off, will make a major contribution?*

The third category Taylor goes for is a specialty item—some-thing unique to his business: one year, that meant telescopes. "Ex-pensive? Yes. Chance of many sales? No. But a telescope makes a very effective crowd-puller for the window display. The profit margin is good. Manufacturers of such items are happy to replace on a one-for-one basis. And there's always the chance that any enthusiasts in the area will keep coming back to the shop." Question five must also be answered: *What unique specialty do you have that marks you out from the pack and helps establish your image?*

The five questions and their correct answers apply, of course, to any marketing business, not just stores (let alone just toy stores). The good marketer follows the Taylor principles: knows what he or she is doing, draws up rules from experience, and works hard at getting results. The great retail chains do no differently. Their national reputation, like Taylor's local one, is founded on being TRUE; to repeat: Trustworthy, Recognized, Unique, Efficient. That's a truth that the best suppliers to the best retailers, as well, have long known to be as much their own best policy as honesty itself.

5. THE CASE OF ANTIFREEZE

Faith, Hope, and Charity are seldom listed among the prime attributes in marketing, but without their abundant display by the consumer, where would marketing be? The *Schloss Antifreezenheimer* scandal, in which Austrian wine growers were found to have sweetened their bottles with poisonous ethylene glycol, was only the latest of many cases that demonstrate in the wine industry alone how, given half a chance, businesses of the utmost outward respectability will violate the consumer's Faith and the First Commandment of marketing: What thou sellest should be what thou saith.

The Commandment and the Faith have been broken so spectacularly in the past that the mass consumer's Hope of finding a totally honest bottle may seem slightly less misplaced than the hunt for the Holy Grail. For years everybody has known that consumption of alleged Beaujolais vastly exceeds the supply of the real stuff, but even when the London *Sunday Times* published chapter and verse for the cheating, nothing diminished the popularity of the label. Such excessive popularity was the very thing that created the chicanery in the first place.

223

Nor did the great Bordeaux ripoff, in which the Cruse booze turned out to be adulterated, lead to any backlash against claret. On the contrary, demand for wine, from the sublime to the unmentionable, has continued to climb—as has its price. With antique wines, the wealthy bibbers paying gigantic sums for bottles show a truly noble trust in the proposition that the contents (often barely drinkable) do indeed bear a relation, after fifty, sixty, seventy, or more years, to what they're supposed to be.

These rare and rarely priced bottles are sold at auctions, and, just as everybody tacitly accepts the fact that falsification is endemic (even epidemic) in wine, nobody doubts that misstatement plays some role in auctions. When a house like Christie's says (as it did in 1985) that unsold pictures have gone for huge sums, it is the size of the lie that (rightly) costs the chairman his chair, not the nature of the lying. Auction houses have been hiding the results of auctions behind veils of deceit since, no doubt, the first hammer ever fell on a lot.

Christie's is no more likely than Cruse to suffer long-term damage from its shenanigans, that being the point where Charity joins Faith and Hope. Whatever fate befell the rich imprisoned antifreeze salesmen, blind eyes would go on being turned by consumers of Austrian, German, and Italian wines (although the last-named will find it harder to survive the methanol adulteration that killed unlucky customers in 1986). Most of the time, the customers are part of the conspiracy. Like store owners, with their allowance for "wastage," consumers accept an element of embezzlement, presumably hoping that the bezzle won't be too big, or that the occasional exposed sinner will repent and live honestly ever after (like General Dynamics after ripping off the Pentagon). Dishonest or half-honest managers can always hope to hide behind such complaisance; honest ones will always pay a price for their virtue. But is half-honesty ever the best marketing policy?

6. PUTTING THE *VALUE* IN VALUE FOR MONEY

The answer to the last question is the most resounding negative in marketing history if you believe what manufacturers, hand on heart, now declare. "Honesty (read quality) is the best policy": that, or something like it, has become the marketing theme of the 1980s, the successor to such immortal lines as "What business are we in?" Today, everybody is in the same business—maximizing customer satisfaction, or offering the highest perceived value for the lowest perceived price. Plainly the trade-off between quality and payment, or value and money, is not only perceived but real. Ask those whose tough but far from thankless task is managing the arts. Opera, for instance, is ludicrously extravagant. Cut it to the bone, though, strike Pavarotti from your phone book, forget that Solti was ever born, use last year's *Rigoletto* set for this year's *Butterfly,* and the public will stay away in droves, thus defeating the object of your economy.

To move from the sublime to the prosaic, reduce the size of the Mars bar enough and one day only a new king-size bar will suffice to restore the status quo. But the value-for-money (VFM) equation has one vicious snag. Although in some instances value can be measured precisely (Mars bars) and in many more can be tested reasonably (by market research), other cases require an act of faith. You don't need monumental credulity to believe that providing more, in all senses, for their money will endear and entrap more users. But how many more? And will their seduction provide enough in extra sales revenue to justify the VFM investment?

The answer to these agonizing questions may never be known. If the up-valuing is followed by stirring reversal of an adverse trend, the betting is fair that VFM-plus takes some of the credit, other things being equal. But they seldom are, especially as it's *RVFM*—relative value for money—that truly counts. What the competition is up to, or isn't, is crucial. Yet the relativity doesn't obscure the absolute virtue of making the very best product (in the VFM sense) in your power—and on the market. The Japanese have long under-

225

stood this philosophical verity, which is often embodied in those statements of corporate ideals that seem so strange, even pompous, to Western ears.

As David Manasian wrote in *Management Today*, "Japanese managers can sound quasi-mystical when describing the goals of the company." But there's nothing mystical about the way in which they seek to obtain and retain customer loyalty: "One of the main reasons for the spectacular success of Japanese cars in the United States is reliability: American customers, fed up with the flashy junk foisted on them for years by Detroit, switched to Japanese models in droves when word of their reliability began to spread."

The statement, confirmed by a mass of consumer reports, certainly contains a good deal of truth. Reliability and VFM generally were the only cards the Japanese could play at a time when in engineering, performance, and styling the cars lagged well behind Western rivals. But other Japanese industries have played other cards, dealt out on the same basic theme: that Japanese engineers "like nothing better than to aim for a specific goal, and surpass it." Marketing, manufacturing, and sales set the goals—and achieving those goals means higher VFM.

For example, the invention of the world's first toy-size but fully functional electronic typewriter by Brother Industries was a little miracle of innovation. But the product's specification defects reduced its VFM to a low level. It was a safe prediction that, within a year, a vastly improved version would appear on the market. And so it came to pass: "Nagoya headquarters repeatedly queried the company's overseas marketing affiliates about the product's size, shape, weight, features and price. Prototypes assembled from off-the-shelf components were circulated throughout the company's network."

In that thorough, goal-oriented way, Japanese manufacturers in businesses ranging from compact discs to copiers, cameras to robotics, personal stereos to excavators, have added and improved features while reducing price, thus improving both sides of the VFM equation. The popular Western approach of producing popular models, stripped down, with fewer features at lower prices, usually reducing the *V* more than the *M,* doesn't appeal to the ethos of leading Japanese companies. And there is indeed an extremely tricky question to answer for those who want to move down the VFM scale. How much VFM can you afford to sacrifice?

Normally, it takes some time before the customer notices its fall —or notices enough for the savings (less chocolate in the chew) to be offset by the losses (less silver in the shops). At times of general stringency or pressure on margins, the temptation to cut VFM thus becomes irresistible, and the savings are often meaty. But they can lead to a fiendish marketing trap. That's when short-run savings lead to long-term erosion in the product's stature in the marketplace.

The solution seems obvious. Just restore the past cuts and boost the present VFM. But (back to square one) you will incur quantifiable costs for unquantifiable benefits. It takes a free-range entrepreneur like Rupert Murdoch to make a costly, bold move like enlarging the London *Sunday Times Magazine*'s page size. But he was very probably right. Kings of the market must be seen as princes lest they become paupers. Anyway, marketing kings can afford to give honest value for money because the more value they give, it so happens, the more money they make.

7. THE BAD NEWS FOR GILLETTE

Everybody knows that it's very wrong to steal secrets the way Hitachi sought to sting IBM—by paying money for their betrayal by company employees. Not only is it immoral but if the caper is found out, the purloined secrets will probably cost far more, in penalties, legal expenses, settlements, and reputation than they were ever worth.

Why steal, anyway, when ordinary, legal spying can be so lucrative? *Fortune* magazine has obligingly listed four ways in which, without recourse to more sophisticated methods like aerial photography, a company can discover competitive secrets within the law—though not without deception.

1. Measure rust on the rails. To find information on the market share and volume of a competitor, measure the rust on the rails of railroad sidings to the plants and count the trailers leaving the loading bays. "By noting the length of the trailers and the dimensions of the cartons carrying the competitor's product, the snooper can estimate how much is being shipped in each truckload."

2. Make plant tours. Have your executives tour competitors' plants to get details of their manufacturing processes and output.

3. Do reverse engineering. Buy competitors' products and take them apart to examine their components. You can determine costs of production and sometimes even manufacturing methods. When one company announced a patented new product, a type of speed-reduction gear, it received fifty orders—about half of them from competitors.

4. Examine competitors' garbage. "While some companies now shred the paper coming out of their design labs, they often neglect to do this for almost-as-revealing refuse from the marketing or public relations departments."

Other activities from the Department of Dirty (or not too Clean) Tricks, says *Fortune,* are:

1. Milk potential recruits. Pay special attention to people who have worked for competitors, even temporarily. "Job seekers are eager to impress and often have not been warned about divulging what is proprietary. They sometimes volunteer valuable information."

2. Conduct phony job interviews. Advertise and hold interviews for jobs that don't exist in order to entice competitors' employees to spill the beans. "Often applicants have toiled in obscurity

or feel that their careers have stalled. They're dying to impress somebody."

3. Hire people away from their competitors—probably the hoariest tactic in corporate intelligence gathering. "Companies hire key executives from competitors to find out what they know."

4. Interview competitors. You don't ask competitors what they're doing directly—you hire consultants. They ask your competitors for information, saying that they are doing a study of the industry and will share the data they develop with all respondents. They do give something back, but it's often innocuous. The good stuff is For Your Eyes Only.

5. Debrief design consultants. Competitors frequently share the same consultants. "While conferring with a consultant hired to help with a product, you can sometimes learn confidential information about products competitors are developing."

You can even, apparently, get customers to put out phony bid requests. Ask a loyal customer to solicit competitors' bids on parts so technically advanced that they can't be obtained from current products. "When the proposals come in, they are loaded with descriptions of technical capabilities or advanced products that the suppliers had been keeping confidential."

On the "Hill Street Blues" argument ("Let's do it to them before they do it to us"), managements can't altogether be blamed for getting their retaliation in first when they know this kind of skulduggery (and worse) is going on. Also, stooping—but not very far—to conquer sometimes can't be helped. *Fortune* thus notes that

In every industry companies show new products to certain key customers because their willingness to buy the product is considered indispensable for success. . . . When Gillette told a large Canadian account the date on which it planned to begin selling its Good News disposable razor in the United States, the date was six months before Bic was scheduled to introduce its own disposable razor. . . . The Canadian distributor promptly called

Bic, which put on a crash program and was able to start selling its razor shortly after Gillette did.

The Good News for Bic was Bad News for Gillette.

8. KNOWING YOUR COMPETITORS

The Japanese passion for gathering information about their competitors and their markets, of which the attempted Hitachi heist is presumably an ultimate expression, doesn't stop them from making mistakes. But it does make far more unlikely acts of marketing insanity such as the U.S. firm that invested heavily in a campaign to sell cake mix to the Japanese—in profound and dismal ignorance of the fact that hardly any homes in Japan have ovens. Japanese houses regularly defeat Western marketers; many have tried to sell domestic appliances that won't even get through the narrow doors. Then there was another all-American hero whose soap ads featured a woman in a bubble bath, when Japanese never allow soap near their beloved bathwater.

As David Manasian reported to *Management Today,* "A top priority of Japanese subsidiaries abroad is to send information home." It was research by marketing people in the United States that inspired Canon's production of the personal copier. In 1984, the drug firm Green Cross became the world's first producer of artificial blood, thanks to scientific work that stemmed from the United States. That's the final outcome of that apparently insatiable "penchant for photographing machinery, tape-recording lengthy meetings, scribbling constantly, and carrying away armloads of technical literature." Gaining competitive advantage by using freely available competitive information is the national pastime.

"Know your competitors" is a standard axiom of marketing; a rider is "Know what your competitors know." *Fortune*'s Unclean

230

Tricks Guide isn't necessary. You don't have to employ engineers who are expert at grilling another company's technical experts and send them to conferences where the latter's brains can be picked; you needn't infiltrate a factory by the back door, lending engineers to a customer to learn from its design staff "what new products competitors are pitching" (that, allegedly, is "how Intel beat out Motorola in microprocessor markets"). What you can and must do is focus your legitimate intelligence gathering on the critical competition.

It follows that a company must first identify its competitors, second, establish what information it wants about the identified firms, and third, decide how to obtain it. In today's markets, competition is more likely than ever to come from unexpected and new sources. Companies hardly ever look for potential as opposed to actual rivals—it's a dangerous error, mirrored by the common practice of basing competitor intelligence largely on taking current offerings to technical and commercial pieces. That only tells you how things are right now, not how they will be in a future which, these days, becomes the present at unprecedented speed.

Academic Graham Kelly tells honest snoopers to monitor the future by doing precisely what the Japanese do: look out for product developments anywhere in the world. In the naked market, a new product or process with a competitive edge travels fast. Like most military spies, foreign agents in the civil field, including your own employees, provide nearly all their useful information from published sources. That's true not just of technology but of marketing information as well. The problem is not the availability of information but its abundance.

In home markets, most companies have a ready-made espionage force in the people who visit their own present and potential customers. Salespeople in the field should be instructed to bring back systematic information. Kelly cites one distributor of house fittings whose representatives have to record retailer stock levels for their own and all competitive products. He then uses a computer to build up an accurate picture of the market. Most firms rely on erratic gossip from salespeople, and even from the most important source of all: the customers' own senior executives.

The closer a company gets to its customer, the more likely it is to obtain invaluable favors like Bic's Good News. But that's just a spectacular example of the constant stream of competitive clues that close customer contact should provide. "Courting the customer" is another standard axiom of excellent marketing. IBM's great strength in supplying the banking business, for example, was based on building up as close a knowledge of banking and bankers as the bankers themselves (if not closer). Electronics is by no means the only business in which, as one executive told Kelly, "customers *expect* us to know all about our competitors." (That man even claims—and he's probably right—that he can tell which competitor a customer has been with by the language the customer uses.)

The foundation of competitor intelligence, though, is published information: all those brochures and technical manuals, all that advertising (for new staff as well as new products), all those annual reports and press releases. Any of them could contain information as valuable as the D-Day landing details that the spy Cicero discovered in Turkey—and which his German employers didn't believe. That often-repeated story (the British likewise ignored their capture of the German invasion plans in 1940) goes to the nub of the problem. Intelligence connotes alertness as well as news. The mighty manufacturers of the West mostly chose not to react to information about Japanese intentions in their markets—ambitions that could not have been clearer or more threatening.

It's no use imitating Xerox, which lost 50 percent of the world market to the new copier competition from Japan in a decade even though Fuji Xerox was perfectly positioned to enlighten its half-owner. Far better to mimic Komatsu, which took its brilliant battle against Caterpillar Tractor to the point of subscribing to the local paper in the giant rival's hometown of Peoria, Illinois. An alert company needs to create the aforementioned problem of abundance before using modern methods of information processing and storage

232

to achieve the stages that follow collection of intelligence: analysis and dissemination.

If sensible conclusions aren't drawn from the data, or if nobody who needs them gets to hear those conclusions, gathering the information is totally worthless. The Japanese gain their strength less from their passion for facts than their willingness to distribute information and to act on what is received. One public relations executive was summoned to Japan by Toyo Kogyo to report on the press reception of the latest Mazda car. He was taken straight from the plane to the factory, where he turned over the clippings, with adverse comments heavily circled, and discussed them with Mazda executives. He was then allowed to check into his hotel to sleep.

The next morning, returning to the factory, he found a prototype incorporating changes designed to meet the press criticisms. Such alertness is even more valuable than the most common form of acquiring a competitor's intimate knowledge—poaching his key employees. The aware response can pay enormous dividends in the easiest way of all, too: putting yourself in the shoes not of the competitor but of his customer. Companies foolishly and frequently ignore what can be learned from their own direct experience of using a competitive product and then honestly assessing what features make it more attractive to a customer than their own.

Worse still, they ignore the equally valuable information that can be obtained by using their own product or service and—with equal honesty—assessing what features make it unattractive to a customer. Failure to do so plays into the hands of the deadliest competitor of all: the Enemy Within.

9. THE PRESSURE ON PEOPLE EXPRESS

The skies of the airlines are spattered with statements that, if not quite lies, are not quite the truth, either. But "oh, yeah?" slogans like "the world's favorite airline" for British Airways, or "We've been the American airline business travelers prefer for ten years" from American Airlines, are as nothing in the annals of self-flattery compared to the contributions of cut-price challengers like People Express.

They needed to keep their courage up. All companies that rely on price alone to penetrate established markets, in the skies or on earth, face the same, classic economic problem—and it's a killer. Initially, the price cutter operates and flourishes under the umbrella of the excessive prices charged by the established giants (like BA or American) whose prices he is undermining. When, eventually and inevitably, they retaliate, he loses his unique selling proposition and with it goes some of the sold-out volume that keeps down his unit costs.

As his costs rise, while his prices can't, the profits get crucified: those of People Express dropped sharply in the first half of 1983 (the corporate semanticists attributed this to tax problems) and then went on falling into horrendous loss, while capacity and revenue soared on regardless. That's the kind of situation when the cutter customarily flails about, trying to escape from his fix. In the process, he takes on commitments (like People's purchase of Frontier Airlines) that, with his highly negative cash flow and mounting debts, he's in no position to sustain.

Yet until the last moment, when Donald Burr's People Express finally crashed into the arms of Texas Air, the People Express founder continued to talk as if he still presided over the wonder airline of yesteryear. In those pristine days, Burr had brilliantly put across the story that People wasn't just a price cutter. It was a crusade, for a better, late-century style of management, as well as for cheaper air travel. The mission was the message. "Fly smart" was People's slogan, "Manage smart" its credo.

Every employee had to buy shares (which seemed a much worse idea when they slumped from $26 in 1983 to the final $4) as part of the all-round participation, the teams, and the self-management, which were supposed to encourage a happy staff to provide happy service to happy customers. "Give people a good deal," averred

Burr, "and they'll use the hell out of it." The ugly truth, however, was that People, with its notorious overbooking, the bedlam at Newark airport, and "no-frills" (that is, minimal) service, offered a bad deal in every respect save one—price. With that single advantage removed, Burr followed the exact downward spiral of Sir Freddie Laker, another great semanticist.

Faced with the hard fact, in his final airborne moments, that paying back his $200 million debt on schedule would involve an insurmountable degree of financial inconvenience, Laker boldly announced a banking innovation: what he called a "release-and-recapture" clause. If the banks were to "release" him from his obligation to repay them on the due date, they could, lucky things, "recapture" the money at some later point.

Those who have difficulty telling the difference between that and asking for a plain and simple extension of a repayment period don't understand the extreme—and basic—importance of semantics in marketing. Every marketer knows that "new" is surpassed in marketing power only by "free" even though most products labeled "new" or "free" are not. Milton Friedman's book title *There's No Such Thing as a Free Lunch* had it right: the New York saloons that once upon a time gave away "free" meals obviously had to recoup the cost in the price of the booze, or go bust.

What Laker was trying to do was place the bankers in an exquisite bind. Heads the banks wouldn't win, because disobliging Laker would do their own balance sheets no good; tails, they lost, because acceding to Laker's "release-and-recapture" fandango would make them seem like reluctant fuddy-duddies dancing to his tune. It can't have been any consolation knowing that the laws of market economics would win in the end, whatever the semantics. Laker and his planes, as did People Express, duly went down, rubbing in the point that management by semantics doesn't work: the words must marry the music just as much as (see section 11 in Step Seven) the package must match the product.

10. MANAGEMENT BY SEMANTICS

Truly winning words have become more important in winning markets than ever before. Winning words have had a semantic boost themselves: what started life as press relations, and then became public relations, is now subsumed under the grander title of *communications*. But the underlying and important nonsemantic reality is that communications means far more than words and goes well beyond the old boundaries of public relations into the heart of marketing—of both the firm and its products.

It actually begins within the firm, with internal programs for spreading information and trying to achieve that unity of purpose that passes under yet another semantic invention: *corporate culture*. To put the matter more bluntly, if a management can't persuade its own people to believe in the company and its products or services, how can it hope to persuade outside customers and all those who influence customers' decisions? Of course, that ultimate audience isn't actually a terminus. Good communications is a benevolent circle: how the company presents itself to Wall Street, for example, feeds back into the perceptions of those who work for the firm and has a powerful effect on their motivation.

Because perceptions are subjective, they can be shaped, modified, or, to use the pejorative word, *manipulated*. There's no real odium, though, in trying to move people's perceptions toward what you sincerely believe to be the truth. That can't be done, however, unless you know the point of departure: what existing perceptions are. Modern techniques allow accurate, objective measurement of subjective states of the public mind. Using these techniques is mandatory, not only in helping a company improve the image of itself or its offerings but because the surveys may well reveal painful realities that can't be glossed over by semantics or anything else. If so, change, introduced sharply, is the only answer.

That's why public relations consultants now demand to enter the inner sanctum of the corporation (quite apart from the fact, naturally, that their fees thus become higher) where its marketing and other strategies are supposedly hammered out. The advertising agencies (naturally) are making the same demand: so are the design consultancies (naturally, again), the research companies, and executive searchers, along with strategy consultants themselves (Natch Three). Here, too, reality lies behind the huckstering. Another dearly beloved piece of soft semantics, *convergence,* describes the hard fact that all these service activities overlap with the same interdependence that unites (or should) marketing, R & D, production, finance, and everything else inside the firm.

Looking after the total communications and the total market, in other words, will make the company smell sweet by any old, incongruous name. Indeed, even an unlikely sounding noise can be forged into a most powerful marketing tool: merely think of Ford, Heinz, Sony, Hoover, Xerox. Note that the last two companies and their names are less powerful than they once were. Names can paradoxically become so well established that they lose all value—becoming generic, like Hoover and Xerox, describing not so much the particular product as what it does. Becoming generic doesn't matter so long as a company continues to dominate growing markets—in these two cases, vacuum cleaners and copiers. What weakened the twain was their inability to maintain their one-time presence and powers in their marketplaces.

If success makes names and makes successful communications possible, though, it must follow that neither names nor communications can make success. That's why corporate name changelings so often don't win back lost glory. The original failure and the subsequent disappointment reflect a single cause: that loss of natural identity and coherence that is fatal in naked markets, and that no Supermarketer ever allows to happen.

Management by semantics can never compensate for mismanagement elsewhere. Calamitous errors reduced Addresso-Multigraph to incipient penury before its name was reduced to AM International; the name change didn't postpone the penury. The ill-concealed weakness beneath its change of name besets conglomer-

237

ates. Because a company isn't cohesive—say, a batch of businesses loosely clustered around a meat-packing firm called Swift—it is repackaged as Esmark in the foolish hope that the new name, if nothing else, will make the corporate image cohere. When it doesn't, retribution strikes.

In Esmark's case, nemesis took the form of takeover and disappearance into another conglomerate, Beatrice Foods, with no great benefit to the purchaser, which ended up on sale (and no return) itself. Change of name isn't always the semantics of desperation or deficiency (although name-changed companies heavily disfigure the lists of large money-losers and bid victims). When a company has genuinely changed direction and nature, or the old name contains some deadly (in several senses) word such as *tobacco, asbestos,* or *lead,* verbal manipulation may be mandatory. The corporate identity, after all, is a brand, and sometimes even a winning brand name may have to be sacrificed, although this go/no-go decision must be one of the most painful in world business.

Analyze a case in which the brand-name decision is go, however, and you will usually find the same hard truth: failure goeth before the fall of a once-proud name. In the British market, however, Ford dropped the name Cortina when it was still riding high above the mid-priced sector, after two decades for most of which no European rival had mounted a convincing challenge. Why did Ford conclude that the years of juggling with the Cortina had run their course? The last of the Cortinas resembled the first about as closely as the Orient Express does the Long Island Railroad; the Cortina was a masterly demonstration of keeping a broad identity and concept intact while radically changing the product as it led and responded to the market.

That's an excellent description of how Supermarketers preserve the semantic and real values of a whole corporation. With a brand, the danger is cumulative loss of freshness, which the marketer can fully recover only with a completely new launch. Yet that wasn't what truly justified Ford's billion-dollar gamble on the new Sierra, rather than running the risks of yet another series of Cortina. Competitors, led by the General Motors juggernaut, had, as noted, been forcing the pace. In the effort to recover lost initiative, so critics contended, Ford went over the top, outdistancing the market with the Sierra's jelly-baby contours and making costly errors in detailing. Maybe so, but the problem was more fundamental.

As I wrote at the time, "The market pressures are intensifying fast: even though the saga of the Sierra is only just beginning, the days of the High Sierra may be doomed." That turned out to be the painful truth for Ford. Peaks do pass for companies and their brands alike, but only when the process of constant renewal and reinforcement has finally failed. In the naked market, even the utmost vigilance, concentration on the lowest costs, the highest quality, and all other virtues, may not avert the vicious and evil decree. But that vigilance is still the key to making a company smell sweet by any name. Names become winners because they are attached to winning brands and winning companies.

11. THE INJUSTICE AT JOHNSON & JOHNSON

All companies would like all the news about themselves to be good all the time. They greatly resent bad news, whether or not it is their own fault. Ford Motor made a notoriously bad attempt to cover up and mitigate the fact that its Pinto car had, through faulty engineering, incinerated some of the paying customers. If the news is really disastrous, the model to follow is not Ford but Johnson & Johnson, whose Tylenol disaster, while great, was an act of God—or, rather, the devil.

It would have done no good for the company to argue (though rightly) that only a minute proportion of the capsules on sale (and then only in Chicago) had been tampered with by a homicidal maniac. The management instead took the disaster on the chin, and withdrew the entire supply. The product then went back on sale in tamper-proof packaging and under the same brand name, with a huge advertising budget. After a recovery that proved how difficult it is to keep a good brand down, the company, at the horrendous cost of $100 million, emerged from its trauma with a strong position in the market and an enhanced reputation—but no better luck.

First its Zomax (another painkiller—it was open season on those in 1982) had to be withdrawn permanently after five deaths, at an initial cost of $20 million. Then the Tylenol devil struck again in 1986, when cyanide-laden capsules cropped up, this time in New York, with one fatal result. Now there could be no happy ending. Tylenol in capsule form had to be removed from the shelves for keeps. Once again, the management reacted in a dignified, controlled, and responsible way.

Terrible, double misfortune aside, the lesson stands. When trouble strikes, any policy other than full, frank, and fair disclosure risks putting future markets at greater hazard than present ones. When trouble isn't striking, though, the lesson is no different.

12. LOW PROFILE AND HIGH

If the first essential is to have an honest company song, the second is to have it sung—and heard. Curiously, these self-evident truths are ignored by many companies. Either the song is a falsehood concocted by the public relations genius in its employ, or the management chooses to leave the music to the great orchestra of public opinion outside. The weakness of the latter oversight is dramatically revealed when a predator produces an unwelcome assault; and the management suddenly finds that it has fewer friends, even among its own stockholders, than it needs.

When the merger steamroller started running over great and once-great companies in 1985–86, past neglect produced an outlandish response. Normally unseen and unheard companies hired agencies to bring forth streams of prose poems to sing their new clients' praises.

Often, there had been little to sing about. In palmier days, companies like U.S. Industries and SCM had happily boasted about achievements that proved to be all too transient. By the time they succumbed to the transatlantic predator, Hanson Trust, both were shadows of their former corporate egos. This was also true of Hanson's largest prize on the other side of the ocean, Imperial Group.

That company had understandably kept quiet during its Howard Johnson fiasco, possibly the worst American corporate buy of the late century. Under attack by Hanson, it started to blather about "Famous Brands Doing Famously." Had the fame been more effectively promulgated before, a group with $7 billion of sales would have found it easier to repel the attentions of the two bidders whose onslaught led to all those famous brands famously changing hands.

The underlying question is of fundamental importance. Should companies make a continuous, sustained effort to market themselves? Waiting for the arrival of a raider set on rape and rapine before stepping up self-promotion can't be right. It's a bit late for the fox to take out life insurance when the lead hound has him by the tail. The answer to the question seems cut-and-dried. Self-marketing is an essential corporate task, to be conducted with the same due care and attention as the main marketing activities. If it isn't, the suspicion is that the company has something to hide—or nothing to reveal.

Yet the suspicion may be unjustified. As a test, and a proof, regard the following list of ten companies: Coleco, Harris, Prime, Fieldcrest, Hasbro, Telex, Sara Lee, Collins & Aikman, Macmillan, Teledyne. How many of the ten can you identify by business classification, naming at least three products or services provided by the company? Even well-versed business readers will fail the test by a wide margin. Yet all ten companies are members of the *Fortune* 500: more, they recorded the ten highest growth rates in earnings per share between 1975 and 1985. Ignorance of the affairs of gee-whiz companies is often no accident. Their managements may simply be content to let a lovely record speak for itself. The media sometimes knock at their doors, anyway, and the management sees little or no need to spend real money on marketing the company.

But catch-22 applies. If the company is successful, it sees no need to promote itself. But suppose the company is *unsuccessful;* it still prefers to keep a low profile in the foolish hope that the media (and eventually the bad results) will go away. At that point, it customarily tries to attract attention to a tale of wondrous recovery, and any journalist knows the ominous implications of a turnabout tale gone suddenly silent. None of this makes any more sense than refusing to advertise a product because it's selling thunderously and doesn't need the ads; and next refusing to advertise because sales have slumped too far to justify the expense.

Bid situations often show up the folly. What made Sotheby Parke Bernet, before its white knight came riding to the rescue from Texas, so pathetically vulnerable to the unlikely combination of three Americans called Feld, Swid, and Cogan? The great auction house had so neglected its self-marketing that it lost many of the large stockholders who should have formed its natural defense. True, Sothebys had plenty of faults it would have preferred to conceal. But if the product doesn't live up to the claims, or to the standards of decent management, that's no argument for silence. Absolutely the reverse: finding out how others see you, and then seeking to correct and improve the perceptions is fundamental; it will inevitably draw management's attention to the corporate sins and omissions—and greatly increase the chances of rectifying them.

Successful self-marketing, like any marketing, is far more than making product claims; it involves public relations and strategic policies, research and identity, planning and integration. For lack of these time- and money-consuming necessities, important companies abound that are little known to consumers, investors, politicians, journalists, even their own labor forces. They can hardly blame fate when it knocks down their doors. It is foolish to forget that fate often does come unbidden—if not in the form of a corporate raider, in the shape of a political body blow or a product disaster, such as Johnson & Johnson's.

As in that case, sometimes market disaster doesn't rain, it floods. No sooner had Eli Lilly emerged from the major mishap (and mishandling) of the forced withdrawal of its antiarthritic offering than the company was plunged into renewed controversy over another of those unlucky painkillers, Distalgesic. No new product, it had been spinning money for years. The drug was under double attack, for being allegedly dangerous and, anyway, no more effective than an over-the-counter product like—well, Tylenol. How should the accused company react?

If a product is accused of being killing (as opposed to just painkilling), the makers must not only ensure that it isn't, they must be seen doing so. Any hint (as General Motors with the Corsair, and Ford with the Pinto) of stonewalling or concealing unsatisfactory evidence will cook your market goose. Thus the asbestos industry, by reacting too slowly to fears about the product, helped create a situation of total distrust in which costly precautions were taken over risks probably no greater than those of sitting in a smoke-filled room. The better the case of the manufacturer, the greater the importance of letting the truth out. Take the Eli Lilly painkiller. It beggared the imagination to suppose that medical practitioners had been gulled or suborned into prescribing expensively and extensively a medication that worked no more effectively than a supermarket pill. But experts on these matters are entitled to their opinions, which may even be right (in which case, you'd better know it). It thus did Eli Lilly no good at all when a subsidiary canceled its advertising in a medical paper that had faithfully reported the adverse opinions.

Such reaction is a time-honored (or dishonored) routine. It inevitably looks like intimidation, and it is an especially pernicious form of lie to suppress the truth, or try to, not because it is false but because you don't like it. The only way to demonstrate truth is by open, frontal assault on the critics, not on those who are merely

243

messengers bearing the lugubrious news. In adverse publicity, there are only three possibilities. The report is false, but not damaging: you may safely ignore it. Or it's false and damaging: sue. Or it's true and damaging: correct the sins—at once and in full public view.

In all three possibilities, management's case is far easier to sustain if opinion has been swung in its favor by a continual, medium-profile self-marketing campaign carried out over the years. That policy, with all it entails, means greater chances of publicity that is true and greatly to the corporation's benefit, not to mention publicity that is false but favorable, which (a long way behind) is the next best thing.

To summarize some of the important points I've mentioned in Step Eight:

1. Resist the temptation of trying to get from government what you can't get from the marketplace.

2. Your advertising will be made ineffective by bad performance anywhere else—from poor product to dire distribution.

3. A chain of shops is a brand, whose strength depends on what makes the shopper come in—and keep on coming back.

4. The best store chains get their results by being Trustworthy, Recognized, Unique, and Efficient.

5. Total commercial honesty always costs something, but total or partial dishonesty will cost much more.

6. You can afford to give honest value for money; because, in general, the more value you give, the more money you'll make.

7. You can learn so much about competitors without cheating that you don't need to.

8. You need not only a passion for relevant facts but also extreme willingness to take relevant action on information received.

9. Don't bend the truth even when the pressure is intense; that's when realism (and honesty) matter most.

10. If you can't persuade your own people to believe in the

company and its product or services, you won't persuade those outside.

11. If the first essential is to have an honest company song, the second is to have it sung—and heard.

12. Corporate self-marketing moves markets—if it's medium-profile and maintained over the years.

Step Nine: Penetrating Markets by Acquisition and Innovation

1. THE MISS AT PHILIP MORRIS

Anyone can see that a multimarket company is inherently stronger than a single-market one, provided, that is, that the multiple markets are all strong. If the only result of diversification is to lose on the swings what you gain on the roundabouts, that provides stability, true. But the steady state isn't the object of business enterprise—especially in markets where competition cannot be beaten lying down.

Many companies, great and small, were forced in the late 1970s to recognize that their bold forays into new markets, by product or geography, had produced so much loss on the swings that the profitable roundabouts were revolving to no ultimate effect. The resulting wave of retrenchment might lead one to speak of a new spirit being abroad in world business—although in one case of withdrawal, *abroad* somewhat misses the point. The case is Gulf Oil's retreat from making petrochemicals in Europe. The invasion of the supposedly rich and growing Continent by the U.S. chemical giants was one of the more striking examples of the famed American challenge of the 1960s—so why was the new spirit abroad taking Gulf, as it were, back home?

A case from quite a different industry provides the answer. In mid-1981 Philip Morris bought a 22 percent stake in Rothmans International (a $350 million puff) because it was dissatisfied with the results of its own diversification away from cigarettes. That bald announcement should have made any marketing professor's Miller High Life beer go down the wrong way—that brand being the key to a saga unsurpassed by any company diversifying into any business.

Using the marketing techniques it had refined with cigarette brands, led by Marlboro, Philip Morris expanded Miller's beer sales by 20 to 30 percent per annum, elevated it from seventh to second place in the industry, shook up the entire brewing industry from top to bottom by its success, and invented the whole low-calorie beer sector. Triumph could hardly have been more spectacular—so what was the trouble? The Philip Morris complaint was that, like Gulf's chemicals in Europe, the marketing game hadn't been worth the financial candle.

In the previous four years Miller's beer assets had yielded only two percentage points more than one-month Treasury bills. With 30 percent of the group's total sales, Miller produced only 11 percent of operating income. At that, it did better than the company's 1978 purchase, 7-Up, which cost $515 million and wasn't making a cent, though even that improves greatly on Gulf's $15 million losses on $450 million of European turnover. Small wonder that Gulf canceled its $150 million expansion project in Rotterdam and thus undermined the business of its existing plants in the one-time wonder Euromarket.

The Morris and Gulf cases differ in that Gulf made a basic strategic error, while the impact of Miller on the market must have

247

gone more than according to plan. 7-Up in turn was given the full Miller treatment (sales force tripled, production capacity upped, prices raised, trademark and packaging revamped, massive new advertising). None of it helped. In the end Philip Morris wished it had never bought the business. All such endeavors, just like Gulf's in Europe, raise the ante horrendously. Buying markets at the price of negative or inadequate returns in capital never makes sense.

2. MAKING DIVERSITY PAY

Once upon a time food was food, and nonfood was nonfood, and never the twain did meet. But just as nonfood companies, like the tobacco giants (including, most spectacularly, the aforementioned Philip Morris with General Foods), have moved into food (on the simple thesis that people have to eat), so food firms (nearly all those of any substance) have moved into nonfoods, because that delicious propensity to eat doesn't seem a good enough guarantee of the corporate future. To quote the *Financial Times,* "In the mature food markets of the West the overall volume growth for food has become virtually static, which therefore encourages rationalisation of processing facilities."

Glossing over the fact that "virtually static growth" seems to be a contradiction in terms, the union of Dart and Kraft, since dissolved, or Nabisco and Standard, hardly rationalized anything at all, since product overlaps were few or nonexistent. So what did motivate the respective managements to merge? The probability is that running a $5.9 billion Nabisco-Standard combine as Nabisco Brands simply felt more comfortable than living lower down the big leagues, especially shortly after its old enemy, Kraft, had jumped to the top by kraftily absorbing Dart.

The old line in prizefighting is "The bigger they are, the harder they fall." In Big Food, apparently, the argument is, the bigger they are, the harder it is for them to fall. It's that same argument of stability all over again. In the case of Dart and Kraft, moreover, that's what seems to have been achieved in the decade to 1982. In earnings per share and total return to shareholders, the company was stuck roughly in the middle of *Fortune*'s annual ranking of the 500 largest U.S. industries, and so was the merged Nabisco Brands before it disappeared (into a tobacco-based giant, of course) in 1985. True, the supposed and expected benefits of the mergers had yet to flow. But that depended on the managements bucking one of the most basic propositions in business: that managing diversity is a business in itself—and one of the toughest tasks in management.

If the diversity has been won by incurring an Everest, if not a whole Himalayan range, of debt, the job may be beyond even the mightiest of purchasers—which is why corporations the size of U.S. Steel, du Pont, and Occidental have become enmeshed, after the billion-dollar oil buys, in selling assets to reduce the interest burden. After the falls in oil prices in the mid-1980s those purchases looked economically as well as managerially misbegotten. But the creations look positively homogeneous compared to many of the collections of brands that today masquerade as food companies.

Again, take Dart and Kraft (which sound like another pair of reindeers for Santa Claus). In addition to familiar comestibles like the invincibly processed slices of Kraft cheese, the Dart side included Tupperware and Duracell batteries. Now, Tupperware is more likely to contain food than anything else, but you can neither chew nor digest a battery. Dart and Kraft during the brief period of their union, significantly sundered in 1986, were not exceptional: after all, under half of world champion Unilever's sales are in human food (though this subtotal still exceeded all sales for the second largest food firm, the virtually all-edible Nestlé, until the latter lapped up Carnation).

The Unilever achievement from its extremes of diversification is not such as greatly to encourage others. In *Management Today*'s 1985 rankings of Britain's 250 companies, Unilever came 166th in growth over a decade, 186th in profitability, and 155th in rise in ten-year, inflation-corrected earnings per share—three facts that suggest that big brand building isn't the best or even the second-best game in town. Yet the brand game's popularity waxed mightily in the mid-1980s. Indeed, Unilever was plainly deeply distressed when deprived of more of the same mediocre medicine—being beaten to Richardson-Vicks by its arch rival, Procter & Gamble; and finally taking Chesebrough-Pond's as consolation for $3 billion.

Its friends had feared that, still slavering for a large American buy, and buying on the rebound, it would exceed even the going prices—which was saying (and paying) plenty. *Business Week* investigated some of the megadeals in brands, and its conclusions were uncomfortable. In terms of enhancing earnings per share, Philip Morris paid around twice as much for General Foods as the cost of PM's own shares—all to pick up a company whose operating margins were a mere third of its own. In no circumstances can any marketing or management magic, whether achieved through synergy or strategy or discounts on advertising, make monetary sense of such mind-boggling equations. In many of the deals, the only rationale lies in the readiness of big banks to finance any bid, no matter how absurd, so long as the earnings of the victim look likely to cover the horrendous interest charges.

Modern takeover techniques have notoriously made any company vulnerable, even to a Mickey Mouse outfit one-quarter its size, unless its brand portfolio has been exploited to the full—and to the full benefit of the share price. Revlon could never have fallen prey to Pantry Pride had Charles Revson's sorry successors shown even half the maestro's skills in making Revlon cosmetics queen of the department stores. Admittedly the magic gets more difficult to sustain, even for a maestro, as time goes on. This problem inevitably afflicts most of the brands in the recently acquired bundles. They are mature, aged-in-the-wood (sometimes literally). While definitely preferable to new brand ventures (only one in three of which even makes the small time), they rarely offer high, rich growth.

From this, it follows that paying billions for such baubles must mean piling up trouble in store—and maybe in the stores, as rusting brands handled by overstretched managements operating from remote headquarters fail to maintain the market shares that made the goods attractive to retailers in the first place. The paradox is simply stated and simply obeyed: don't diversify unless or until the core business is so strong as to be *nearly* invulnerable—that being the highest degree of strength known in the naked market.

3. THE CONSOLIDATION OF SARA LEE

"It is a very dangerous way to build a company—scary, too. It is logical that top management cannot sit in an office and build a company that way." John H. Bryan, Jr., chairman and chief executive of what was then called Consolidated Foods, was speaking about his own company, which in 1974, to quote John Thackray in *Management Today,* "was no less than 125 different businesses, and its $2,500 million-worth of sales all sprang from independent divisional fiefdoms which cared naught for headquarters direction from a scant staff of just 45."

The divisional bosses were predominantly self-made men who had sold their businesses to Consolidated without relinquishing a shred of personal power. Bryan's family meat-processing business had the same character and origin, but he was subsequently forced to launch a mighty effort to reshape Consolidated into something more akin to Procter & Gamble, a unified corporation expert in making and marketing fast-moving packaged goods.

Consolidated got rid of something like sixty businesses in toy trains, curtain rods, men's shirts, women's clothing, furniture, and so on. But unloading trifles like these is not the answer to the problems of diversified management. It can build successfully only around "core" business: divisions that, paradoxically, are strong enough to stand on their own in markets they dominate and that are worth dominating. Bryan simply didn't have enough of these—so he

251

bought two, one of which, Hanes, is a fully fashioned illustration of the point.

Hanes makes women's and men's hosiery and underwear, and had $100 million in annual operating profits in 1983: half what Bryan paid for the entire company in 1977. The key products are L'eggs panty hose. Sold from store racks in egg-shaped containers, L'eggs propelled the company into the top position as a mass marketer of hosiery. The packaging, the promotion, and the merchandising (the stockings are sold like paperbacks, with Hanes filling racks at no cost or risk to the retailers) were brilliantly innovative, and rocketed Hanes clear away from direct competition with the encroaching cheap private labels. In no time L'eggs had half the market in supermarkets, drugstores, and discount stores, a market it proceeded to segment carefully into support hose, high-fashion items, and heavier-knit winter legwear.

Bryan was proud of his efforts to achieve similar breakthroughs with the division after which the whole corporation has now been named, Sara Lee (frozen croissants as well as cakes), and the Capri Sun soft-drink-in-a-pouch idea from Germany; less proud of the flop of L'eggs-style cosmetics. But the efforts only emphasized the paradoxical task of the diversified corporation. It can rise only on the undiversified success of significant units.

4. CREATE, INNOVATE, AND GROW

The success of significant, concentrated units inside a diversified conglomerate like Sara Lee can be built in two principal ways:

1. Product innovation aimed at finding gaps in the market or opening up new market areas.

2. Finding gaps in the distribution system peculiar to their markets, and sending the innovative products into the gaps (at Sara

Lee, for example, the soft-drink business undercut the market leaders by shipping, not to retail outlets, but directly to retailers' warehouses).

Yet for all its efforts, Sara Lee's six main activities, though accounting for 93 percent of sales after Bryan had completed his surgery and reconstruction, couldn't have had much less in common without completely destroying any semblance of corporate rationale: frozen bakery products, processed meats, coffee (European, mostly), soft drinks, hosiery, and door-to-door sales of vacuum cleaners. Bryan has complained that the same kind of criticism can be leveled at Procter & Gamble—which, before snatching Richardson-Vicks, was already in peanut butter, diapers, health-care products, coffee, and more—or at any other big packaged goods company. So it can; that's why Wall Street has "a clear view that companies like us have parts which are worth more than the whole corporation . . . which implies that we as managers bring nothing to the sum of the parts."

They do bring something, of course. But is it enough? That's the huge question lurking behind every bid battle, every friendly purchase, every transfer of assets. It isn't the basic financial query, Is the fat price justified? (Answer: generally, no.) Nor is it the usual issue of public interest (antitrust, for example). It's the unusual question. Would the economy in general, and companies in particular, be better off if acquisitions (as in Japan) were out?

Put that way, the question almost writes its own answer. Japanese companies can't, and therefore don't, acquire; Japanese companies have outperformed Western counterparts on almost every criterion: thus, acquisitions are bad. Or, Western companies acquire others as squirrels do nuts; Western performance has been deeply inferior: thus, acquisitions are bad. Neither chain of thought is as logical as it sounds; other factors entirely could explain the performance gaps. Yet it is hard, in any management terms, to justify, logically or illogically, the vanishing of a General Foods into a Philip Morris.

True, the latter's base will be broadened. But that overworked

253

strategic argument has applied to most disastrous or disappointing mergers since the war (which means a good half of them). The objective, time and again, isn't truly strategic, anyway—not if strategy is truly defined as the pursuit of enhanced performance. Many a deal has been slung together in the way that Rupert Murdoch acquired 20th Century–Fox and Metromedia: not because the acquirer has calculated the impact on the corporate bottom line and found the sums rejoicing his heart, but because that heart lusted after other aims—in the Murdoch case, that of owning a large TV network.

In many cases, it is left to a later generation to make sense of such ambitions—to heirs who often find the creation splitting at the seams. Heroic, even near-total dismantling of the previous management's "broadening" purchases generally follows, and then, more often than not, the new hero launches into his own orgy of broadening. Organic diversification on Japanese lines, building on real corporate strengths to create genuine and lasting new businesses, not only sounds better, it probably is better. But there's a catch: Catch-C5.

The failure rate of new ventures is fearsome. For every 3M Post-it Note Pad or Sony/Philips compact disc there are countless Sinclair C5s, the weeny and weird British electric buggy that short-circuited in 1986. Companies acquiring other firms are at least purchasing an existing positive cash flow, an extant management, and a quantifiable risk (but not always, fools being born every minute). Had they tried to launch from scratch, *à la Japonaise,* the risks, the time scale, the cash outflow, and the management task would all have been greater, maybe intimidatingly so. Yet, just as bad money drives out good, the easy alternative reduces the incentive to capitalize on the company's human, financial, and technical assets to *create, innovate, and grow.* That's the most thrilling threesome in Supermarketing. And that's where the nonmerging Japanese rightly excel.

5. THE DAMP SQUIB OF SQUIBB

THE BOTTOM LINE IN TEN BIG MERGERS ran the headline in a 1982 issue of *Fortune* magazine. Good or bad news for the whale-size corporations that are still so avidly swallowing the smaller (and bigger) fry? Alas, for all the experience that should have been garnered in three decades of mounting amalgamation, it's still thumbs down—even though half the cases actually did have better earnings per share in 1981 than they would hypothetically have made without their 1971 acquisitions.

In four of the cases, the acquiring managements could say, hands on hearts, that the buy and its consequences had been genuinely good. But two of the four sounded less encouraging notes. Drug firm Squibb, which in 1971 couldn't even "spell out" the wondrous "growth opportunities" that lay ahead of the Lanvin–Charles of the Ritz cosmetics business (a $206 million buy), admitted, "We made some mistakes because we didn't understand the business." Another drug firm, American Cyanamid, also went into cosmetics, with Shulton (for $106 million), and confessed that "synergy in research took too long to come." Funnily enough, relative failures said much the same, as in: "We made our share of mistakes; we took too long to move down the learning curve."

That was Heublein, the brewers, talking about Kentucky Fried Chicken ($237 million). Another drug maker treading the same route as Squibb and Cyanamid into cosmetics, Schering, found that its "international people didn't adapt well to consumer products. That synergism took longer than we thought." Its $644 million purchase of Plough knocked 19 percent off hypothetical 1981 earnings. Plough was the most expensive of the ten buys, both absolutely and as a percentage of the purchaser's book value (815 percent). But expense, absolute or relative, has no visible correlation with success or failure. Nor does closeness of fit with the acquirer's own business.

Thus drugs and toiletries don't sound impossibly far apart—but look at Schering. The answer, which is no surprise, lies in management, in the speed and skill the acquirer applies, or makes sure is applied, in its new market. Even so, the task of managing unfamiliar markets brings no bonanzas. Relating net profits in 1981 dollars to the purchase price in good old 1971 bucks gives yield figures for the four successes ranging from 7 to 13 percent.

Merely think of what those 1971 purchase prices were really worth in buying power ten years later, and the old lesson is doubled or redoubled. A purchasing company is buying one of the toughest management tasks, as four of the ten proved in the hardest possible way. Three of the businesses they bought in 1971 had been sold, with one more allegedly up for grabs. If you can't manage 'em, sell 'em, is a sensible policy; but it is, of course, an admission of failure. The failures, note, were not failures of the acquired companies but of the acquiring managements.

That diagnosis is made clear by studying the many large, merged failures formed out of competitors. Postmortem analysis usually reveals that the union had not been properly consummated until years after the parties formally became one. The problem wasn't that of managing diversity (the problem that lays low most major companies that try to buy their way into new markets); rather, the problem is one of just managing *tout court*—of imposing the common direction, common controls, and common sense that any operation needs.

6. MAYHEM IN MEGAMERGING

The dismal score in the *Fortune* survey—five acquiring companies worse off, in terms of earnings per share, than if they had never merged, the other five improving the shining hour—has an interesting symmetry. Evens are not especially attractive odds in themselves when such great sums are at risk (or even with lesser amounts). But when the standard is return on investment, measuring 1981 earnings against the price paid in 1972, the case for these ten deals becomes weaker still: all the companies underperformed the 13.8 percent median return in the *Fortune* 500 of 1981.

The picture is borne out by British experience. Five years later, *Management Today* conducted a random survey of ten significant mergers of recent years. All but one had been friendly. Three could be called clear successes; three definite failures; four, to use the Scottish judicial style, were "not proven"—either they were too recent or the figures weren't decisive either way. The odds were, however, that the not-proven quartet would divide equally on opposite sides of the line that separates the sheep from the goats. The odds seem to be evens on both sides of the Atlantic.

Motivation has much to do with determining on which side of the Great Divide a merger falls. Most of those present at the nuptials of the classic car manufacturer, Rolls-Royce Motors, with the overdiversified defense contractor, Vickers, no doubt felt much the same as commentator Sir Patrick Sergeant, who wrote at the time: "The two chairmen spoke like old lovers, all passion spent, who can think of nothing better to do than get married." Even after a relatively fast drive in U.S. markets, with car sales fueled by the soaring dollar that disappeared from sight in 1985–86, the merged group was still earning well below the merger year figures in real terms.

Unspent passion is an essential ingredient of marketing and merger success. Its presence and absence must be a major part of what explains the strange saga of Exxon's attempts at new ventures. According to Hollister B. Sykes, who ran Exxon's program for eleven years, his company did marvelously well when it invested money outside the group. It backed eighteen ventures that began beyond the reach of the corporate embrace. The cost was a mere $12 million, but within a dozen years, the reward in cash and the value of securities was $218 million.

The Exxon management was so pleased with half a dozen of these little darlings that it took them out of the cold—or rather, into it. Once merged into the world's largest oil company, the half dozen, along with the ventures that had always been internal, produced a completely blank scorecard. As Sykes tactfully told the *Harvard Business Review*, the whole bundle "did not provide Exxon with a profitable major new business diversification." You couldn't ask for stronger proof that concentrated managements left to get on with their own affairs achieve much better results than sprawling ones, which give only intermittent attention to their acquisitions.

This principle underlies the remarkable ease with which concentrated and concentrating managements absorb other businesses and make them pay far more handsomely than the previous owners: successful buyouts make the identical point. Often the recipes are astoundingly simple. One store tycoon, luxuriating in a 90 percent postpurchase profit rise in sales higher by only half, said blandly that "If people are offered well-designed, well-made products at a sensible price, they will like and buy them." That isn't one of the world's great insights. But it takes a great retailing manager to apply such truisms effectively—especially in a newly acquired firm.

The purchase of another business, diversified or complementary, can only be justified by its effectiveness. It is just another commercial venture, no different from a new factory or product. Its justification hangs on the planning, the cost, the execution, and the results—in that inevitable order. Ignore marketplace realities, allow a gap to emerge and grow between the real-life potential and the still more real costs, and deserved disaster will follow, even without mangling the execution (as you probably will).

There are no other factors, macro- or microeconomic, that can ever justify a merger, not even the effort to turn back the Japanese tide. Japan's businesses, as noted, compete and grow without benefit of mergers and acquisitions, ruled out by both social custom and the tough antitrust laws laid down, ironically enough, by the U.S. postwar occupiers. The true path to beating Japan can lie only in equal efficiency and innovation, and equal use of new technology, not just to lower the costs of production but to develop new products and defend the competitive status of the old ones.

Relative inefficiencies on these scores can't be improved by either mergers or diversification. In terms of the Japanese challenge, for example, General Electric's massive acquisition of RCA for $6.3 billion looked not at all persuasive. Neither of the colossi has been able to use domestic production to resist the surge of Japanese imports in light electronics. The main attraction of RCA, its ownership of the NBC network, gave GE's already enormous business portfolio a still broader base. But the broadening argument for diversification is just that: an argument, not a return on investment.

Neither did GE's biggest buy say anything for its willingness to compete beyond the bounds of the American domestic market, into which Japanese money, as well as Japanese goods, has been flooding. Real concern surfaced among thinking financiers about the potential for monetary mayhem in this flood of billions seeking employment in the financing of megamergers. The anxious included none other than Felix Rohatyn of Lazard Frères, who played matchmaker for GE and RCA and who took a leading role in the hundreds of mergers that created the largest, most notorious conglomerate of them all, ITT.

That corporation became the most conspicuous realization of Peter Drucker's fear, expressed long ago, that the conglomerates of the 1960s would become the beached whales of a later era. Will the explosion of corporate gigantism in the mid-1980s beach many more whales in years to come? The only way to dodge that fate is to concentrate on the matter at hand, the maximization of discrete businesses in their own markets, and to concentrate that matter in the hands of capable managements who understand the markets and have the power and authority to exploit them. Otherwise, to the extent that Japan's money and Japan's competition have generated the merger boom, Japan will have the last laugh—as well as the first.

7. THE MASHING OF MATTEL

"Beware of being Mattelled" or Warnered is a warning that should be engraved deep on the hearts of the new entrepreneurial companies. Few firms have ever expanded so explosively as Mattel, whose electronic games doubled to $556 million in a single year, while Warner's Atari division multiplied its sales ten times in five years to an incredible $2 billion. Yet both crashed into horrendous losses— and the warning is that their calamities were not beyond control.

Indeed, *control* is the key word. Rapid growth of highly profitable business (Mattel had $67 million of electronic earnings in 1982–83) customarily covers up a multitude of sins. Though Mattel won its rapid success by leapfrogging Atari, it then failed to upgrade its game player; missed out on video game cartridges; and came to market with a $150 computer—$50 above the competition's. Exit computer. Exit Mattel, back to toys, out of electronics altogether.

The toy company had failed to build up management to control and match the explosive electronic growth. At Atari, lack of control showed most conspicuously as disorganization: a dozen separate, uncoordinated divisions in forty-nine scattered buildings, five finance departments, terrible overlaps, no pay structure, too many products, and too many people. Apple showed much the same syndrome: its Macintosh white hope, for example, was produced independently from and without any reference to the now-abandoned Lisa computer, which used identical technology.

Explosive-growth companies need to be reminded that they are mortal, and that the management basics they blithely ignore in boom time will be desperately needed when market conditions change —and change they will. What makes the Atari and Mattel horror stories so striking is the speed and severity of change, as the bottom dropped out of games and home-computer markets and prices. Mattel's Intellivision in 1984 was fetching a sixth of its 1982 price—and that should be a dire warning even to much better controlled players in the naked market.

8. FIVE POINTS FOR COMPETITIVE PROWESS

Do today's corporate essentials represent a break in continuity? Has management in general, and marketing in particular, been changed radically by the brave new markets? According to an article in *Fortune,* the answer is a resounding Yea. It quoted one academic to the effect that "all of a sudden, industrial products are like Hula Hoops." Without a doubt, the pace of markets has heated up to relative frenzy; product life cycles have shortened by as much as a third; product innovations follow hard on each other's heels; no price structure is safe.

All very true: but more important by far than events is how management reacts to them. In the reactions described by the magazine, the starting point is that everywhere the customer is king. One man at Hewlett-Packard told *Fortune* that "we'd never heard of" focus groups. But once they had, getting a bunch of computer purchasers to talk proved invaluable—surprise, surprise. Over at Texas Instruments, the example cited is the $660 million collapse in home computers, blamed on inadequate observance of the marketing injunction, Know Your Competitor; when it launched a price war, TI just didn't know that Commodore's costs were decisively lower.

The third point is Know the People Next Door. You can no longer afford to let design, manufacturing, and marketing operate as separate, sometimes warring, factions, especially when it comes to innovation. In a move led by IBM, companies are thus even putting design and manufacture under combined command. Speed is the fourth point: speed in development, speed into the marketplace. You can get it more easily by simply stopping engineers from making the big changes they love *after* the initial process of market identification and product design is complete.

The fifth point, and obviously vital at a time of fast change: cannibalize, even supersede your own miracle before some other swine does. If necessary, join the other swine—form joint ventures (as AT&T has with Olivetti, say) rather than go it alone, however rich you are in money and technology.

Through all these five points there runs a note of impending doom, an "or else" based on the hard facts of rapid corporate disaster in the naked markets. In the light of events like those at Mattel and Atari, nobody could accuse *Fortune* of scaremongering. The pace of change in markets is so fast today that even growth companies have little time to repair their basic deficiencies—after, that is, those errors have found them out.

Nor are only the new growth companies affected. In an industry where RCA was mature to the point of gray hairs, the management created one of the biggest hashes in marketing history. The three-year, uncharmed life of the video disc cost the company a $550 million loss. The disc players sold only 550,000 units, all told: a humbling 2.75 percent of the total of rival videocassette recorders that had been sold by the time the disc died. What went wrong? Where did RCA so miserably misread the mass market that, from radio to color TV, it had virtually created?

In fact, its consumer electronics people divined the auguries correctly: they wanted a VCR, according to an in-depth study by Margaret Graham of Boston University. But the corporate management was dead-set on finding a new mass-market miracle, capable of producing no less than half of corporate turnover by 1990. The $500 disc player would be much cheaper (VCRs cost $1,300 when first put on sale); it would be much simpler to operate; and the discs, costing much less than prerecorded cassettes, would not have to be rented.

Against that seductive case, a management desperate for new consumer success could muster only three apparent counterarguments. The discs couldn't, unlike the cassettes, be used to record programs off TV sets; the VCRs were already firmly established in the marketplace; and there would be problems selling players until enough recorded discs were available. The RCA bosses ignored these objections, which they knew full well, partly because they were ignorant on three other counts.

They didn't know that the price of VCRs would drop to $900 by the time the first disc player reached the market, or that reaching the market would take much longer than planned. Neither did they realize that dealers would prefer to sell the higher priced and thus more profitable VCRs. Well, RCA should have known those three things. The car and computer markets offered ample precedents for the propensity of dealers to push costlier items. Products nearly always do take longer to develop than big-company managements expect or want. The prices of new electronic consumer durables have always tumbled rapidly after introduction.

Because of its blindness to the forces in its own market, RCA ended up with a selling proposition that was unique, all right, but fatally weak. Promotion spending and price cuts couldn't make up the deficiency, because a full frontal assault on somebody else's market hardly ever succeeds without a three-to-one advantage in resources. RCA had no such advantage over the Japanese individually, let alone collectively. It couldn't outspend and undercut them indefinitely. The lesson is that today a giant barging into a new market is subject to many of the same limitations as a relative midget.

The unavoidable nature of these limitations, the fact that nobody can buck the market, emerges clearly from a study of the rampant retailers who have won on both sides of the Atlantic by identifying new market trends, and adapting strategies and products to match, at full speed ahead. As one successful out-of-town discounter explained, he had to move swiftly because he was frightened that "if we didn't do it," an established supermarket chain would. Differentiate, specialize, and segment—and fast—is the new formula for retail riches, and it has an oddly familiar ring.

It's precisely the policy that the gurus and the pundits have been trying to force down the throats of the manufacturers of the Western world—along with the warning (to quote the same discounter) to "give the customer what he wants or go broke." That is nothing but the oldest of business basics. Yet hark back to that list of the new five-point management necessities as established by *Fortune*. Any old marketing hand should experience a sense not of brave new management but of déjà vu. Isn't this what marketing has always been about?

Keeping close to the customer, watching the competition tigerishly, bringing the functions together on coordinated product development, getting products through development at top speed, beating the competition to the punch—these are among the very oldest rules of the game. They have also, it is true, been honored more in countless breaches than in dutiful observance. But there is something new under the sun: the fact that, because of the newly ferocious pace, rule breakers may expect (like TI, RCA, Atari, and Mattel) to get broken.

9. THE BLUMKIN BUSINESS

"Our evaluation of the integrity of Mrs. B and her family was demonstrated when we purchased 90 percent of the business: NFM had never had an audit and we did not request one; we did not take an inventory nor verify the receivables; we did not check property titles. We gave Mrs. B a check for $55 million and she gave us her word. That made for an even exchange."

What kind of nut buys a business in that casual manner, for $55,000, let alone $55 million? The nut in question was Warren E. Buffett, probably the most successful investor in postwar America. The assumption must be that Buffett knows what he's doing: his company, Berkshire Hathaway, has appreciated so spectacularly since the fall of 1983 that Buffett profited personally to the tune of $2,390.14 every minute for three years and one month, according to *Forbes*. That is the result of a series of stock purchases of which the Nebraska Furniture Mart is a small, but juicy example.

The Mrs. B who gave Buffett her word was the ninety-one-year-old Rose Blumkin, matriarch of a family management whose performance easily outshines the country's biggest independent retailer in home furnishings, Levitz Furniture. Buffett had carefully evaluated NFM's market performance. Where Levitz operated at a gross margin of 44.4 percent, NFM ran at "not much more than half that": not because the Blumkins were less eager for profit, but because all

NFM's "operating expenses (payroll, occupancy, advertising, etc.) are about 16.5 percent of sales versus 35.6 percent at Levitz."

In other words, NFM was able to charge exceptionally low prices, which attracted customers to the single store in Omaha from a much wider catchment area than could normally have been expected. The subsequent large volume enabled the Blumkins to negotiate high-volume discounts on their purchases and to record annual gains in sales, which, according to Buffett, in themselves exceed "the annual volume of many good-sized successful stores."

Not surprisingly, Buffett is often asked about the Blumkin secrets. "These are not very esoteric. All members of the family: (1) apply themselves with an enthusiasm and energy that would make Ben Franklin and Horatio Alger look like dropouts; (2) define with extraordinary realism their area of special competence and act decisively on all matters within it; (3) ignore even the most enticing propositions falling outside of that area of special competence; and (4) unfailingly behave in a high-grade manner with everyone they deal with."

Buffett thus had every reason to suppose that, in acquiring NFM, Berkshire Hathaway was adding a business that obeyed the strongest precepts of modern marketing (note especially points 2, 3, and 4, above) and that fully lived up to founder Rose's splendid and splendidly simple business plan: "Sell cheap and tell the truth." But there's another little fact that helps explain Buffett's pure pleasure in that simple transaction.

His $55 million bought nine-tenths of a business with $115 million of sales and $14 million of pretax operating profits. . . .

10. HOW TO BUY COMPANIES

The quickest way for a company (and its owners) to grow rich, and the quickest way for a company (and its owners) to destroy its fortunes, happen, unfortunately, to be one and the same: buying another company. However noble it is to talk of growing "organically," by developing your own markets and products, that process always takes much time and trouble. Managements can save a great deal of time through acquisition. But how can they avoid the trouble?

Mergers can make magic, for those who follow four very simple rules. In one U.S. study, after investigating over 600 buys, Dr. Roland Burgman came to the following conclusions for those who sincerely want to be rich through acquisition:

1. DON'T overpay. The lower the premium, the better the buy.
2. DO restrict buys to businesses you know something about.
3. DON'T buy a business with a management so incompetent that you'll have to throw everybody out. The chances of success are enhanced when the sitting management stays in place.
4. DO buy big. The bigger the buy, the more you are likely to succeed.

Companies can disobey the commonsense DON'Ts and neglect the obvious DOs and still succeed, but they do so at great peril. In general, the classic buys work brilliantly when they follow the rules. In one case, for instance, the target was a money-losing business that had been declining for years. It was up to its hairline in debt. Consequently the purchase price was abysmally low (Rule 1). The purchaser had recruited, well beforehand, a top-class entrepreneurial manager who knew the acquired business inside out (Rule 2).

The former family owners departed, but the professional management left behind, once given proper direction, proved fine (Rule 3). And the company they managed was a big one (Rule 4). The result? In the latest financial year, the bought company made more in profit than its purchase price had been seven years back. The price had been $82 million; the turnover at the time of purchase was $637 million. The mastermind, a Czech-born frozen-food pioneer named Alex Alexander, has an excellent recipe for getting the best out of buys.

1. Determine what businesses you want to build on, and get out of the rest.
2. Concentrate capital and human resources on areas you want to bring on.
3. Produce quality products.
4. Provide excellent service to customers.
5. Improve efficiency so that you are competitive.

These rules make sense whether the buy is good or bad, expensive or cheap. Many buyers believe that they can manage expensive buys so brilliantly that they will become cheap and good. Don't believe it—the turnaround effort is always enormous, and you'll be lucky to escape like Britain's Midland Bank, by finding somebody who, after your long and losing travail, is willing (as Wells Fargo was) to take the crippling burden off your back (in this case the Crocker National Bank in San Francisco).

What's more likely to happen in expensive buys is illustrated by a saga very different from the one above. In this case, the buyer, desperate to buy a particular business (a good one), kept raising the price he was prepared to pay over two years until he won (breaking Rule 1). The purchaser knew nothing about the business (breaking Rule 2). The entire top management that had built up the buy so brilliantly walked out (breaking Rule 3). True, the buy was big (Rule 4). But that was no consolation as group profits fell and fell, pulled down by the poor profit performance of the buy and its colossal financing costs. If the rules are broken, the price is unlikely ever to be right.

How to pay the right price is the basic question. First, remember that you don't *have* to acquire the company. Bide your time until the right opportunity comes along at the right price. Second, do your homework, starting, of course, with how well the proposed buy obeys the four rules. Third, look at how much you're paying for sales. As a rough rule of thumb, never pay more than a dollar for a dollar: a dollar of purchase price for a dollar of sales. Try to do far better—

like Alexander with his purchase and Warren Buffett ($55 million for $115 million) with Nebraska Furniture Mart.

The low-price-for-sales logic is the essence of corporate raiding. Say that $300 million of turnover is valued in the market at a footling $9 million. Suppose you pay double the market price—$18 million —and then find that, say, half the turnover isn't worth having. You dispose of those unwanted parts of the business (note Alexander's wisdom above). On the rest of the turnover, you earn a miserable 6 percent before tax—but that's $9 million, or a stunning 50 percent return on capital from a low-margin business.

Push that yield up to $15 million (still by no means a stiff target), and your return is dreamy. By following the logic of paying cheap for turnover, so that even low margins equal high reward, you kill two birds with one stone. The disposals that remove the loss makers also generate capital with which to repay the debt. A heavy preexisting debt is always likely in a cheap buy, and very possibly debt will be necessary in the buyer's own financing. Play your cards properly, though, and you can emulate Hanson Industries North America, which, after recouping the entire purchase price of SCM by disposals, ended up with a rump producing $200 million of profits. That approach explains a return on shareholders' equity that, in 1985, was the second highest in the *Fortune* 500: no less than 47.5 percent.

A good buy, or good sale, for one party isn't necessarily a bad sale or buy for the other. You may, of course, be dealing with one of those fools born every minute; it's also true that one company's poison may be another one's meat—provided, that is, that it takes the trouble to have an excellent digestion.

11. THE CASH FLOW OF COLUMBIA

You shouldn't always believe what companies say, even if the words have the effect of pillorying them. For instance, Roberto Goizueta, promoted in a spectacular personal leap to revitalize Coca-Cola, promptly ran into heavy flak for bottling up Columbia Pictures with a $765 million bid. What, the Wall Street critics wanted to know, did peddling pop have in common with films such as *Annie,* Columbia's $40 million musical?

The answer is nothing at all, except that Old King Coke reckoned to know a thing or three about marketing, especially promotion and merchandising, a field in which, by comparison, movie moguls are babes in the woods. At least, that was one of the arguments adduced by Goizueta. But the analogy between encouraging people into cinemas and into pop bottles doesn't bear much examination; films are essentially one-offs, and the universal, long victorious, Coke franchise is based on continuity and repetition.

The salient fact, though, is that even Coke is not ultimately unbeatable. The reason Goizueta won his promotion was that Pepsi-Cola had been fizzing all too fast for the peace of the royally rich clique of Atlanta businessmen who are Coca-Cola's time-lords. Just like Jacques Bergerac, plucked from ITT by the legendary Charles Revson to run Revlon, the new Coke boss plainly saw that one quick route to financial targets (growing faster than inflation in Coke's case) is to buy the growth.

Funnily enough, Revlon did precisely that in one field, health care, that Goizueta had examined and found wanting (apparently rightly, given the lackluster record that led Revlon into Pantry Pride's parlor). Why? Because it involved high technology—and that was one of Goizueta's diversification no-nos, along with high capital investment in plant and inability to grow rapidly without dramatic increase in market share. That last stipulation, obviously enough, would rule out Coke itself. After all those years of massive consumer bombardment, its chances of fast outgrowing the whole soft-drink

269

market are hardly high. It's a problem that eventually comes to all successful firms, even on far smaller stages: when you and the market have matured, what next? The movie market, of course, is even more aged in the wood than Coke's; the behavior of audiences around the world has been as discouraging as the failure rate of feature films. Finally, as Goizueta pointed out in his own defense, Columbia is only a tenth of Coca-Cola's size; which means it can hardly make a mighty difference to the Atlanta giant's performance.

The drinks market was where Goizueta's cause had to be won or lost. The real reason for the Columbia buy was to provide a rich cash flow that would underpin the greatest shake-up the U.S. soft-drink empire had ever seen: distributor reorganization and executive revivalism went hand-in-hand with an unprecedented flow of new product launches, in which Diet Coke sprang out of nowhere to beat all comers in its sector; including Coke's own Tab. The purpose of diversification must always be to add strength to the basic business, never to dilute the drink. As Goizueta's new slogan (eventually sadly outmoded by the bifurcation of the main brand) rightly said, "Coke is it!" The basic business always is.

12. TRIUMPHING IN TURBULENT MARKETS

The commotion at Coke, Columbia buy and all, leading up to the twin-Coke contretemps of 1985 as reported in Step One, section 1, of this book, is symptomatic of the destruction of old certainties by new developments. In naked circumstances, nothing is sacred and very little is safe. *Turbulence* is the word used by Bill Ramsay, a General Foods executive, to describe these conditions in world markets. He pointed out in a paper on brand marketing that the world economy had gone from growth through crisis to flatness; that brand marketing had passed from proliferation through rationalization to polarization; that consumer requirements had moved from choice to price/value to identity; that the source of profit, market expansion in the 1960s, had become margin improvement in the next decade —now the profit lies in winning the battle for market share.

This all means that management has had to switch its attention from diversification through resource allocation to competitive strategy. The huge competitive pressure felt by U.S. companies has consequences for management that run right through the business. Ramsay's conclusions on what these consequences are for brand marketing alone are emphatic and far-reaching.

1. Recognize that the brand is in a state of flux and transition. The conditions of the 1960s have disappeared forever. Anticipate the changes to come.

2. Build a strategic view of your brand adjusted to the new realities. Learn and relearn the key leverages that affect the market you are in. Look for segmentation opportunities. Think about how you would enter your market if you were a new competitor.

3. Analyze your consumers. They are no longer conformist and uncomplicated. The behavior of women consumers, in particular, is changing. They are smarter, less predictable.

4. The manufacturer and the trade are strategically interdependent. The manufacturer needs a detailed trade-marketing plan; the trade needs a brand-marketing plan.

5. Invest heavily in advertising when you have a new brand, a new item, or a genuinely improved product (or service).

6. Use research and development to improve or at least maintain your competitive quality.

7. Accept innovation as a necessity for your category and organize accordingly. New products need to be technologically driven as well as market-driven.

Once again the wisdom is ancient but the urgency is new—and powerful. Ramsay quoted a passage from a *Harvard Business Review* article that should be engraved in every marketer's mind: "The key to long-term success—even survival—is what it has *always* been: to

271

invest, to innovate, to create value. Such determination, such striving to excel requires leaders." So there *is* strong continuity; the difference is that the lessons of what has always been true have to be observed in a setting so strongly discontinuous that what is old can look frighteningly new.

Anyone who thinks that diversity offers an escape from this discontinuity has never diversified; or has been very lucky, very good, or both; or is being fooled. The Ramsay Rules apply in all cases. And the prime task of a diversifying, Supermarketing management is to see that the rules are applied. If not, the turbulence will run within the firm as well as without.

To summarize some of the important points I've mentioned in Step Nine:

1. Buy into markets only when you can see the certain prospect of adequate returns on capital.

2. And don't diversify unless you are also making the core business so strong as to be nearly invulnerable.

3. You can only win diversified success through the undiversified achievements of significant units.

4. Don't let anything reduce the incentive to capitalize on the company's own assets to create, innovate, and grow.

5. The odds on mergers succeeding are evens; motivation makes the difference between the sheep and the goats.

6. If you want to beat the Japanese, or anybody else, you need equal efficiency and innovation and equal use of new technology— to lower costs, develop new products, and defend old ones.

7. "Differentiate, specialize, and segment" is the formula for business riches—in retailing and manufacturing alike.

8. Know your customers, know your competitors, know the people in your own company; move fast, and keep the product line ahead of the competition: do these things, and you must win.

9. When buying companies, don't overpay; do stick to businesses you know about; don't buy bad managements; and do buy big.

10. After buying, get rid of what you don't want; concentrate hard on the good areas; go for quality; give excellent service; improve efficiency—and do them all fast.

11. Winning in the markets of the 1980s means overwhelmingly winning the battle for market share.

12. If you want to succeed in turbulent times, meet discontinuity head-on; but do so from a base of exploiting your continuous strengths.

Step Ten: Keeping Ahead in Fluctuating Markets

1. THE RAH-RAH OF ICI

All managers must answer two very simple questions: Do you know what you're doing? Are you doing it properly? No less a company than the $10 billion Imperial Chemical Industries came to the conclusion that it couldn't give an honest yes to these questions. Its proposed retreat from its fortress in London to a far smaller head office nearby was a landmark idea in the history of big business. Indeed, *big* is an operative word; small has become fashionably beautiful, and ICI has always had a penchant for following management modes—raising its hemline rather late, but with enthusiasm.

Its new organizational rah-rah, though, reflects more than modishness. For that matter, so does the whole worldwide reaction away from the centralized mammoths that once dominated the industrial

274

scene—those 300 that, in the popular scenario referred to earlier in this book, should have been ruling the international roost by now. No doubt the 300 would have included, on any reasonable projection, the near-bankrupts International Harvester and Massey-Ferguson. Size has been no protection against the intensified, segmented competion that rules now and demands companies organized at the sharp marketing end.

Certain businesses will never be successful again in anybody's lifetime. Steel is already a shadow of its former self. In ICI's business, many bulk chemicals hold out the same sad prospect of eternal oversupply and low returns, but in such large volumes that few managements have yet dared to shed what is in fact the baseload of their corporations. What they can shed, though, is the baseload of management, the funguslike growth of second-guessers and satellites that multiplied in the days when size dominated.

ICI carried this to an unusually baffling extent, because the real power of command over people and resources always lay with its mighty divisions. The efforts of the executive directors to execute, given this essential powerlessness, were cramped. The millstone in the Millbank HQ's nickname of Millstone House weighed especially heavily around the necks of some of its own higher inhabitants. Pity the poor director impossibly responsible at one and the same time for a function, a geographical area, and a division.

The alternative method of management, by performance, is now well established as faster and far more effective, with a small center exacting and monitoring results from separate, market-oriented operations headed by individual chief executives, and with the growth markets separated out and properly, profitably exploited. But the retreat from millstone management must fail if it is merely organizational. The force that drives the engine is all-important, and that force can only be marketing.

275

2. WHAT THE MARKETING CONCEPT MEANS

How on earth is it that the marketing concept has failed to penetrate all managerial minds? As noted in an earlier chapter, Colonel Lyndall F. Urwick expounded the concept a half-century back. He warned that "the main job of distribution is not to get rid of what production makes, it is to tell production what it ought to make." Splendid stuff, and obviously true. But set that 1933 quote against this 1984 one from *Business Week,* on Edwin H. Land, the founder of Polaroid:

> Land believed that success depended on coming up with innovative products, then persuading people to buy them, and in his day Polaroid used little or no market research. . . . By contrast, Land's successors are looking outward to the market. They are taking their cues from potential customers . . . and are tailoring their technology to meet the need, not the other way round.

The reason for this conversion was not the retirement of Land (although that helped) but three years of declining sales that turned Polaroid from wunderkind to has-been.

This great innovative company was not alone in ignoring market research; to take just one other example (the biggest you could find), so did General Motors. In describing that company's effort at a turnaround, one of its top engineers was moved to remark that the company is now "trying to find out what the customers want." About time, too—but what explained a neglect so long and so grave that these mighty managements proved, by their awful results, how right Urwick was?

Nor should the question be asked only of U.S. leaders. At the aforementioned ICI, in the darkest days of the fiber division's attempt to cut losses by cutting back, one move (incredibly) was to dismantle the marketing department; the new, far more promising strategy is marketing-led, using technology to develop special fibers that the end-user wants, and employing marketing razzmatazz to exploit these desires. "The biggest fundamental thing we have done is to stand our business on its head and ask 'What does the market need?' rather than produce the goods and tell the salesmen to go out and sell," said one executive with pride.

There's Colonel Urwick's wheel being invented all over again—note, once more under the duress of desperately bad results. But strength can flow from weakness. It takes strong management for the company that was first, and famously so, into polyester filament yarn, to be first out, or (another example of ICI daring to dare) for the company that invented polyethylene to abandon the product. Today's naked markets have stripped even giants of their clothes. Those prepared to re-dress themselves in the marketing concept can truly hope to capitalize on the innate strength of both the company and the modern marketplace. Riches, as well as naked competition, lie in the market's variety. The riches can be won only by companies that can organize a varied and vital response to match—but in the full knowledge that half a century of mounting discontinuity has made no difference to the basic elements, the continuous framework, within which the Supermarketer reacts.

Nobody can market successfully in changing times without carrying out all the duties, functions, and roles that Urwick pinpointed in the 1930s. In the 1980s, too, everything starts, as he wrote, with "determining what the business shall make and sell, how many different lines and how many different sizes and patterns."

First fix your mix, then price it. Is it more profitable, for example, to sell x units at \$10 apiece, or x plus 50 units at \$8 each? As an earlier chapter showed, many firms still make the countless decisions needed on pricing policy in a fog of misapprehension and misconception. Many are no better when it comes to deciding "to whom the business can and should sell," which involves the systematic use of market research and imaginative exploration of "new avenues and methods of distribution."

The longest part of old Urwick's catechism concerns the addition or withdrawal of lines. This goes to the heart of modern marketing—the study of demand, the provision of the right quantity and quality of production, the winning of new markets, and (the real crunch) "all the detailed arrangements necessary to ensure that when a new line is launched, the efforts of all departments in the business, design, production, advertising and selling, are united behind the new venture, focused as to time, quantity, and range of effort." As the guru noted, this meant "constant and systematic study of the products and methods of competitors."

After observing that another prime job of the marketing function (which he insisted should be a separate, parallel department, not placed over production and sales) was to work out the volume sales targets for each line, Urwick urged as a final duty "Determination of the standard of quality which the business should seek to maintain." Like the rest of the catechism, the quality stipulation has a familiar ring in the 1980s. Look back at the whole program, at the Supermarketer's code of conduct, and you're looking precisely at the approach the Japanese world-beaters used to crack their Western markets. Those foreign markets were far stranger in many respects than any discontinuity that Western marketers have had to absorb. It was because the Japanese built their advance on a marketing platform that was tried and true that they succeeded in times and circumstances that were untried and full of hazard. It's the only way.

3. THE EIGHTEEN PERCENT OF IBM

Corporations don't come any prouder than Intel. Its Robert Noyce was the first living legend of the semiconductor industry, father of the integrated-circuit design that became the industry standard, creator of the company that gave venture capital one of its first and greatest successes. The company's first memory chip, the 1103, tripled sales in the single year of 1973—and that was before the advent of the Intel microprocessor, an invention that set the computer industry on its ears and took sales up to $700 million by 1979.

At that point, Noyce stepped aside. As Michael Orme wrote in *Management Today,* Intel was "no longer about gee-whiz engineering, but more and more about customer support, software, production prowess and marketing." Still, the Noyce successors, chairman Gordon Moore and chief executive Andrew Grove, adapted to the new environment in just as legendary a style. Grove even wrote a book *(High-Output Management)* to put across the hard-driving, hard-driven ideas of executive motivation that promised to take Intel onward and upward under its own powerful head of steam. Yet in 1983 the one-time wunderkind of Silicon Valley seemed to surrender to the Big Daddy of data processing, IBM.

The $250 million with which IBM purchased its first tranche of Intel shares (on its way to an 18 percent holding) made short-term sense against the background of static sales and soggy profits— especially at a time when Intel had to invest $100 million in twelve months just to stay competitive. The longer-term reality, though, was that even as inventive a company as Intel, selling essential building blocks of modern technology, had run into the marketing trap of the 1980s. Maintaining market leadership means sustaining a product advantage: in industry after industry, that costs more and more to achieve, carries rising risks of inadequate returns, and demands increasingly large amounts of money to put new products into production. And if you can't afford that, one day you won't be able to afford anything at all.

4. GROUPING THE INTERESTS

Nobody, but nobody, can afford everything in the naked market. One of the most striking signs of change is the new currency being given to a management maxim of noble antiquity: "If you can't beat 'em, join 'em." The new twist this is getting in the remarkable evolution of today's markets is the same in many different contexts, whether it's IBM buying into Intel's microcircuitry, or VW teaming up with Renault to make an automatic gearbox, or Glaxo initially placing its U.S. wonder drug in the hands of Hoffmann-La Roche. Even the greatest of companies can't hope to cover the whole gamut of products and marketing requirements imposed by fast, specialized markets.

The old received idea was that the giant used its financial and marketing muscle to get mighty economies of scale. These days, the economist of scale has to cope with much greater variety; and needs far more flexibility than of yore. Scale costs too much for one company to manage all the scales on its own. Thus Renault and VW competed on body shells, but combined on automatic transmissions. Thus Glaxo and Hoffmann-La Roche raced each other to the marketable patents—but the former decided, for a time, that the latter's American marketing strength was worth more than its own patented exclusivity.

By similar tokens, IBM has perhaps the most powerful marketing image of any company in the closing decades of the century. But even in a relatively confined market like data processing, IBM lacks all the specialized expertise that moves the market. Hence it wisely turned to Intel, the archetypal Silicon Valley venture, for the vital innards of its sure-to-succeed (with its IBM label) personal computer, the PC. Hence, in turn, Intel, now dependent on IBM for huge chunks of business, found it advantageous to take in a senior partner. The strategic IBM stake underwrites Intel's ability to go on satisfying the market, while Intel's microcircuit skills should guarantee that IBM won't fall behind the Japanese.

Of course, there's many a slip between cups and lips. Maybe Intel would end up as a wholly owned subsidiary of IBM. Glaxo's deal with Roche didn't end in tears, as other such joint ventures have, but it did end with Glaxo taking its U.S. fate into its own hands. Whatever the risks, the principle is plainly right. Even the effective, high-growth specialist like Intel will come, sooner or later, to a point of no return—where, to guarantee its progress, it needs more marketing outlets and more money.

Preserving independence, though, is highly desirable. As always, the French have a word for it—or rather a few words: *groupement d'intérêts économiques*. It's the legal term for a combination of parts that isn't a merger (with all the familiar disadvantages thereof) but a union. More and more, sensible firms are seeking economies of scale in this way. For those that don't join 'em may very well be beaten.

Like so much else in modern marketing, this is a lesson that came naturally to the Japanese, no doubt because they started too far behind the West to make their own headway. In the process, they have become past masters of interest grouping. For instance, Fujitsu made none too bright a decision when, unlike other Japanese computer aspirants, it teamed up not with an American company but with Siemens. Even in the 1950s, the West German giant's lag in computer and electronics technology was evident. But as Simon Caulkin reported to *Management Today,* "One reason for the decision [which meant in effect developing its own computer capabilities] was Fujitsu's characteristic reluctance to break a long-standing commitment to a business partner."

An executive explained that "Siemens was our grandparent. We learned our technology from them [starting in 1923], but now the positions are reversed." The Siemens brand today goes on Fujitsu computers, whose development has been enhanced since 1977 by another arrangement built on friendship, that of Fujitsu's computer guru with the vastly respected American Gene Amdahl. Fujitsu's original 26 percent stake in Amdahl's firm mirrors IBM's first bite at Intel; maybe the later development of Fujitsu's stake (now 48 percent) will also be paralleled one fine day.

Peek into any great Japanese company, and a web of such cross-deals and cross-fertilizations materializes. Canon is cooperating with Sony on the filmless still camera, for instance; and Canon is one of the most articulate exponents of the necessity of taking *groupement* beyond the traditional, limited deals into a whole new concept of the high-tech corporation. In this grand design, each giant concentrates on developing its own exclusive and excellent technologies, not only for its own purposes but to use as bargaining counters for the inevitable moment when it will require the technology of another company.

The commercial world has always been crisscrossed by joint ventures and other alliances, from East to West. The French, in recent times, have been peculiarly adept at using trans-European deals to help them accomplish nationalistic aims like staying in civil airliners against Boeing (with the Airbus) and competing with NASA in satellite launchers (with the Ariane rocket). But only the Japanese bring to bear a whole philosophy of *groupement:* the idea that a commercial relationship can be like a friendship, founded on mutual interests and respects, and lasting until death do us part.

In the adversarial world of Western commerce, the idea sits uneasily. Yet even so independent-minded a firm as Philips, after an abysmal failure with its own design of videocassette recorder, has seen the error of its ways and formed a *groupement* with Sony for laser discs and their players. The basic imperatives of *groupement* make clear the necessity of a relationship based on this kind of mutuality. What you cannot do alone, you must do with others. That means giving them your trust, and expecting them to trust you. Intel's other customers have perforce had to trust IBM to maintain the integrity of their supplier: to the point where Compaq actually leapfrogged IBM in personal computers by being the first to use the latest Intel microprocessor.

However grudgingly, IBM's rivals have been propelled toward the position that the British computer maker ICL found had been naturally established by its Fujitsu partners. Once trust had been achieved, "they have never looked at the agreements. It's all been done on a shake of the hand." Very Fujitsu, very Japanese; but also very much the collaborative way to survive in the naked market.

5. THE RANDOM ROLLS-ROYCE

Can the principle of "grouping interests" be applied within the firm? The management of Rolls-Royce Motors, the people who brought the world's most famous maker of luxury cars from the dark of perennial loss into the bright uplands of high profit, should be compelled by honesty to answer no. The issue is less their own merger with the one-time armaments giant Vickers than what they were joining—a collection of unjoined bits and pieces.

There were warning signs in abundance. Vickers is one of those companies that seem to be born unlucky, with every step forward followed by at least half a pace back. Before the 1983 dividend-cutting plunge of a third, the company's earnings per share had declined in a decade by 7.8 percent annually on an inflation-corrected basis. Yet in the early 1970s, as again in 1980 when the Rolls merger took place, Vickers (not for the first time) had promised, under reformed management and with reformed ways, to come right. So long a run of bad luck—with the American setback in Rolls-Royce sales the blow of the early 1980s—cannot be attributed to fate alone.

Look at it this way: what do luxury limos, lithographic plates, health care, and bottling machinery have in common? The only answer is that Vickers was in all four markets when, yet again, the profits collapsed. Its interests were grouped in about eleven diverse main activities, which at the time showed the following pattern: profits up, five; profits down, five; unchanged, one. No doubt even an infant statistician would spot this as a typical random pattern. The randomness is typical, too, of this kind of accidental conglomerate, held together not by any marketing unity or deep-laid financial strategy, but mostly by the weak cement of history.

Some theorists would argue that the resulting blend, in which even the magnificent machines of Rolls account for only 28 percent of sales, provides greater balance and safety than an organization with too many eggs in one basket. But that's merely another way of

283

saying that the group just doesn't have the market base that helped BOC (once also seemingly luckless) get lucky under the thrusting management of the American Dick Giardano, who proved to be a prime asset won in the company's unluckily drawn-out purchase of Airco. Despite Giordano's diversifications, even in 1982–83 BOC's traditional core in gases accounted for half of sales and four-fifths of operating profit. Very typically, one part of all activity does account for the lion's share of all useful results, in any diversified company.

That was true of Rolls-Royce cars in 1984, when they turned in 43 percent of group profits. But those motors needed to generate at least double the sales to give Vickers the bread-and-butter single-market base required, not just by every diversified business but by any company that, like Rolls-Royce, has found its niche. Porsche, for example, has over $1.3 billion a year in sales, compared with the $224 million rolling out of Rolls. What might the latter's management (who moved into the driving seat at Vickers after 1980) have done if their strategy and control hadn't been spread over more than a dozen different businesses? A feeble nothing of profit came in 1982 from $75 million of "activities each with under $23 million sales." No Supermarketer would tolerate "activities each with"—not in the age of the Niche.

6. NUGGETS IN NICHES

Never before have markets offered so many rich nooks and crannies. Never before have so many pundits, echoed by so many managers, agreed so unanimously on the virtues of the same strategy: exploiting the nook, the cranny, the niche. High technology in particular, by its very progress, has created niches. An inventor or group of inventors doodles on a tablecloth (which is said to be how Compaq was born); the bright technical idea, performing uniquely, forms a new segment, in Compaq's case, the IBM-compatible portable. Hundreds, probably thousands, of businesses have been built on such foundations in the last couple of decades—and more are being born every month.

If you're competing with a giant of the prowess and spread of IBM, there isn't much option (as rival giants, such as GE and RCA, who tackled IBM head-on found to such ruinous cost). The niche is a metaphor for the flanking action that wins most military campaigns. Yet the most celebrated and successful attempts to go around IBM's side have often ended in either defeat or dismay. Control Data took the macro-mainframe route; Digital Equipment, in contrast, went beneath the giant's belt with minicomputers for nonbusiness markets; Apple went lower still, with personal computers sold primarily to individuals. All three have had their toils and troubles, although DEC in particular has struck new gold, and new blows at IBM, with its VAX range of minis.

For years the niche profits just rolled in, until the day when competition, not just from IBM but from others attracted by the rich niches, became more and more intense. Because of the ease of entry, personal computers in particular have become an arena for some of the most prolific competition ever seen. In consequence, few analogies have caught on faster than that between the dawn of the automobile and the age of the personal computer. The similarity that has received most excited attention, though, is not just the proliferation of makes, but the possibility of computers emulating the fate of American cars in massive brand extinction. Are the failures of lesser computer firms, led in the United States by such as Osborne, the precursor of the collapses that left GM, Ford, and Chrysler in command?

It can be argued that, unlike the car of the 1920s, the computer of the 1980s is strictly an assembly job. Far from making its own engines, gearboxes, and axles, even IBM buys in the entire kit and caboodle for its personal computer. Thus the economies of scale don't work in favor of the integrated producer, there being no such thing. This argument contains an incontrovertible truth that applies to many markets. Ease of production, often for reasons akin to those

285

in home computers, has resulted in ease of entry; and costs of production, being roughly equal, in many cases no longer rule the roost.

What does? Technical strengths (like logic arrays and software) may still give a mighty advantage to the big battalions. But so, above all, does marketing. Given the vastly greater spending power of the IBMs and Apples, let alone the Hewlett-Packards, Wangs, and DECs, and given that these companies, despite their technological power and financial muscle, have all had much trouble in the personal-computer market, the chances can't really be good for weaker firms with minority sales.

There is, of course, a rich market for those serving genuine minorities with special products that suit particular purposes. In the computer market the profitable survivors will include both those who reap the economies of marketing scale and those niche sellers who play DEC to the great man's IBM—and sometimes (like DEC with VAX) steal the show. Every marketing company must make this strategic choice between specialization and generalization, and it's no use choosing the latter without the necessary general strength.

The truth is doubly and triply confirmed by the interesting study from McKinsey consultants Richard E. Cavanagh and Donald K. Clifford referred to in Step Four, section 8. It shows that America's profitable mid-size companies wisely shun mass markets in favor of niches. Nor are the fast-growing U.S. middleweights exclusively technological, as noted; the likes of Dunkin' Donuts stress that low tech can create a rich niche just as readily as can high.

To cook up niche success, however, not only must you first catch your niche, you must fatten it up for the long-term pot. As disastrous declines in the stock market valuation of high fliers have often shown, precise targeting on defined market niches, which is supposed to yield consistent and rapid sales rises, together with the lofty margins won from proprietary technology, works brilliantly but not forever. Characteristically, the high-tech niche yields its ripest rewards when the exploitation is least mature. The low-tech segment, on the other hand, may well make its mints as it ripens, with economies of scale (as in fast foods) countering the proliferation of competition.

The enthusiasm with which the fast fooders have spread across the globe holds the clue, as do the fortunes of high-tech successes like Microsoft, which on going public made its thirty-year-old progenitor, Bill Gates, worth $350 million. Gates makes the software that runs the IBM PCs and clones. Within the profitable niche, the would-be Supermarketer must likewise achieve international spread and clear leadership to be reasonably (but only reasonably) sure of success everlasting. Far better to be Japan's Epson, with half the market in printers for computers, than to rely on slugging it out with the champs in personal computers, or, in any market, to get stuck in too tight a niche and too narrowly confined a world.

7. THE BRANIFF-BENDIX SYNDROME

Consider the sad fate of four companies, each of which suffered from the same deadly disease: Datapoint, Bendix, Braniff, and Continental Illinois, the bank that nearly busted the entire U.S. banking system before its federal rescue. Braniff, once the highest flying airline (multicolored planes and all), actually did go bankrupt. Bendix, after its bizarrely hectic attempt to take over Martin Marietta, ended up taken over itself. As for the common disease, the Datapoint case reveals its identity.

This corporation "suffered considerable embarrassment and loss of reputation . . . because of managerial actions apparently taken in response to enormous internal pressures to maintain a string of 39 consecutive quarterly profit increases." The same illness—the urge to grow at all costs—also afflicted Bendix in its takeover bid and Braniff in its move into "a great many cities, several located far from its established routes" in the sorely mistaken belief that airline deregulation would be withdrawn. Continental Illinois just wanted to become one of the three top banks for corporate customers—and so unjustly stuffed itself full of bad, high-risk energy loans.

Two Rutgers professors conclude from all this, and from some

287

earnest thought about who is supposed to benefit from expansion, that "growth *per se* is not an appropriate corporate objective." For a start, which dimension of growth are you talking about? In profits and profitability? In the market value of the firm? In sales? Or how about market share? Not to mention physical measures like the number of employees, the wages bill, and total expenditures—but nobody in his or her right mind would use those as measures of anything meaningful in terms of efficiency or prosperity.

Actually, the professors have no trouble showing that the other measures all have drawbacks, too. They call every single one of them a "rubber yardstick." For example, take growth in return on investment. B. F. Goodrich "dramatically increased its ROI over the past decade by casting off low-profit elements of its tire operations without experiencing fully commensurate sales declines. Does this constitute growth?" Similarly, if unit sales decrease but prices rise, so that the value of sales goes ahead, is that growth or contraction?

All the reasons for not having growth as an objective add up to just one: "growth appears to be an effect, not a cause, of a company's success." So what should you aim at? "Corporate goals should be based on the 'find a need and fill it' philosophy. Firms should identify legitimate opportunities to serve a market's needs and then do so effectively and efficiently." That sounds a bit like advising children how to be good—by behaving well, of course. But there's a very valuable lesson in there.

Use growth figures by all means to monitor progress, but don't just pluck some growth target out of the sky and make it your primary goal. Listen rather to the great guru Ted Levitt: the goal of business (any business) is to "create and keep a customer." The only question is, How?

8. HOW TO PLAN SELLING

Creating and keeping a customer are in one sense two sides of the same coin. The loving care and attention paid to a customer during courtship, if continued into the married state, will go far toward preventing divorce. But selling, like everything else in marketing, has been subject to change and discontinuity. Far from disappearing from sight (the fate many expected), individual selling has become more important than ever—and its general mediocrity has become increasingly insupportable, on grounds of both expense and ineffectiveness.

To the extent that selling fails because of sloppy technique, it can be corrected by training, using all the modern psychological jargon and gimmicks. If motivation is at fault, that can be magnified amazingly by better designed financial incentives. But what if the whole sales effort is misdirected? What if you're employing the kind of salesman who proudly tells a seminar that he called on one outlet 135 times in a year because the account was worth $500,000, and the client was so loyal that he "needed to reciprocate"?

Marketing experts Simon Majaro and Malcolm McDonald quote this foolish fellow to make their point that customers come in different shapes and sizes as well as in markedly different types, each of which, for maximum cost effectiveness, needs different treatment. As they point out, salespeople are human. They like being loved and hate being rebuffed. But it's as wasteful of time, money, and selling effort to lavish undue attention on a loving, loyal customer as it is to devote yourself to pursuing one who clearly won't buy from you in this century.

From this commonsense observation, the Majaro-McDonald Matrix emerges. It divides clientele into three major groupings: "those who literally love the supplier (the 'Philes'); those who are totally indifferent to the supplier so long as the offering is right (the 'Promiscuous' companies); and those who are hostile to the selling company and reluctant to buy from it at all (the 'Phobes')." Plainly,

289

how you sell and communicate to each of these groups needs to vary greatly to maximize the chances of obtaining their business or retaining it—and without incurring excessive cost in either case.

Like all good matrices, though, this one has nine boxes, for exactly the same need for variation is created by differing size. A large Promiscuous customer needs different treatment from a medium-size one; a medium Phile should be handled differently from a small one. The consequences can be very obvious: "A small Phobe is probably not worth bothering about, since the results of even a successful combating of the phobia will not justify the effort involved. A small Phile, on the other hand, will probably buy from the supplier, anyway."

You shouldn't exploit this small potential by large sales effort but should call infrequently and concentrate on protestations of undying love. Don't spend more than the absolute minimum of time on small clients if you want to achieve real sales productivity. The argument can't, of course, apply with equal force to the large, loyal, and important Phile. But even here the experts recommend "a maintenance policy, under which a representative should do only what is necessary to maintain the business," say, one phone call a week. You have to be wary of competition, true, and that's what will determine how often you judge a personal visit to be necessary.

The medium Philes, too, qualify for maintenance. But it's the conversion of the Promiscuous into the Phile that offers the most profitable field for customer creation—and the larger the better. These difficult people are fickle by definition and tough on price. The experts suggest a four-pronged attack. It starts, like all good selling, with analyzing those who actually make the decisions and then analyzing their motivation. Second, concentrate on showing the fickle fellows the cost/benefit and "value-in-use" of what you're offering. Third, watch and record carefully everything in the marketplace that is likely to affect your selling chances. Finally, fall over yourself to demonstrate how able and willing the company is to respond to problems and queries at all times. If salespeople do succeed in converting the Promiscuous into the ever-loving, what's more, you reward them specially under the appraisal system.

That leaves just one other class of customer who is too large to ignore: the Big Phobe. You may not even know why it dislikes your company, or even whether there's any way of breaking through the hostility. But keep in low-profile touch, if you can. Try to answer that initial question "Why won't they buy?" to find out the reasons for the hatred and to see if you can remove the problem. Look for chances, like changes in top personnel, that might open the door. Above all, make sure that failures in supply or quality or service don't turn other customers into Phobes.

The same principles apply to other classes of customer in the matrix. Relate effort to potential. Analyze the reasons for difficulties and eliminate your deficiencies. Develop a clear strategy and plan for every type of customer, and don't let salespeople deviate from the plan without good reason. It can't be a completely cut-and-dried process, naturally. For instance, small customers, whether Philes or Promiscuous, should always be nurtured in case, one day, they become larger, perhaps very large. As for the small Phobe, "This customer is more trouble than he is worth. Allow him to indulge his phobias in happy isolation."

Note that the victims of the Braniff-Bendix Syndrome never seem to have considered these vital aspects of creating and keeping the customer. Bendix sought to buy its way to growth; Braniff built the network but couldn't drum up the business; Continental Illinois, instead of searching for the desired top-class customers with the bait of top-class services, took on easier-to-win, low-class business; Datapoint put the cart (earnings) before the horse (building larger, profitable customers). You should, instead, cherish the Philes, seduce the Promiscuous, and convert the Phobes—by creating products they can't refuse—and growth will follow, as night does day, in any market.

9. THE GREAT EUROPEAN BUY-IN

The European takeover surge in the United States can be looked at from different angles, but most of them give a similar view: that of the relative loss of power of many giant U.S. corporations. The loss has been considerably redressed by the Reagan economic recovery and the subsequent megamerger surge, but the fall from grace was still substantial. And it was not merely financial—the relative marketing failure was on such a vast scale that the astonishing became the commonplace.

In a single week in the spring of 1982, for instance, a huge British conglomerate bought one of the most famous names in U.S. retailing, while a British advertising agency, of modest size internationally, became positively immodest by purchasing a far larger American firm. Not so many years ago the idea of BAT paying $310 million for Marshall Field, or the Saatchis pocketing Compton for a $29.2 million down payment (let alone, in a mere month of 1986, buying two other U.S. agencies, to become the world's largest), would have bordered on the unthinkable. Now nobody raises an eyebrow—although these deals symbolize one of the most extreme turnabouts of modern times.

America is still the world's leading marketplace, the largest by far, the most varied, the most competitive, the one most likely to innovate and to accept innovation—but no longer right across the board. In retailing, for instance, one-time leaders, such as Gimbels, Saks, and the Chicago-based Marshall Field, steadily slipped through lack of the aggressive, enterprising management that had created them in the first place. The decline of the once-great supermarkets of A & P (now headed by an Englishman) has also been stupefying to behold.

The universal spectacle has been that of Europeans using retailing techniques imported from the United States to greater effect than the originators. The process just described should sound familiar to followers of the Japanese miracle. In the major beleaguered industries (like cars, where the Americans have been so tortured by Toyota and others), Western manufacturing mammoths have been similarly hoist with their own petards. The giants of the 1960s in many cases either lost touch with the markets or relied on money rather than management to diversify away from their basic market troubles—only to find peripheral ones instead. In the 1980s, buying your way out of a gross marketing error has become an even less promising course of action, because markets themselves are in a fascinating flux.

10. PROFITING FROM MARKET CHANGE

The recession from which the world emerged as the 1980s progressed was in one respect the strangest in history—deep in its impact on production and employment, but shallow in its effect on consumption. Throughout the years of high and mounting unemployment, the world featured market after market with a buoyancy that was evidence of plenty amid dearth. The plenty is buying power; the dearth, jobs of the traditional variety. If an article in *Fortune* is right (and it's very hard to refute), the phenomenon won't disappear with recovery—no matter how vigorous. As its headline says, "The mass market is splitting apart." Not only is the gap between rich and poor widening, visibly and substantially, but the middle class is also polarizing (defined as families with annual incomes of $15,000 to $35,000).

While the number of these solid citizens as a proportion of all families fell, the percentages earning above $35,000 or below $15,000 actually rose. The explanation isn't far to seek. Nearly all the new jobs created in the United States have been in services, while manufacturing's share of employment has fallen. Service jobs are usually lower paid, except in the management and professional classes. Hence the $35,000-plus proliferation, the $15,000-minus increase, and the obvious conclusion for marketers that the top money lies at the top end of the buying spectrum.

This plainly means going up-market, tapping the purses of the new class that can afford to change cars often, to gobble up home computers, and to guzzle increasingly expensive wines. *Fortune*'s conclusions for those "used to selling millions of their products to middle income folks" are thus bleak—and the prospects are dark as far as the eye cares to see.

For the smart retailer, though, the prospects could hardly be brighter. Supergrowth has come to retailers who have exploited the newer mass-marketing techniques of reaching the more affluent consumer. In the age of the car and the selective purchaser, of onerous wage costs and omnipresent price sensitivity, the retailer with car access, or takeout goods, or central, computerized warehousing, or cut prices has a huge advantage over the traditional retailer when cashing in on the demographic trends.

Toys 'R' Us, the U.S. chain that created four of 1983's five highest paid Americans, specializes in offloading toys in lavish quantities from warehouselike premises, a technique being tailored to several other trades, including computers. In the computer market, companies like IBM have been brought face-to-face with the consumer for the first time, as products such as the IBM's PC are pushed through dealers rather than being hawked by the company's own sales force.

To some degree, the same rethinking is now required practice for all comers hoping to sell through the new retail powers. They must build even more powerful consumer franchises to force the retail titans to stock their products. In U.S. computer retailing there are already fears that the strength of IBM, Apple, and a very few others will drive out the smaller fry simply through lack of shelf space. In the economic society now emerging, not so much postindustrial as consumer-dominated, access to the consumer is increasingly critical. Most companies have no choice but to become consumer-dominated in step, a move that will take them a long way from their old industrial bases.

294

By the same token, the omens are awful for companies that haven't moved from that base—or won't move. Look at the sunset or smokestack industries: steel, much of chemicals, a good deal of construction equipment, many textiles, and so on. Contrast them with the recent successes in Japan, which have lain in the high-volume, high added-value end products of mechanical and electrical/electronic engineering—exploited by managements driven by the identification of strong markets and the stop-at-nothing creation of world leaders within them.

For companies with a Western, as opposed to a Japanese, base, that is far easier said than imitated. Farsighted companies on both sides of the Atlantic, true, have been thinking in global terms. Beecham is one example: it raised U.S. turnover to 28 percent of its total, closing fast on the share coming from a British market where the company's main brands were distinctly mature—and also offsetting some of the sluggishness from another ripe line, antibiotics.

Beecham's U.S. buys in toiletries, pharmacy products, home care, and perfumery were several and reasonably solid. But early in 1984, *Business Week* pointed out one mighty snag (along with the predictable, lesser ones of marketing and takeover problems in the seething U.S. market): Beecham was "butting up against consumer product companies that dwarf it in revenues and resources," which can therefore presumably bring backbreaking and possibly overweening market pressures to bear. If that is true of a company as vast, vigorous, and victorious as Beecham (with £1.7 billion in 1982–83 sales), the world prognosis for smaller and/or less sturdy firms looks dismal, whichever way they turn. And that applies even to the exploding new high-technology and information-technology markets.

Every company, of whatever size, has to take a cold, clear look at itself and its changing markets, to discover those in which it can achieve some kind of dominating presence—and that's where flux helps. Bye-bye, Middle America can also be Hello, Opportunity— but only for those firms that seek it.

11. THE SOFTER LANDING AT DELTA

No matter what the game or market is, it's getting tougher. Take Delta Air Lines, renowned in 1979 for its management performance —as well it might be. Operating revenues had doubled to $2.4 billion, after-tax profits had risen by almost half, and return on stockholders' equity was the best in the business at 16 percent. Delta had cashed in strongly on the basic strategy of feeding passengers from outlying cities into the central hub of Atlanta, from where its long-distance flights took people on.

In 1979, though, deregulation changed the game. In the airline market, the shock came from government; in other markets, the mold-breaking force has been less artificial, but no less shattering in its impact. Delta resisted the deregulation blow well enough for a while. But when cut price and other competition hit, on top of its own less than successful efforts to create a second hub at Dallas–Fort Worth, Delta in 1982–83 made its first loss in sixteen years.

The best managed airline was still best in everything—except in the marketing and pricing skills that had suddenly become decisive. In the 1984 and 1985 fiscal years, though, Delta flew back strongly, and the explanation given to John Thackray by a First Boston analyst, Mike Derchin, tells the story (my italics): "One, the success of its commuter airline *marketing* program; two, increased penetration of the Dallas–Fort Worth *market;* three, the aggressive *marketing* programs against People Express, Eastern and Pan Am in the Northeast-Florida *markets.*" . . .

Only the fourth reason, additional services in the Atlanta hub, fits into the traditional pattern of Delta success. Otherwise, as the italics show, it's marketing all the way. The computer's ability to allow airlines to create in the passenger the illusion of paying less while receiving more has been one of the main instruments of profitable change. So has the emphasis on customer service—"the name of the game," the phrase used by Delta president Ronald W. Allen in explaining why Delta reserves customers' seats on another airline if necessary. "It builds loyalty. The next time the customer flies, which airline do you think he's gonna call first?"

But this is one war in which victory is never won. The attack could come from some future variant of People Express, which is why financial strength is so important in what Delta's vice chairman, Robert Oppenlander, rightly calls "a marketing war." Money "permits you to create an unprofitable price to fight off interlopers in a market." But still they come: "This is an environment in which we are constantly reacting to the competitive threats from others—every day, it seems, a major competitor is invading one of our routes for the first time, or coming out with a new schedule, or new prices." This is the story of the naked market: and that market demands continuous and vigorous adjustment to change that is at least as effective as Delta's softer landing.

12. DOING A DOUBLE D

The logic of intensified competition, of segmented, niche markets, and of rapid response to change in all markets explains why one management doctrine above all is spreading so swiftly, even among the beached whales of the business world. The notion is that large companies should be divided into profit centers built around clearly defined markets, and placed under the equally clear leadership of managers who are instructed to get onward and upward, or out.

It's the antithesis of the once equally fashionable idea of packing a skyscraper with superminds who would coordinate, compel, and control everything—but couldn't. The new trend doesn't only reflect such past failures, which are legion. More important, it's a response to the fragmentation of markets into segments, often dominated by unique technologies, techniques, and trading patterns. That now gives the old Double D (Decentralize and Delegate) a far better chance. At the corporate center, he who doesn't delegate is lost in the complexities of markets he can't hope to manage from afar.

The extent to which this logic has been taken up by the best-managed companies is remarkable. IBM not only set up an independent group for the PC, but allowed it to place the crucial work (chips, software, and all) outside IBM—an action that once would have been rank heresy. In Japan, Canon based a corporate turnaround in part on a division by products, which gave the new groups their own reorganized factories and R & D facilities. Again, the results were spectacular.

It would be a mistake, though, to attribute these results solely or even principally to the Double D. Decentralization and Delegation should be slaves to the master plan of the corporate center—whose role is made more, not less, important by the development of niche markets. The Achilles heel of the new segmentation could be failure at the center of companies to grasp that the vital central role includes imposing the common culture that makes an IBM even stronger than its parts and strengthens the parts in turn. The market niche has become a necessity, but it offers no hiding place from the other corporate essentials.

Of these, one above all has been made paramount by the very competition the Double-D approach is designed to meet. Continual competition of today's (and tomorrow's) intensity has changed all the rules—including those of competing. Relativity is all as the competitive firm seeks a discontinuous advantage over its rivals. That's even harder than it sounds. The competitive marketer needs eyes in the back of the head—and on both sides—so as not to miss dire dangers like these:

1. Rejoicing over a competitor's poor showing while some tariff or other restrictive barrier is in force. Behind the screen, the competitor may be gathering strength and preparing to pounce, as did Japanese car and other firms during "voluntary" quota restrictions.

2. "There is an idea that most businesses can be brought back to profit simply by cutting out the rotten pieces to leave a pristine core. But a competitor may very well slip into the market segments

that are vacated and gain even more in relative strength." The words are those of Ken Simmonds, a marketing professor and former accountant who has some severe words about the discontinuous impact the new competition is having on his former profession: "Competitive marketing is about maximizing the present value of the net cash flow from a business, not about maximizing an annual accounting profit."

Simmonds's strictures apply to one obvious target: cutting back on advertising and other marketing expenditure to avert a short-term fall in profits. The much less obvious target is closely linked: the seemingly laudable effort to produce a steady, continuous advance in earnings. Simmonds warns that "steady profit targets can thus end up producing fluctuations in market share, and lower profits than would have been achieved by maintaining a consistent competitive strategy and allowing fluctuations in annual accounting profit."

What does a consistent competitive strategy demand? It begins with that all-around vision, continually reviewing which individual foes to defend, get into bed with, and which to attack, the latter being "perhaps the most difficult step." Do you, for instance, go for the jugular of an aggressive close competitor, who is offering much the same goodies, or fight to stop a distant competitor from muscling into your territory, or attack whichever competitor seems least likely to retaliate?

As those three questions show, the problem is where to start. Study the leading competitor, a close competitor, and a laggard, advises Simmonds, and you have the basis for assessing how well or badly you're doing and for plotting a strategy that makes sense for the business—even if it means throwing out the window (it probably won't) such hallowed doctrines as "Never start a price war," "Withdraw from any market in which you do not hold a 15 percent share," "In the early stage of the product life cycle, set market share as the key objective and ignore profits," "Attack head-on only if you have superior resources."

The pursuit of the highest possible market share, as advocated by PIMS and the Boston Consultant Group, and as practiced by the Japanese, may not always work out best. You might prefer to wait for the other competitors to knock each other out and then pounce (actually, a favorite Japanese gambit). Simmonds notes that "in the early growth stages of both calculators and computers, Hewlett-Packard's high-price, low-volume strategy seems to have paid off far better than the Texas Instruments alternative of a price-cutting race for a high market share."

His rules for rough and tough competitors are:

1. Guard your adjacent territory. Let competitors occupy it, and that may give them an advantage.

2. If you're competing globally, think globally.

3. When deciding for or against an investment, take into account its impact on the competition.

4. Measure your market share relative to (a) the firm most likely to do you damage; and (b) the firm you can most easily outdo.

5. Insist that all plans clearly specify target competitors and what the manager is trying to achieve in each case.

6. Measure the achievement of competitive objectives against the plans.

7. Review a business's achievement against competitive targets in public—before its management peers.

In other words, Double D demands three more initials: KYC, Know Your Competitors. That's the essential preliminary to Knocking Them Down.

To summarize some of the important points I've mentioned in Step Ten:

1. All managers must answer two very simple questions: Do you know what you're doing? Are you doing it properly?

2. Everything in marketing starts with determining what the business shall make and sell, how many different lines, and how many different sizes and patterns.

3. These days you cannot afford to sustain product leadership across the board—not without a little help from your friends.

4. If you can't beat 'em (and you can't beat everybody), join 'em, by any and every means within your power.

5. Precise targeting on defined market niches yields rapid sales growth and lofty margins—but not forever.

6. The bigger and wider the niche, obviously, the larger and more stable the profits.

7. If growth is your corporate objective, it isn't enough. You must define exactly what kind of growth you have in mind.

8. Concentrate your selling efforts where they will be most rewarded, and minimize your efforts where they won't.

9. If you rely on money rather than management to get you out of trouble, you'll only end up in a worse situation.

10. Fluctuating markets give you a better chance of finding what you must have: some kind of dominating presence.

11. If you're constantly having to react to competitive threats, that's today's norm; only unusual sensitivity to change will cope with it.

12. Delegation and decentralization aren't just the fashionable answer to today's marketing problems: they're the only answer.

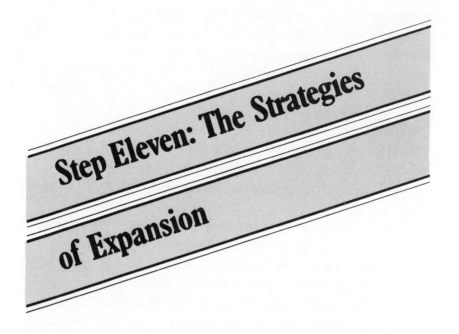

Step Eleven: The Strategies of Expansion

1. THE DREAM OF HONDA

Marketers must have vision. The formation of dreams is romantic and thrilling, and their realization is the foundation of futures. Honda's first successful bike wasn't called the Dream for nothing. But for anybody but an entrepreneur of Soichiro Honda's supremacy, what followed would have ranked as the Impossible Dream: using that little, low-powered machine as the foundation for conquering not just the market in Japan but a world market dominated at the lower end by the Italians and in larger machines by the British.

True, anybody who had studied the British companies and assessed their innocence of marketing, their hidebound technology, and their lack of ambitious dreams would have given even little Honda a sporting chance. But that wasn't true of the great Dreamer's second vision: cracking the Japanese and world car markets in which he had never competed. Even Japan's mighty MITI, the ministry that Westerners wrongly identified as the powerhouse of Japanese growth, thought the idea wildly misplaced, and any economic pundit would have argued that creating a brand-new mass-market car company in a crowded national economy and a competitive international arena was a mathematical impossibility.

In proving the doubters wrong, Honda repeated the invaluable late-century lesson that there are degrees of impossibility, that an improbable target can be achieved, provided that the dreamer is also a supreme realist. One former oilman has never forgotten the first Japanese appearance at the world motorcycle championships on the Isle of Man. When they approached his company, it expected to pay the newcomers, in the normal way of promotion, for using its oil. Not at all: the Japanese wanted to pay the oilmen for the privilege of drawing on their expertise.

The Eastern seekers after Western wisdom were there in droves, observing and noting everything that happened in a championship in which their machines without exception performed miserably. The next year, though, the Japanese returned and won, and they haven't stopped winning in world competition ever since. The real point of such successful dreaming lies in realism itself. Managers whose future dreams are unrealistic are at grave risk of pursuing dangerous policies in the present.

Often, impending failure can be smelled in words before it is verified by deeds. A senior executive once urged would-be wage strikers at the BL motor group, Britain's last survivor in the mass market, not to impede the company's progress toward becoming "the best car company there has ever been." At that time, it would have been an economic miracle for the company to have broken even on schedule. If breakeven is "best," how would making a profit rank?

In rough reality, BL stayed stuck in the red. In early 1986, the Thatcher government, BL's far-from-proud owner, was determined to dismember the best car company there had never been. Jaguar, the jewel in the tarnished crown, had already been privatized. When

General Motors expressed warm enthusiasm for buying the money-losing trucks and the Land Rover business, it seemed like manna to the Thatcherites. Ford, with their active encouragement, was also nibbling hard at the mass-car side, all that would have been left of the breakup and of the dream of creating a mini–General Motors in Britain.

Like that insubstantial dream, the breakup collapsed (political opponents being understandably reluctant to see $3 billion of previous public investment lead nowhere). That left the unhappy company clinging to its one white hope in cars: the new model being developed in collaboration with a Japanese company far superior in technology, marketing—and realism. It was, of course, Honda.

2. GETTING DOWN TO EARTH

Realism is the foundation on which enthusiasm can work managerial and marketing miracles: hard, cruel, merciless realism. Retiring behind clouds of self-deception makes a company desperately vulnerable. One victim of a corporate predator prepared its own destruction by, among other masterpieces of mismanagement, persisting with spending only 1 percent of sales on research and development. Was that because its board of directors thought 1 percent a realistic level of spending in marketplaces that were highly technological? Or did they keep reassuring themselves that theirs was the best of all possible companies marketing the best of all possible products in the best of all possible ways?

Time and again, some such thesis is swallowed hook, line, and sinker—usually making a vice out of necessity. The necessity is often that the company can't afford the required spending. Caught between incompatible necessities, the management allows its marketing strength to ooze away as underinvestment saps the ability to compete. Anybody can see that slowness to take up new end-use possibilities, adopt new processes, or use new materials must be fatal in fast-moving markets. Whatever the excuse (uncertainty about demand, poor returns on investment, restricted availability of funds, or whatever), it won't make the competitive facts go away or avert the inevitable consequences for the future of the business that lags behind.

But these slow horses put on their own blinkers. And the blinkers are made of delusions like (in the extreme cases) becoming "the best car company there has ever been" when you lack all the requirements in volume, quality, cost, and model range that determine the ability to penetrate any market. The realism that is the only safeguard begins and ends with the market: its dimensions, its competitive structure, its susceptibility to new offerings.

The degree to which that market is or isn't satisfied always calls the tune. If ever a business appears to be successfully ignoring the logic of markets, don't believe it. Nine times out of ten, if not ninety-nine times out of one hundred, logic will win. The falling apart of IBH, the construction-equipment colossus stitched together by Horst-Dieter Esch, was just such a severe blow to those who had hoped that circles could be squared. The Esch theory was that by sewing together firms that have separately failed in weak markets, you end up with a group that is strong—strong enough to compete with the likes of Caterpillar, once one of the most admired marketers on (and in) earth.

But in an era when Caterpillar was crawling through heavy losses, how could an accumulation of feebler competitors hope to survive? True, Esch got most of his companies for next to nothing from owners (ranging from General Motors downward) who were only too glad to offload these burdens. But the process gives a new twist to Lord Duveen's famous advice to art-buying millionaires: "If you're buying the priceless, you're getting it cheap." In commerce, the valueless is probably expensive—it would have taken miracles to make a silk purse out of Esch's collection of sows' ears.

In fairness, some of his companies were much better than others. But in the aftermath of the IBH receivership, the truth emerged that in several vital respects IBH had done too little to make marketing or manufacturing sense of its acquisitions. For instance, similar IBH products with different brands were still being sold through the same outlets. While Esch had shown a pan-European vision that was admirable, and financial dexterity that was prodigious to the point of utter recklessness (as the courts duly decided), his weaknesses in the basic business of making and selling would have worked against IBH in better markets.

But in a world where construction equipment demand was down by 30 to 50 percent, IBH hadn't an earthly chance. Not that Caterpillar's fate has been shared by everybody—its Japanese competitor, Komatsu, stayed profitable, taking advantage of the recession to make huge inroads into the U.S. firm's market share, which as recently as 1981 came to around three times that of Komatsu. The latter's sales were only 38 percent behind Caterpillar's by 1983. Further tribute to Japan, Inc., you might think.

But you'd be wrong. The nonexistent Inc. (in the shape of MITI) actually let Caterpillar into Japan by way of a joint venture with the ultrapowerful Mitsubishi. Confidently expected to crumble, Komatsu did nothing of the sort. Instead, it set its sights squarely on the giant, making *Maru-C* (or "encircle Caterpillar") its motto and fighting ferociously to undercut Caterpillar on price (by 10 to 15 percent) while surpassing it on service—and challenging very strongly on technology.

The Japanese were also quicker to anticipate the Middle East construction surge, whose reversal explains so much of the subsequent world market collapse. In comparison to Komatsu's concentrated, centralized, comprehensive drive, the overexpanding Esch empire had little to offer. But, then, who can compete with a Japanese company whose boss once said, "You can't get by just doing your best"?

3. THE COMEBACK AT COORS

Not knowing when you're beaten (unless you really are) is an indispensable element of the Supermarketer's armory. No less than Komatsu, the Colorado brewery of Adolph Coors seemed to have fallen off the bandwagon. Once a byword for high-quality beer and profits (the two qualities being intimately connected), Coors made a legendary botch of its efforts to expand outside its native preserves. *Business Week* included Coors emphatically among nineteen business strategies that had "failed, ran into trouble or were abandoned." The brewery's attempts to regain lost market share had been vitiated by lack of marketing smarts.

Small wonder that a marketing professor called Coors a prime example of "marketing inertia," of failure to replace old, inappropriate ways with ones that might actually work. The numbers could hardly have been more damning. In 1984, Coors sold about the same volume of beer as it had in 1977—after having expanded into another twenty-three states. Worse still, its lead brand, Coors Banquet, had steadily lost market share. Yet in 1985, Coors suddenly picked up its bed and walked. Its sales climbed by 12 percent in a year when only one other brewery (the able industry giant, Anheuser-Busch) recorded a rise. Coors' market share consequently moved up from 7.1 to 7.9 percent, as $53 million of profit came from the $1.3 billion of sales.

What explained the comeback? Jeffrey, the presiding Coors, told *Fortune:* "We've gone through years of troubled times, but it seems as if the public is accepting us more than in the past." The consumer reaction obviously played a part, especially the high acceptance of low-calorie Coors Light. But the cardinal factors were a decisive invasion of the Northeast, coupled with the highest advertising spending in the business: $10 a barrel for the company's first-ever national campaign.

Now, extension of the product line, diversification into new geographical markets, and massive advertising (plus what amounted to $650 million of public relations expenditure to heal wounded black and Hispanic feelings) don't exactly add up to a new magic formula for marketing supersuccess. The recipe could hardly be more obvious, tried, tested—or true. If failure has resulted from doing the basics badly, then success should logically follow from doing the basics well, like the two young Coors now in charge.

4. LEARNING FROM LAPSES

In any market, any company can make mistakes. Some mistakes are part of the normal learning process, and their correction will in turn form part of the company's marketing strength. But the "out of weakness came forth strength" routine is even more important when the error is abnormal and gross. The greatest error, in fact, is to perpetuate an offense, especially if the main reason is that managers gang up to defend the status quo.

The example of Waterford Glass should not be ignored. Few companies in the British Isles, let alone in Eire, could have matched the performance of a company whose figures, in an unbroken series of rises, took it from $2 million of profits in 1970 to $17.5 million in 1979. The series was broken in 1980, when, on a 13.7 percent rise in turnover, the company's pretax profits fell by 31 percent. The managing director reacted with the following comment: "It's about time. The group needed a shock to get itself back into line."

He could quite easily have rested on some statement like those of other big groups weighing in at the same time with far more dreadful figures. "All the economic factors have been very adverse," one of the bleeding mammoths said. But it's not what hits you, or even why, that counts—it's what you propose to do about it. Waterford should have been shockproof, occupying a marketing stance as near to perfect as this imperfect world can offer. World demand for its cut-crystal wares was unabated even while the economic climate worsened. Year after year the product has been on allocation, the prices have been wonderfully elastic (in the upward direction), the competition virtually nonexistent. So what went wrong?

Managers in Waterford's wonderful position have to maintain a delicate balancing act, keeping the market undersupplied but not by too much. The balance was disturbed in the first half of the bad year by a drop in productivity, blamed on absenteeism. Whether the cause is delinquent workers or deficient management, the moral is the same. Effective, reliable production is the foundation of marketing success—a truth Waterford has turned to great advantage down the years.

It's no surprise to learn that Waterford, like so many other firms, had diversified into other activities to reduce its potential overdependence on one product. All that usually happens, of course, is that, far from acting as an extra float, one or more of the diversified interests becomes a dead weight. In Waterford's case, the 1980 villain was retailing, where profits all but disappeared. None too bright diversifications are among the errors with which groups tend to live too easily, while otherwise enjoying twenty-five years of continuous and immensely profitable growth. That's why a little misfortune may indeed be an almost necessary blow—provided that the shocked management follows Waterford (1984 profits twice those of 1980 on two-thirds higher sales) in one other respect: it really does get itself back into line.

The magic of realignment is just as effective in a wholly diversified company as in one that, like Waterford, is built around a dominant and clearly identifiable core. Lack of such identity in the diversified conglomerates was a prime factor in turning Wall Street off the whole breed. The idea of growth by growing—of acquiring businesses hell-for-leather—died with what writer John Brooks memorably called "the Go-Go Years." But the conglomerates didn't.

As one close observer explained, "Conglomerates have gone through three metamorphoses since the go-go days. First there was the buildup through acquisitions; then they rationalized and became more like operating companies. The third phase was the shrinking phase—because they'd gotten too diverse and unwieldy." The speaker, Lawrence Klamon, knew whereof he spake. His company, Fuqua Industries of Atlanta, shrank between 1979 and 1982 from $2 billion in sales to $607 million; yet the stock moved in the opposite direction, surging by 400 percent between its 1982 low and the summer of 1983.

Founder John Brooks (J. B.) Fuqua was initially far from enamored of shrinkage. According to John Thackray, writing in *Management Today,* Fuqua first reacted to Klamon's plan by demanding, "How are we going to grow the company this way?" Klamon's reply was curt: "How are we going to grow without restructuring?" Although clever financing played a considerable part in the turnaround, the basic force behind Fuqua's new fortune was the switch from a mistaken, outmoded strategy (that of assuming that any growth was growth) to one of recognizing that profitable growth, even at a lower level of activity, has infinitely higher value.

The re-formed, far smaller structure allowed the marketing virtues of Fuqua's better businesses to shine through; like Snapper, which in fifteen years rose from $10 million of sales to $230 million as it grasped 40 percent of the driver-lawnmower market with its better margins, and 12 percent of the walk-behind type. The 17 percent growth rate maintained by Snapper since 1975, nearly three times that of the industry, reemphasizes the gold-plated truth that high growth can be wrung from low-growth markets—even inside conglomerates.

The conglomerates' claim has always been that their ownership can indeed generate prodigies of growth from market-oriented components. Fuqua can also point to wholesale photofinishers Colorcraft (acquired with $3 million of revenues, but doing $150 million in 1984, even with 60 percent of the United States still left to cover), and a small galaxy of sporting goods (exercise equipment, golf carts and golf bags, boat trailers, and camping gear). "We have major market shares, and because of good management we've had consistent increases in our results for twelve consecutive quarters," noted Klamon early in 1985.

But whatever prodigies this marketing clutch had achieved, it would have been submerged in the previous $2 billion of sales in trucking, petroleum distribution, movie theaters, retail farm stores, TV stations, and so forth. What Waterford and Fuqua both learned, in their very different fixes, was the same healing lesson: the larger the lapse, the greater the leverage in abandoning vice and embracing virtue.

5. THE STOLEN BASE OF SINGER

In mid-1985, the conglomerate BTR briskly completed a management buyout that relieved the vendor of Dunlop's tire interests in the United States. With that deal BTR more than covered the entire purchase price of what had once been Europe's proudest tire-maker, founded by the inventor of the pneumatic wheel. The sale also spelled the end of Dunlop as a tire-maker—the previous management had already bowed out in most parts of the world, selling the tire business to the Japanese Sumimoto in a last, forlorn attempt to retain the independence of the rump.

Less than nine months later, Singer let it be known that its sewing machine business—like Dunlop in tires, the foundation of the industry—was no longer wanted on board, after 135 years. Singer was dealing from a position of far greater strength than Dunlop's. Government purchases of its high-technology aerospace and shipboard electronics products would account for four-fifths of sales with the consumer incubus removed. *Business Week* commented that "Singer has steadily been moving toward higher growth businesses protected from global competition."

That sounds pretty good until you ask two questions. What kind of business has to be sheltered from global competition? And how did Singer get into a noncompetitive position in the first place? The truth is that while Singer was beginning its quest for reduced dependence on sewing machines in the 1960s, an effort that cost it $411

311

million in writeoffs, mostly on an abortive foray into business machines, the company failed to develop new products, failed to maintain the quality of its production facilities, failed to keep its retail stores up-to-date—and blew the sewing machine business, to the eternal gratitude of the Japanese and other competitors. The copout leads to the dropout.

6. EXPLOITING MARKET LEADERSHIP

To get some idea of the enormity of Singer proposing to withdraw from sewing machines and Dunlop quitting tires, merely think the impossible thought of IBM copping or dropping out of computers, Ford deserting cars, or Sony, audio recorders. To be fair, tires are among those markets that, through no fault of any individual firm, have soured. Not that the individuals were faultless, though: to be overstaffed, overborrowed, and undercompetitive in a strong market is a sorry burden; in a weak market, it's a catastrophe.

Dunlop's besetting domestic weakness, visible as long ago as 1969, was its overdependence on original equipment sales to UK car firms, not a particularly good idea even at the time. In the replacement market, selling to car owners direct, Dunlop's lack of all-round marketing wizardry showed up in a notably lower share. Far more serious, however, the group's very early European and world expansion didn't feed back into greater domestic strength. On the contrary, the hand of Fort Dunlop, Birmingham, lay heavy on the Continental interests. Dunlop first lagged fatefully behind the radial revolution launched by European rivals, and then, after belated conversion, opted wrongly for textile cord instead of steel.

All that, however, is in the gory past (to the tune of $180 million of group losses in four years). What lessons does hindsight teach? Or, rather, what would due foresight have predicated? First, the basic objective of a market leader must be prowess in productivity, with the lowest costs in the least factories. That championship goes hand in hand, obviously enough, with (second) cornering the most wondrous production technology money can buy. That in turn links intimately with (third) the absolute and burning need for the brightest and best product technology. Fourth, all of the above must be cemented by unbeatably strong branding, of the corporation and its product lines; Michelin has been very effective in this department, as in its radial technology. Fifth, you need the rare big business courage, when all around are generously expanding capacity, to restrict yours parsimoniously to what can realistically be utilized at a truly ripe return.

Finally, the company must be marketing-led to the last detail. Even in sporting goods, for one small example, ads for Dunlop's running shoe seemed to appear far more than the shoes themselves; Adidas, Nike, New Balance, and other brands monopolized shelf space. Generally, in Dunlop's non-tire rump businesses (a billion dollars of 1982 sales), there was urgent need for transformation, judged by their measly $30 million of operating profits. Those big base businesses, alas, easily breed complacency, and that's a hard habit to break, save in desperate adversity—and by then, it may be too late to save the ravaged vitals. As, indeed, Dunlop found—forced to surrender to that takeover bid from BTR, at one time a rival with only a tiny proportion of Dunlop's sales.

Clearly there is no safety anywhere—not even with products whose reputations have been on top of the world for generations. Throw in quality and luxury, too, and there may still be no protection. Take Wedgwood, Rolls-Royce Motors, and the previously mentioned Waterford Glass. All three, very obviously, depend on the American market for their health and strength. When rich U.S. consumers are off their feed, no marketing power on earth can protect a luxury china, glass, or car business from feeling undernourished.

But what happened? In 1983, to recover U.S. sales, Rolls-Royce had to cut its prices—an unheard-of act of self-inflicted *lèse-majesté*. Waterford's long years of uninterrupted profit growth, as noted, had come to an abrupt end in 1980. Wedgwood also ran out of growth with a bang; it produced profit figures that would have seemed wan in 1973–74, when total sales were a mere quarter of their level of ten years on. Only with the aid of a temporarily mighty dollar did profits recover (and then with some splendor).

The breakdown of Wedgwood's sales had changed markedly over the period. The people who run top-of-the-market companies are not blind to the obvious: overexposure to America is only the most glaring aspect of a market situation in which, by definition, saturation can never be far away. After all, nobody needs these costly goodies; purchase is indefinitely postponable; and it takes only a relatively small number of postponements for growth to cease entirely. The prudent company thus diversifies, going down-market in its main business, or striking out geographically, or adding entirely new markets—as Waterford did with things like greetings cards and fine china, but with those far from brilliant results.

As for Rolls-Royce, it sought shelter in the hugely diversified embrace of Vickers, thus utterly and evidently changing the nature and scope of top management's problems, but making them no easier. The same is true of the other luxuriators. Running a business concentrated on one basic, strong, and clearly identifiable theme is a different game entirely from trying to make financial sense out of a clutch of companies or countries.

The strategy adopted by Moët-Hennessy proved to be much more promising: stringing together the leading champagne house by far with a top name in brandy and with other upper-crust marques like Dior perfumes. Recession in luxury markets will still hit the whole company, but probably unevenly—and at least the management problems will be in the same language. Such is fate that it is almost certain that interests bought to counterbalance the existing base business will reserve their nastiest surprises for the moment when they are least welcome: when the long-loved luxury is also down on its luck. The real safety lies only in learning the lessons of failure and repeating those of success. A management with its eyes open will find plenty of both in its own experiences.

7. THE WAR WITH *THE WSJ*

In today's naked markets, investing is success. If a company can't afford to finance investment in new products, processes, and markets, it is already failing—and it will fail still more in the future (if it has one). If there's a single lesson that Western business needs to learn from the Japanese, this is it. But even those Westerners who have seized hold of the lesson have sometimes grasped it only dimly.

Consider this observation: "We have a five-year perspective to break even. It's what I'd call a Japanese approach." Thus spoke the Frankfurt marketing director of the *Financial Times,* adding a new phrase to the marketer's lexicon of useful euphemisms. All over the West, companies in similar positions, losing money on projects that were either misconceived or mistimed, have consoled themselves with the thought that they were really dynamic thrusters *à la Japonaise,* breaking into new markets on a long-term strategy.

Even the Japanese reality doesn't bear out this engaging myth. The most celebrated breakthrough is probably Toyota's penetration of the U.S. market. It took seventeen years for Toyota to topple VW off its peak as leading importer. The first Crowns blew up on the California freeways—only the grisly start of a long saga of blood, sweat, and tears. What the Japanese had seen as a potential Pearl Harbor became the equivalent of Mao's Long March. Nobody goes voluntarily into that kind of torture. Given its time over again, Toyota would have done very differently—and so, I doubt not, would the *Financial Times.*

How much the *FT* has truly suffered in following its "five-year perspective" is known only to the keepers of its books. But its managing director once observed that it cost the paper some $3 million a year "to print in Frankfurt rather than distribute from here." Assuming that all its 33,000 overseas sales came from West Germany, that adds up to over $3.00 a week per extra subscriber to the paper (sales abroad had doubled since printing in Frankfurt had begun). And who is to say how many of these extra sales could have been obtained from London printing? Or how much of the extra $24 million of (presumably) European advertising revenue the *FT* really, in its spokesman's words, "wouldn't have gained if we hadn't been there"?

Frankfurt was (in truth) a greenfields project, a new venture in its own right, in which the management was not, like its lately discovered Japanese models, breaking new export ground for established products. The *FT* has striven to create a new market for English-language, trans-European business papers. In those pioneering circumstances, it's lucky, to quote the Frankfurt man again, that the pioneers' "view has not been to make money very quickly." They didn't.

It's no secret that the *FT* was inspired less by the example of Japan than by the fear that *The Wall Street Journal* might possibly come to Europe. Possibility became actuality—and it certainly took Japanese, if not Dutch, courage for the *Journal* to launch in Europe in the middle of a world recession, and at a time when the wind bore grisly rumors of collapses among the very banks on which it had to depend for much of its advertising. But that was only one of the myriad acts of commercial bravery that first made it clear that, while the smoke of deep recession still obscured the battlefield, the Western economy was on the march. The important thing for would-be Supermarketers is to march in the right direction.

8. TEN TRAPS FOR STRATEGISTS

Identifying the main competitor, the enemy, and taking the fight to him is a basic approach for those who want to win in naked markets. Military language is appropriate; analogies between military and marketing campaigns abound. As companies battle to preserve and enlarge market share, they wittingly or unwittingly face many of the same strategic and tactical problems confronted by generals as they seek to gain territory and positions of advantage against a determined foe. As G. James Barrie wisely said in *The Journal of General Management* "The study of military strategy and tactics cannot guarantee success, but it can help avoid obvious mistakes."

The *Financial Times*, for example, may have been guilty of "choosing the wrong enemy at the wrong time in the wrong place." (Its real foes were the printing unions that ferociously blocked modern technology.) That's the seventh of Barrie's "ten traps to be avoided":

1. Preparing to fight the last war rather than the next.
2. Concentrating on fighting for the objective rather than on fighting the enemy.
3. Underestimating the magnitude of the task and overestimating your capabilities.
4. Relying on size and resources rather than speed and mobility to win battles.
5. Being unprepared for combat.
6. Following traditional, rather than new and creative, strategies.
7. Choosing the wrong enemy at the wrong time in the wrong place.
8. Staying in static positions that invariably lead to neglect of combat efficiency.
9. Being discontinuous in the conduct of combat.
10. Being unable to concede an engagement.

Legions of disasters demonstrate the perils of each trap. But one case covers the whole corpus of failure: the reaction of Western car manufacturers to the Japanese threat. Some reacted faster and more effectively than others, but the mass-market companies all, to greater or lesser degree, fell into all ten traps.

In general, they concentrated on the competition in their home markets, especially from domestic rivals, although the rise of the Japanese industry and the disappearance of tariff and nontariff barri-

317

ers to car exports had transferred the action to the global theater (Trap 1). Looking only at their immediate market objectives, and struggling for the odd percentage points of market share in this or that calendar period, they didn't anticipate or seek to preempt the Japanese plan for a long-term buildup of overseas market share (Trap 2).

They had a thoroughly exaggerated idea of their own strengths and played down their own weaknesses (blaming higher labor costs, about which they could do little, and ignoring the production deficiencies that greatly magnified the wage cost disadvantage), while continuing to believe that the competitive task would be quite easy —because of an assumed product superiority that was, of course, rapidly diminishing (Trap 3).

None of them, especially the Detroit giants, did much to speed up their responses to a changing marketplace; they trusted too fondly in their own vast scale and deep purses. Thus the development of smaller American cars was halting and haphazard, while in Europe companies such as Fiat and Renault allowed their model ranges to become rambling and obsolescent (Trap 4). Levels of investment in production facilities, marketing efficiency, and management practice were woefully inadequate for the wars ahead (Trap 5), which meant that a hugely expensive catchup program became essential at exactly the point when, because of earlier failures, the industry was short of the profits required to finance its efforts to overtake a moving enemy.

In clinging to outworn styles, both of product design and manufacture, the Western makers failed to capitalize on their initial product lead, and lost the advantage in innovation. Worse still, several makers stuck to expensive errors that could no longer be afforded (like low commonality of parts among different models in the range, or the Detroit practice of separating design from marketing) (Trap 6). In Britain, the manufacturers—Americans as well as natives— chose to continue shunning TV advertising, arguing that it was an unsuitable medium. This allowed the Japanese (an enemy the industry chose to ignore—Trap 7) to use heavy advertising in what is actually and obviously the most powerful medium available. Neither did the British realize, any more than did the Continentals and the Americans, that nondomestic markets had become the vital arena—indeed, General Motors did not set up a European headquarters until 1986, two whole decades after Ford.

As for static positions (Trap 8), the fixation on traditional strategies led to atrophy of the competitive instincts: every major manufacturer failed to follow up on initiatives that could have developed into major strategic advantages. The Americans introduced compact cars only to inflate them in size and price, thus deflating their market appeal; the British pioneered transverse engines only to neglect the need to develop the theme by continual aggression with line extensions and model upgradings; the Germans didn't capitalize on a dominating position in the lower-priced sector; the Italians flopped in executive cars; the French threw away a whole range of unique market positions.

That chronicle of error represents Trap 9. By the same token, many of the mass competitors fell into Trap 10: not quitting when the market had turned irrevocably against them. Already the American endeavor, exemplified by GM's cutdown Saturn project to build a small car profitably in the United States, is being widely seen as yet another, and hideously expensive, instance of not knowing when to disengage, so as to conserve resources for the battles you really can win. All the same, the car giants, American and European, have shown many signs of learning their lessons and finding the right path. To find that right direction, ask (or rather answer) the following questions:

1. Are you sure you're fighting the next war, as opposed to the last?

2. Are you concentrating on fighting the main competition, as opposed to fighting for the objective?

3. Have you correctly estimated the size of the task and the extent of your own capabilities?

4. Are you relying on mobility and speed for victory, instead of just trusting to size and resources?

319

5. Are you fully prepared for competition?

6. Are you following new and creative strategies, rather than relying on those that have worked in the past?

7. Are you sure you've picked the right enemy at the right time in the right place?

8. Have you avoided the trap of staying in a static position?

9. Are you continuously carrying the fight to the enemy?

10. Are you capable of conceding a defeat in order to win a victory elsewhere?

If the answers are all in the affirmative, the business is capable of beating anybody, even the Japanese. In competition with many Western companies, only a small number of positive answers will be enough to deliver a large advantage and, given continuing positive action, a lasting one.

9. THE PAYOFF FROM PLOWBACK

The Big Squeeze of the early 1980s proved yet again that adversity is an excellent teacher. In the food industry, for instance, with one arm of the Iron Maiden of recession throttling revenues and the other pressing on costs, the nature of the struggle was clear. Only higher productivity could open the door to higher margins; manufacturers duly became intent on cutting labor costs. One survey showed that 85 percent of food manufacturers intended to raise or maintain their spending on plant and machinery, mostly to boost productivity, for which, alas, read unemployment—almost two-thirds expected their investment spending to cut the numbers employed. Sad, but in food, as in other industries, investment in de-staffing has become an essential ingredient of the productivity mix—and thus of the marketing one.

But investment means goodies as well. In the same survey, a

nourishing 82 percent of the food companies planned to invest more than replacement needs, and over half included new product work in their plans. The opportunity to cash in on product differentiation has scaled new peaks in recent years, as consumers switch to nutritious, unfattening, starch-free, and exotic foods. Not only do these lissom qualities offer the hope of higher prices, they are one way to break the hammerlock that, given half a chance, the retailers apply.

Supermarkets can exert their own version of the Big Squeeze even on a supplier who has 65 percent of the market—vastly more than the national share of even the biggest retailer. In fact, a manufacturer's 65 percent may only be a tiny fraction of a supermarket's total trade, so advantage over the retailer can be gained much less easily by muscle (of which the latter has plenty) than by innovative, irresistible consumer appeal, which is aimed at raising margins and return on investment. In marketing, money is the root of all virtue. Without putting enough of it into innovative investment, a manufacturer will be in the Big Squeeze forever. In fact, 2.7 percent of the above sample thought they would be, anyway. They were wrong. The future is bright with naked, unsqueezed opportunity—but only for those who are prepared to create, grasp, and finance the opportune investment.

10. INVESTING IN MARKET SUCCESS

The need for investment is not, of course, confined to fast-moving consumer goods, as every high-tech marketer knows. In the last few years every week has seen report after report of brave new ventures in such things as pay TV, computer graphics, identification systems, and scientific graphics computing. The waters of the higher technology are spreading to engulf all of traditional engineering while offering those segmented opportunities for which the bravest and best marketers have been searching everywhere.

321

But new technology doesn't mean new principles—or even new industries. The guiding principle is challenge: investment in technology, like investment in marketing, is the powerhouse from which to challenge the established position of others, or to challenge the market itself by creating new dimensions. On this criterion in what later won that ugly name of fast-moving consumer goods, there was only one real contender for the title of "best manager in Britain" in the 1960s: H. G. Lazell, architect of the Beecham Group, who died in 1982 at the age of seventy-nine. He was the exponent of a style of management that, if it had only attracted more imitators, would have rewritten much of Britain's deeply disappointing performance after 1968 (the year Lazell retired).

Here are some of the great man's major themes. First, if you want to beat 'em, fight 'em. Seeing correctly that American companies would try to set the pace in postwar Europe, Lazell decided that Beecham could never compete at home unless it could challenge and succeed in the United States, as it did with Brylcreem and Macleans. Second, Macleans had become the cornerstone of Beecham's growth after Lazell, who had become an accountant the hard way, supported Sir Alexander Maclean, with pen and paper, by showing that he was winning even more gigantic profits by selling his own brand than by supplying druggists with private-label toothpaste. Lazell thus established two principles: in modern marketing, the pen is mightier than the hunch; and branding is the true name of the game.

Third, Lazell hated his challenges to fail, but never let failure deter him. The disaster of Silvikrin shampoo in the United States (the name killed it dead among a nation of macho males who dreaded gray hair) was taken in broken stride, and a later generation of his managers did well in the United States with Aquafresh toothpaste. Fourth, such triumphs were founded on the fact that Lazell, a professional manager himself, staffed his group with trained people who followed the same canon—whether in the toiletries, food, or pharmaceuticals businesses—that he had developed so powerfully.

Fifth, in pharmaceuticals, Lazell never allowed his belief that investment in research was the key to success to be shaken by decades of no reward. He was finally vindicated by the synthetic penicillins that underpinned much of Beecham's post-Lazell growth. But that was only after mastering a sixth principle: concentration is the key to success in R & D, as in most of management. The lesson applies to advertising, too. Lazell used to say that he didn't mind what the advertisements said about Macleans, so long as they said that it made teeth whiter. More foolish marketers have forgotten that advertising is in part (in major part) about repetition, just as they have forgotten (or never knew) that investment is the key to marketing success.

11. THE KICKER IN KIWIFRUIT

Once upon time, there was a plant known to botanists as *Actinidia chinensis* and to a few happy eaters (a very few) as the Chinese gooseberry. As such, the fruit had no commercial success or prospects worth munching over—which only goes to show that a rose (or a gooseberry) by any other name can smell much, much sweeter. Renamed the kiwifruit by some inspired hand, *Actinidia* swept the world, to the extent of 62,000 tons of the stuff in 1984.

The first guideline for aspiring marketers is that if you think your product is good but the market doesn't, look at the packaging (verbal and visual) to ensure that the presentation, rather than the content, isn't at fault. Ever since the 1950s, when New Zealand's embryonic kiwi industry sent its first tentative shipments to London and Australia, the money has multiplied, thanks overwhelmingly to German and Japanese consumers.

Every silver lining has a cloud, though, and in high growth markets, from computers to kiwifruit, it's generally the same one. The large profits and lush growth attract new entrants while encouraging the established forces to increase their strength. The result is to subject the laws of supply and demand to continuous test, and the common mistake is to forget that these laws change the rules of the game.

Since, according to John Cherrington, who writes about such matters for the *Financial Times,* it takes six to eight years for *Actinidia* to do its stuff, refusing to oblige without perfect leaf cover and lavish spraying, the first symptoms of the kiwi disease affected not the fruit but the land. The more costly the acres, obviously, the lower the financial yield, unless the price of the produce can rise. But catch-22 applies. The planting mania that causes the land boom guarantees that produce prices won't justify those being paid for the land. Far from rising, the growers' kiwi price flopped by 38 percent between 1980 and 1985.

The local supply potential swelled fivefold, to 367,000 tons by 1992, so you can see that the kiwi disease had reached a virulent stage. Like all plagues, it was spreading worldwide. Other countries have been fatally tempted into planting still more acres by the *Actinidia* boom, which raises the fascinating prospect of actions like those brought against imitators in other lands on behalf of French champagne or Spanish sherry. Somehow, kiwifruit from Hungary doesn't sound right, but Magyar fruit sounds even worse.

While the kiwi farmers pursue their destiny, other marketers should ponder the strategic conclusions. One, obviously, is that first is best. But the second could be, first in, first out. The shrewdest and richest player, in this game, makes the fattest operating profits and, when the product life cycle passes its peak, takes the optimum capital gain before the suckers catch on. Those who think the joy ride is eternal, though, may become suckers themselves.

12. TIDES ALWAYS TURN

If the quadrupling of oil prices was the most significant single economic event of the 1970s, their undermining is just as significant for the 1980s. The oil shocks, after all, were estimated to have, in effect, removed one machine in twenty from Western production, a dramatic representation of the awful impact on output and employment. In theory, but only, alas, in theory, one machine in twenty would now come thundering back into use thanks to the jellylike wobbling away of OPEC as a price-fixing cartel. That is certainly not a price shock, but rather the further development of powerful tremors that the laws of economics made inevitable.

The inevitability, true, was obvious to almost no one except Milton Friedman. Nearly everybody else believed that energy shortages and price rises would persist even further than the eye could see. The blindness of the collective eye, though, isn't just a failure of economists and forecasters—although few facts in life and markets are more established than the twin truths that undid OPEC.

Twin 1 lays down that the greater the price rise, the larger the impact on consumption. Its twin, or corollary, is that what goes up must come down: OPEC-style price rises act as the catalyst by discouraging the consumption and encouraging the supply of golden eggs, which (like microcircuits in 1985) can addle almost overnight. Why, though, are such obvious, axiomatic truths ignored? The psychology of markets is to blame. Whichever direction markets are taking, people are reluctant to believe that the tide will ever turn. Exactly the same mentality grips companies at the sight of a booming sales graph: they look at the internal whoopee without checking to see what's happening, and likely to happen, in the great world outside.

The tricky words are *likely to happen*. Notoriously, every single team of economists that forecast oil consumption in the wake of the price surge, from the CIA down, got it wildly wrong. They all, for a start, still foresaw rises in demand. The idea of an actual and marked fall in oil usage never entered their minds for the simple reason that it had never happened before. In much the same way, the computer industry was totally unprepared for its first recession (and, far less excusable, for its second).

325

The moral for marketers is not easy to follow, but plainly they should always ask themselves what event is the least likely to happen. They should then ask how unlikely it really is. In fact, nobody should have been surprised by either the sudden death of the microcomputer boom or the virtually simultaneous eclipse of several electronic giants, as saturated, oversupplied micromarkets produced secondary (though equally powerful) effects for the component suppliers. But the profit problems of the latter had little in common with those of Apple or the imperial IBM—except for one thing.

All these companies compete in crowded civilian markets that are full of giant companies that are used to monopoly, oligopoly, duopoly—in other words, having it all their own way. All, too, have scented the seductive aroma of convergence, of the technological trends that are melding computers with phones, copiers, typewriters, even televisions. Each giant has reasoned separately that unless it joins the great game, it will lose not only opportunities but very possibly existing sales. Thus even the seemingly invincible IBM bulldozes ineffectively into arenas like telecommunications. *Bulldoze* is the word; remember these heavyweights come from worlds where they are used to winning—and heavily.

This is the perfect setup for imperfect decisions. Still worse, the ambitious plans of most players demand huge spending. Massive R & D is only a beginning, but one for which large profits—the very joys that must evaporate in such competitive circumstances—are indispensable. Of course, some of the many and varied market conditions that explain such evaporation are bound to improve as the cycles turn upward. In 1985 the computer business was surely set to burgeon again as the industry got its products and priorities right, and as customers recovered their breath. But that would still leave too many giants chasing too few sales. The sane policy would be for more players to retire promptly—as Xerox has in computers—from games they cannot possibly win. But, as happened in synthetic fibers around the world in the 1960s, pride and stupidity will doubtless result in fatal delays.

326

One of the toughest questions in marketing, though, is what you do with a worst-case answer in a market currently enjoying a best-case boom. Plainly, only a mad manager would base his investment on something he doesn't expect. The exercise becomes more useful when considering a project with the odds stacked against it, like a personal computer that can't succeed unless the whole market goes on booming. If that's the deal, learn the lesson of Sheikh Yamani: forget it.

To summarize some of the important points I've mentioned in Step Eleven:

1. If you want to achieve the impossible, obtain a thorough grasp of the possibilities first.

2. If ever a business appears to be successfully ignoring the logic of markets, you're better off not to believe in it.

3. Most failures result from doing the basics badly; therefore, doing the opposite is the straightest path to success.

4. Every marketer makes mistakes; Supermarketers learn from their errors, all the time.

5. Don't seek shelter from competition; rather, ask why you need the shelter.

6. Even in luxury markets, efficient production, top product technology, strong branding, controlled output, and being led by the market are the necessities for success.

7. Losing money on misconceived and mistimed projects isn't courageous—it's crazy.

8. To succeed in competition, first make sure that you're fighting the right enemy at the right time in the right place.

9. Create, grasp, and finance the opportune investment in new production methods and new products if you want to survive through lean years and fat alike.

10. Compete vigorously, build your brands, bounce back from failures, develop expertise, concentrate efforts, and finance research —that's the way to get organic growth.

327

11. In a new market the richest profits usually go to the first in —and often to the first out.

12. If your marketing project can succeed only if the whole market continues to boom, forget it.

Step Twelve: Opportunities in Changing Times

1. THE INERTIA OF TEXAS INSTRUMENTS

Failure may have few friends, but it has plenty of remedies—so many and so well known that nobody attempting a turnaround from disaster lacks examples and precepts. But how do you tackle what is usually a far more difficult problem? How do you cope with success?

The problem is twofold. Not only does a smash marketing hit, like a personal triumph, often go to the head, but the winning company, bumptious or not, will sooner or later face the real and agonizing questions of how to build on and sustain its success. Thomas V. Bonoma, writing in the *Harvard Business Review,* came up with a telling phrase to describe one aspect of this potential crisis: "marketing inertia"—the title of an article that takes a swipe at some U.S. names famous for getting stuck with ideas of their own marketing brilliance, even though the ideas were founded on enormous market success.

Thus Texas Instruments passionately believes that "low prices lead to market share dominance." Sounds OK. But TI followed this philosophy when marketing its cheaper calculators at discount prices through department stores and other mass outlets. It thus neatly poleaxed its standing with the office equipment specialists, who had been selling Texas Instruments' more expensive, higher-margin machines. In 1981, after similar pursuit of the cheap and dominant, TI had to withdraw in disarray from the watch market. A couple of years later, exactly the same fate overtook its home computers. Low-priced, mass-volume consumption goods just aren't its bag.

Then there is Coors, a beer that became famous for the quality ("product superiority") to which the family management attributed its success. Bonoma points out that "quality is determined more by customers' preferences than by family formulas"—and, in the case of Coors, customers preferred a beer that they could actually buy. Poor distribution made the quality quite academic. At Coors, as at TI, marketing actions were attuned not to the market, but to preconceived notions of how it would or should behave. As described in Step Three, section 11, two younger Coors family managers had to break with the past to set the brewery on a new course of profitable growth.

At that, Coors was lucky to have a pair of insiders who could recognize and conquer the corporate inertia; and the two were lucky, in a sense, that the facts of market share and profitability made an overwhelming case for change. If a company is held to be wholly successful by most of its own management as well as everybody on the outside, and by the family shareholders, the victory of inertia might seem inevitable. Surely nobody will see the need to jolt the business into reforming its inert ways? The favored jolting technique in a family-dominated firm is to appoint a chief executive who is not a family member. And, in a rare reaction to incipient inertia, that is exactly what happened at one of the very few retail businesses that's as famous outside its country as inside: the mighty and once-marvelous Marks & Spencer.

2. GOOD IS NEVER GOOD ENOUGH

"Anatomy of Britain's most efficiently managed company": so ran the subtitle of a book by a Hong Kong manager named Dr. K. K. Tse. Ask any informed Brit which company that is, and the answer, nine times out of ten, would be Marks & Spencer. Whether the judgment is correct, of course, is a matter of opinion, and a prickly one at that. *Efficient* is a difficult word to define; "efficiently managed" almost suggests that there's some discrete activity, like abstract painting, that exists in its own wondrous right.

Efficient management without efficient results sounds contradictory. But the book musters an array of reasonably objective financial counts, on all of which M & S leads, and often dwarfs, its retail competitors. The genius of its business, though, is that it actually has little head-on competition. The M & S principles have profoundly influenced retail businesses all over the world: build dominant shares of consumer markets on limited ranges of products (in its case, clothing and food), all carrying the chain's own brand, all produced to the chain's specification and under its tight control, and majoring on high VFM—the value for money being achieved by combining superior quality with moderate prices.

Its closest rival on financial measures is the British supermarket chain J. Sainsbury, but the M & S food-and-drink business overlaps only part of Sainsbury's spread—and the higher margin portion, at that. The real similarity between the two is their brilliant (and certainly efficient) use of the house brand. Against Marks's one-third of all British bras, Sainsbury boasts one-seventh of Britain's wine sales —maybe the more remarkable statistic of the two, given that competitive bottles are distributed more widely than uplift.

Speaking of uplift, Sainsbury does outscore M & S heavily on one financial count that Dr. Tse doesn't use: growth. From 1973 to 1983, the St. Michael's brigade raised sales by 338 percent and profits by 209 percent; the Sainsbury figures were 518 percent and 637 percent. Moreover, the 1981 supremacy of M & S on other scores is no longer complete—Sainsbury easily outdid the champ in 1985 for return on shareholders' equity (18.9 percent versus 13.9 percent, pretax).

You could (and should) argue that growth isn't relevant to the "most efficiently managed" title, as Sainsbury was expanding from a regional to a national base, which M & S had long occupied; and this very process of rapid expansion has helped to generate the supermarket chain's rise in profitability. All the same, that doesn't dodge the fact that, while Marks's margins have remained commendably stable (never higher than 12 percent or lower than 10.2 percent since 1977), the productivity of its capital has slumped. A fall from 36.1 percent (1974–75), or 31.4 percent (1978–79), to the recent 22.2 percent isn't what is generally meant by efficient management.

Thus, when the chief executive torch at Marks & Spencer passed to a nonfamily manager, a case for fundamental change could certainly have been argued. But M & S's new leader, Lord Rayner, was no newly made broom. After his long years in the country's most admired retail chain, he was as thoroughly indoctrinated in the group's culture as any of the ruling Sieff family. That corporate culture, in turn, is among the most powerful ever created, as you'd expect with so many forceful men concentrating on so narrow a front for so long.

But was the front, for all the product diversification of recent years, including the crucial postwar food expansion, still too narrow? A business whose shops are obviously good, by subjective and objective standards, is desperately hard to criticize. But if you adjust the group's rise in earnings per share for inflation (as *Management Today* does annually), the result turns out to be negative over the decade to 1982: a 2.4 percent annual *decline*.

True, that was better than 127 other companies in Britain's top 200, and by 1985 the decade's figure was up to a positive 8 percent, against 21 percent for Sainsbury. These figures don't dispel the nagging feeling that so intensively managed and superbly integrated an operation should have generated greater rewards. The reasons why it hasn't are obvious. Britain's sluggish economy has inevitably cramped the style of a group that was confined largely to those stagnant shores, that has near-saturation shares of mature markets, and within which that all-powerful culture was dead set on organic growth, not acquisition. When these characteristics were described to an American financier wanting to know if Marks might like to take a billion-dollar retail bauble off his hands, he listened in silence, then said: "I seem to have picked on exactly the wrong company." He sure had.

Maybe the missing phase in the great chain's development would have made it the *right* company. After all, Sears Roebuck in the United States would be a mere smidgen of its $39 billion size (seven times that of M & S) had it stuck to mail order. The evidence is that Marks has long been pressing against the natural and national barriers to the expansion of its magnificent patented method: the vertically integrated, limited catalogue variety store, stocking own-brand merchandise and steadily expanding the lines and sidelines. The way out is either to export the method (which Marks began, only to find the overseas sledding slow and sometimes painful), or to follow Sears in adding other consumer-based operations.

In the great Marks and Sieff eras, the company did not bring its usual scrupulous intensity to exploiting the base asset: its unique experience of the consumer. This could be because M & S has, in a sense, created its own consumers. The genius of its founders was to change people's buying habits and thus turn a store into a national brand. But serving mature markets in mature ways with a mature corporate culture is unlikely to produce rich growth.

There couldn't be a more conspicuous example of the fact that managing efficiently carries a hidden price: that of creating a hard act for yourself to follow. Markets (like bras, in a manner of speaking) get saturated. New areas are less rewarding, at least initially, than are old. And the harder the cost lemon is squeezed, the less juice is left. Whoever said that nothing succeeds like success didn't know what he was talking about. Success is only the beginning; building on it is the tough, and vital, part.

3. WHATEVER HAPPENED TO BABY HOOVER?

In some cases neglect of a business is so extreme, so puzzling, and the results so drastic as to raise that doom-laden question, Whatever happened to . . . ? For example, whatever happened to Baby Hoover? This British company, child of an American parent, grew so strong that it became the brightest jewel in the parental crown. In 1960 few companies seemed better poised for rich and lasting success: multinational, Europe-oriented, leader in unsaturated consumer markets with weak domestic opposition, proud possessor of a great household name, famous for productive efficiency, blessed with access to American know-how and market developments through its U.S. ownership. How could it fail?

Yet success didn't come. The closing of Perivale, once the focal point of the whole British appliance industry, was only symbolic of a long and sad two-stage decline. From 1971 to 1981, on cumulative sales figures of $2.5 billion, Hoover earned a total net profit of $80 million—a pitiful 3.5 percent. That followed a desperately dreary decade in the 1960s (1969 sales were only $4.5 million up on those of 1959). In the early 1970s Hoover did smartly pull up its socks and its sales, but the rot set in again. In 1980 turnover was only 27 percent up on 1975, while the accompanying five-year plunge in profits had reached the vanishing point. By contrast Black and Decker had tripled its British profits and sales between 1973 and 1979.

Even if you argue that Black and Decker's markets for electrically powered appliances were better ones, who deserves the credit for that? It was an Englishman, Robert Appleby, who built this UK subsidiary of an American parent into an intensively managed model of how to conduct and develop a fast mover in consumer durables. Another Englishman, Sir Charles Colston, had created Hoover's enormously strong position in Britain and Europe in an earlier era. But whereas Appleby was rewarded with honors and the number-two spot at the parent organization, Colston was awarded the boot —kicked out by Herbert Hoover, Jr., himself.

That wouldn't have mattered if, after an affronted U.S. management putsched Herbie himself in 1967, the UK operation had sustained development either on B & D lines (as a crack, independent subsidiary) or on those of British Ford (as part of a U.S.-controlled, trans-European, locally and strongly coordinated organization). Perhaps the critical moment was the 1965 success in breaking the back of a challenger who sold awful cut-price washing machines door-to-door, but who proved, before his crash, that he was more in touch with Hoover's market than was Hoover itself. As far stronger challengers arrived from places like Italy, it's small wonder that the Princes of Perivale found themselves being bashed in turn by the Borgias of the appliance industry. Machiavelli could have told them what to do. If you hold mastery in the marketplace, you never, never let go.

That truth was one that Hoover's parent back in the States had cause to rue, as it succumbed in 1985 to takeover by Chicago Pacific. By that time, Western Europe was producing only $13 million of Hoover's total operating profit, on $270 million of sales. The United States, with only $30 million more in revenues, generated $30 million more profit. The price tag on the Hoover deal wasn't low, at $530 million, but how much more would the company have fetched if the European business had emulated the efficiency and inexorable rise of Sweden's Electrolux? Had it done so, would Hoover have lost its independence at all?

The *Financial Times* noted at takeover time that Hoover's European picture was brightening up: "Within the past three years, virtually every product manufactured by Hoover has been changed or radically redesigned, to take account of improving technology and make more profitable use of Hoover's market shares. . . . Its new Turbo vacuum cleaner, for example, has a completely redesigned engine as well as other novel features such as an incorporated air freshener."

Better late than never, maybe. But Hoover's fault was the same

335

as that which turned the future of Westland, the helicopter company, over to United Technologies and its Sikorsky managers, after a political fracas that cost two British cabinet ministers their jobs and brought Prime Minister Margaret Thatcher into some peril. Westland, like Hoover, had been mismarketed for two or three decades. And in the main theater of that failure there's a vital lesson. In the 1960s and 1970s, it paid to innovate; in the 1980s, it kills not to.

Even if Westland had been better at production (it was poor, and not much better with its financial controls, either), it would have been brought low by its failure over all that time to come up with profitably competitive models of its own design. Licenses from Sikorsky were Westland's mainstay—and also its main weakness. Effectively the company was shut out of the world's best markets, led by the United States. Every company needs its USP: the unique selling proposition that's yours and yours alone, which nobody else can better, and which you can sell in all markets.

That's the reality that lies behind innovation. Not only must a business possess that unique product or service (which is the starting point for most businesses), but the edge has to be constantly sharpened. If you don't achieve that sharpness, you'll be Hoovered: after establishing an apparently invulnerable market position, the company failed to keep pace with the significant changes and improvements in its markets. If you don't even develop your own successful line, you'll be Westlanded.

4. QUESTIONS OF INNOVATION

How can a company avoid the fate of either a Hoover or a Westland? There is no single answer, but a dozen highly suggestive ones were given by four hundred top businesses and six hundred of their executives. This is how their answers ranked, in order of importance, the actions that a company can take in the essential effort to obtain innovative success:

1. Increase or improve market research efforts or capacity.
2. Get top management commitment and support or leadership.
3. Increase rewards or establish a reward system for innovative groups and individuals.
4. Encourage risk taking and avoid penalizing mistakes.
5. Improve or establish a positive, more entrepreneurial climate for innovation.
6. Increase creative, entrepreneurial, farsighted thinking and behavior.
7. Establish separate or small organizational units responsible for innovative activities.
8. Establish clear priorities, goals, objectives.
9. Delegate authority and responsibility—decentralize.
10. Develop differentiation in products or services.
11. Use innovative strategies and formulate an innovation plan.
12. Persist in innovation efforts.

One important point: don't imagine that innovation is only about products or even services. The survey, absolutely rightly, defines it as "any new product, service, process or organizational activity through which a company expects to solve a problem, satisfy a need, or achieve a goal." The barber shop chain, cited by Peter Drucker, that used time-and-motion study to reduce haircut time, while opening in several locations at once, was innovating just as much as the publisher of free magazines who got recipients to register if they wanted to keep getting the publications—and both were just as innovative as the man who gave Sony the Walkman.

Why? Because the barber chain could afford to use local TV advertising, offering a short maximum wait—or you got a free haircut. Predictably lucrative results ensued. The publisher could not only prove the demand for his giveaway but could deliver far more information to advertisers about their audience. Every business needs continual review, formalized in regular meetings, of the key activities that generate costs or income to see if there are new ways in which either or both can be improved: in other words, innovation.

It's *never* trouble-free, though. Doing new things is the most exciting and often the most rewarding part of business, but it's also the most exhausting and nerve-racking. Also, the innovator has to face a number of man-made obstacles. If these are in your path, do your utmost to remove them:

1. Red tape; cumbersome "decision and review" structure or process
2. Lack of funds for innovation
3. Preoccupation with current operations at the expense of future opportunities
4. Failure to engage in innovative thinking; insistence on tradition
5. Lack of top management support, commitment, or innovativeness
6. Organizational structure that discourages innovation.

Plans to surmount these obstacles may run into more barriers. The following list ranks the barriers in their most common order of occurrence. Note that these are all very closely akin to the sales objections you receive from people who don't want to buy, but prefer not to say so. The arguments are shot through with illogic and emotion. They can be overcome—but you need good sales skills and persistence to achieve your end.

1. Cannot afford; inadequate return on investment
2. Tendency to protect an existing investment or livelihood
3. Fear of failure or risk taking
4. The "not-invented-here" syndrome
5. "Let's postpone it, give it some more thought"
6. Opposes custom, habit, fashion, taste

7. "That product won't work," or "It didn't work last time"
8. We are basically followers, not leaders.

Suppose you sell yourself and your innovation over all the barriers—your troubles still aren't over. The novelty may fail (the majority actually do). Westland came out with civil helicopter projects of its own, but totally failed to win the sales the company desperately needed to offset its dependence on orders from the good old Ministry of Defence. The following are the hard questions you have to answer in the hardest-nosed manner possible before plunging into the unknown—for that describes the future of any innovation in a product or service. Again, the questions are ranked in order of importance:

1. Has our analysis of market and customer needs been full enough, thorough enough, and accurate enough?
2. Has the competition been fully, thoroughly, and accurately assessed?
3. Is the offering sufficiently different—that is, not too much of a "me-too"?
4. Are we straying too far from our real areas of corporate and marketing expertise?
5. Are we allocating the proper amount of time to development and marketing: not too little, not too much, but just right?
6. Is top management sufficiently involved and committed?

All these questions are important, but the first, judging by the responses to the survey, is crucial. Over 60 percent of those replying gave insufficient or faulty market or customer analysis as the prime reason for failure. Certainly, one new venture in publishing was shown by postmortem to have failed this test. Because of fears about security, the research concentrated entirely on the size of the market, paying no attention to the buying patterns of the customers. Because of this basic defect, the product's ability to take market share from the competition was greatly exaggerated.

The stupidity is that independent market research, given time, could have solved the problems. But the companies responding to the survey (conducted by Arthur Young and reported in *Advanced Management Report* by the firm's Cesar L. Pereira and William K. Foster) often had a low opinion of their research abilities. Only half of them thought themselves "relatively strong" at research. Given that companies generally overstate their strengths, that is a dismal picture. It's one, however, that's not only easy to improve but that will pay richly in both mistakes avoided and masterstrokes made—and not just in innovation.

5. THE DOUBLE WHOPPER AT VW

Every success carries within it the seeds of its own potential destruction. Successful managements ignore this truism precisely because they are successful. It explains how one great company let sales of its most important product in its most valuable foreign market halve in a single year. The company was Volkswagen; the beleaguered market was the United States; and the product was the Rabbit. The year was 1982, and one reason for the collapse, of course, was the general U.S. recession, courtesy of President Reagan. But the Rabbit run-down also raises two fascinating questions:

1. Had VW kept the Rabbit running too long because it thought of it as another Beetle?
2. Had VW's decision to assemble its cars in the United States, and to promulgate that fact assiduously, backfired—because, to quote an analyst, "people were willing to pay more for a foreign car, [but] . . . it became hard to convince consumers that there was something unique about a car made in Pennsylvania"?

On the first point, VW got in the deepest possible trouble with the Beetle itself. It had lived on far, far too long, with the entire company's fortunes pinned to its snub nose, because the management couldn't bring itself to admit that its beloved Beetle was obsolete— or to agree on how to replace it. In today's world market, you can't afford to run a Rabbit (launched in 1974) indefinitely, certainly not at a time when Ford had launched its three leading lower-priced ranges in 1977, 1980, and 1982.

As for that "made in America" label, the advertising stress was making the best of a bad job. VW felt that U.S. assembly was essential to counteract the strength of the deutsche mark. But once the boot was on the dollar's foot, the Rabbit, despite price cuts, cost notably more than its Mazda or Toyota rivals. As in its calamitous purchase of Triumph-Adler's business machines (offloaded on Olivetti in 1986), VW simply got its strategy wrong, but this time in its base business and key markets.

The company had come back from the edge of the grave famously before. After record-breaking losses, new management pushed through a total revamp of production facilities and model range in a single amazing year, as Rabbits ousted Beetles. But some journeys back are too long ever to be made. Note three vital statistics: 500,000, the American sales of VWs (mostly Beetles) in 1971; 150,000, the sales in 1984; and 560,000, the U.S. sales figure for Toyota in 1984. Clearly nothing short of a new Beetle, probably not even the excellent new Rabbit, could restore VW to the palmy American days of eleven years earlier. In marketing you can get away with one whopping error, but seldom with two—especially if it's the *same* error.

6. STARRING, EUROPEAN-STYLE

Gigantic companies like VW seldom face the ultimate sanctions of total collapse or private takeover. This is not simply because they are so gigantic and their debts so huge that banks and governments won't let them go under, but also because of the regenerative powers of any company that has retained a real hold over large volume markets. What VW lost for keeps in America, it won back in Europe thanks to the launch in 1985 of the new Golf, an obvious winner from its first appearance. By early 1986 the West German company had over $16 billion in sales and was on course for a $600 million profit in 1988, a performance strong enough to win an honorable mention in *Management Today*'s roster of Western Europe's best companies.

The key to that assessment (and to the turnaround itself) was VW's 12.8 percent of the European market. That pushed sales value just above those of the European paradigm, ranked head and shoulders above all competitors in esteem: Daimler-Benz. The very fact that the latter is a long-running saga, a prime case, says the magazine, of "taking a long-term view of the market, rigorously building up its presence and steadily increasing its economies of scale," explains the accolades. But the most striking aspect of Europe in the mid-1980s was less stamina than resurgence, of which VW is only one conspicuous exemplar.

In the same motor industry, Italy's Fiat staged an equally impressive comeback, based on a massive revamp of the model line. The same style of rejuvenation also explained the nomination of Peugeot, whose troubles had been created not only by model obsolescence but by the troubled takeovers of Citroen and Chrysler's European interests. The auto renaissance, though, was outshone by the dazzling performance of Olivetti under Carlo de Benedetti, lauded by *Time* magazine in 1985 as "an inspiring example of a fresh entrepreneurial spirit that is beginning to rustle through Western Europe."

That quotation marks an emphatic change of mood in American attitudes toward the Old World economies. Until quite recently U.S. reports had concluded that Europe, plagued by conservatism and heavy unemployment, had run out of manufacturing and commercial vitality. The running in international reputation had been made by Japanese and, to a lesser extent, U.S. companies, as their leaders pushed steadily into new markets, Europe among them. These powerful competitors rebuked European complacency with

their efficiency and productivity in the Japanese case, and their entrepreneurial high technology in the American one. The dollar's fall
and the oil price collapse have prompted some of the swing in mood
back in Europe's favor, but the evidence of European corporate
resurgence has also been compelling.

There's a common thread binding the fifty-odd stars listed by
Management Today, whether they are comebacks like VW, golden
oldies like Daimler-Benz or Siemens, new companies sprung from
the imagination of a postwar entrepreneur like the late Heinz Nixdorf, or reassembled, rejuvenated old-line groups like Moët-Hennessy ("the ultimate Yuppie company," according to one admirer). All
have sought to build or rebuild market share by reliance on products,
new or old, that offer the purchaser a strong perceived advantage
over the competition's entry. Most important, though, is the combination of this basic strategy with another quality: high ambition.

De Benedetti, for example, aims to make Olivetti "the IBM of
Europe" (a position IBM thinks it already occupies). That may
sound grandiose, but Olivetti's current European position is founded
on a relatively small base in the Italian home market, and the small-
base syndrome can be a source of strength. It explains why several
European stars have been forced to pick targets that sound overambi-
tious to anybody except a Japanese. Like the latter, the ambitious
European has created his own definition of impossibility. Thus a
German maker, Heidelberger Druckmaschinen, makes "more printing machines in Japan than all the Japanese companies combined";
the Swedish firm Tetra Pak supplies "nearly all the milk and juice
cartons *everywhere* in Western Europe"; the Danish compressor-to-
hydraulics company Danfoss exports 90 percent of its production to
105 countries.

Even for companies based in larger and richer markets than
Italy, Sweden, or Denmark, the achievements are often out of proportion to reasonable expectation. West Germany's Robert Bosch,
praised for a "bull's-eye strategy, excellently executed," has three-
quarters of the rapidly growing and lush market in fuel injection. It
pioneered this market so successfully that its chairman could boast

343

to *Fortune* that among European car makers, "the only alternative to Bosch is Bosch." It's much the same approach, applied business worlds apart, as that of Louis Vuitton, the fine luggage makers, whose management has at all costs "maintained the exclusivity and quality of the products."

In the 1980s the quality of ambition is as vital as that of the product or service being marketed; in neither case does the Supermarketer settle for second-best. From the narrow Swedish base, Hans Werthen of Electrolux (whose own choices of top European company start with Siemens and Bosch) expanded the company into Europe's largest white-goods producer by excellent engineering-based management and judicious takeover. One recent foray, the U.S. purchase of White Consolidated, not only went a long way toward making up for a deficient presence in the richest market but gave Electrolux world leadership—reinforced by buying Italy's Zanussi.

From the equally narrow base of West Germany's data-processing industry in 1968, Nixdorf built one of IBM's few forceful and profitable competitors. By 1984, Nixdorf had multiplied revenues thirty-one times and stockholder's equity by forty-nine, thanks to gearing its business not to computer hardware but to computer solutions, giving IBM a ferocious race in selling computers and terminals to European banks. The Nixdorf emphasis on close cooperation with the customer, rapidly assimilating new market trends and new ideas, with swift translation into innovative products, backed by superior service, is the classic niche recipe. But like Electrolux before buying White, Nixdorf has a Western weak spot: a mere 1 percent of U.S. minicomputer sales.

In general, the Europeans' record in the American market compares badly, not only with the Japanese penetration but with their own ambitions. Another weakness is that post-1950s start-ups that have achieved world status in the 1980s are thin on the European ground. Yet the best Europeans have added to continuity (the traditional strong point) an unexpected resilience in adversity and a readiness to embrace new ambitions that have produced some evidently

344

lasting achievements, often out of unpromising circumstances. In doing so, they have demonstrated the extraordinary diversity of late-twentieth-century markets and the even greater range of marketing strategies with which ingenious Supermarketers can create winning positions from vaulting ambitions—even when they start from ground as soggy as Europe's in the wake of the gone, but not forgotten, oil price shocks.

7. THE INDUSTRY OF BIG MAC

There'll be plenty more opportunities, but they won't be in traditional industry. Indeed, what is industry? This sounds like a silly question, until you consider a fact like this: the fifth or so largest employer in the United States isn't in cars, or oil, or steel, or computers. It's in hamburgers—none other than Big Mac itself.

If industry means converting raw materials into consumable products, McDonald's is as industrious, so to speak, as General Motors. True, the product isn't durable, and the materials consist entirely of food. But food manufacturers count as an industry—so why is a fast-food processor a mere service? Anyway, why are services "mere"? For that matter, how many of the people employed in industry, such as marketers, are much more remote from actually making things than a short-order cook?

The definitions matter for both the economy and the business of management. What's traditionally defined as *industry* notoriously employs far fewer people than it once did—especially at the blunt end. At the sharp end, where the product meets the customer, industry employs more and more, directly and indirectly. The analogy is with agriculture. Numbers actually working on the land have become minute, but great hordes are now occupied in transforming farm produce and delivering the results, often in fantastical guises, to waiting mouths. Really, the staffs of Carnation, General Mills,

Kellogg, Heinz, and McDonald's are all part of the agricultural industry.

Agriculture's dwindling away as an employer of labor is an optical illusion. The action has simply moved downstream. True, in some cases (like steel), the action has moved away from a whole industry, for reasons that won't be reversed. In others, though, like cars, the action has moved from blunt-end companies to sharp, market-oriented ones; the extraordinary results of BMW and Mercedes, growing rich yet again while rivals groaned, rest on superbly efficient service of defined market segments. Similarly, Sweden's L. M. Ericsson won an absurdly high world market share in public telephone exchanges, which was a just reward for starting at the sharp end and setting out deliberately to provide customers with their hearts' desire in electronic switching.

That is the sharp clue to nearly all Supermarketing success in the 1980s: the sharp end. Acute knowledge of acutely defined markets not only separates the sheep from the goats, it divides the high returns from the low.

8. WINNING THE AMERICAN WAY

The Supermarketers of the 1980s don't think of themselves as operating in broad industries. They flourish in specific product sectors—sometimes many more than one. But the number doesn't make any difference to the principle: whatever they are, the best companies specialize. They possess, in their segment, sector, or niche, the offerings that are most wanted; and they serve its public devotedly to sustain the high market shares and high yields from which continued leadership can be financed.

Consider this list of corporations: American Home Products, Dow Jones, Mitchell Energy, SmithKline Beckman, Kellogg, Deluxe Check Printers, Worthington Industries, Maytag, Merck, Nalco

Chemical, IBM, Dover, and Coca-Cola. Ostensibly they share nothing, but they are bound by a common statistical excellence. In April 1984, *Fortune* found that these thirteen companies, and they alone among the magazine's list of 500, had averaged at least a 20 percent return on year-end shareholders' equity over the decade to 1983, without ever dipping below 15 percent. Look again at the list, though, and a nonstatistical similarity emerges. By and large, these are older-line, conservative companies. Each has a strong and generally leading position in a desirable market. But the strength and the leadership spring from solid virtues applied over a sustained period.

That follows axiomatically from the acid test. No company can earn such high returns over a decade without being built for the long haul. But there's more to it than that. Only the energy business, Mitchell, financed its performance with heavy debt (and later fell out of bed in consequence). The others succeeded in large measure in self-financing their market leadership. Again, that outcome is axiomatic. The higher the return on current capital, the less the need to obtain additional capital from outside. The axiom is not that straightforward, however. Other things being equal, high leverage is supposed to lever upward the return on shareholders' equity. So why were these companies the supreme exponents on that vital score?

Clearly other things aren't equal. Is there a connection between the kind of marketing management that farms its territory most assiduously for long-term yield and the mentality that dislikes deep entry into hock? Maybe so. The fact is that customers, like these companies, are fundamentally conservative. They flock to the genuinely new, whether it's a videocassette recorder or a new munchie or an anti-ulcer drug. But once flocked, they tend to stay with the supplier who, year in and year out, gives them what they want, as they want it, when they want it.

Even better, they are willing to pay more for the privilege. *Fortune* cites two highly relevant examples to show that, when market leaders risk losing business by raising prices, "a strong brand name or a rock-solid reputation for service will usually carry the day." Thus Kellogg didn't rescind all of its earlier price rises, neces-

347

sitated by mounting cereal costs, when those costs fell. Return on equity soared joyously from 20 to 26 percent. At Dow Jones, continual increases in the cost of paper, excused by rising costs, were readily absorbed by readers who found *The Wall Street Journal* irreplaceable at any price.

Mind you, it greatly helps if the product has an absolute or virtual monopoly, such as the *Journal*'s. The objective of the long-term Supermarketer is to achieve, if not an actual monopoly, the benefits of absolute market ownership. Even in a commodity business like check printing, the determined company can achieve incredible market shares, like Deluxe's better than 50 percent, a figure that is claimed to rise slightly each year. The key was a Japanese standard of error-free service (99 percent perfect, with over 95 percent of orders delivered inside two days) based on Japanese-style adoption of the best technology—without which Deluxe would have run out of the supplies required to meet the demand.

That's another characteristic of the champions. They concentrate on the supply side as much as on the demand. Maytag's boss, Daniel J. Krumm, started expanding plant capacity for its appliances by three-quarters in the recessionary conditions of 1974. The $60 million he put at risk paid off triumphantly with capacity that Krumm expected to last out the 1980s—and to deliver high quality at efficient costs. High investment of that nature can pay off even when demand disappears. Dover's Norris division tripled its capacity for the "sucker rods" used in oil drilling. When their prices crumbled, Norris might have looked a sucker indeed, but, so chairman Thomas C. Sutton told *Fortune;* "When the circus comes to town, you rent every room in the hotel, at the best prices you can get. . . . Norris totally capitalized on the marketplace. We earned an awful lot of money for the shareholders."

The common themes of reliable supply (in both quantity and quality), deep understanding of markets, low costs (combined with premium prices), and conservative finance are no coincidence. A similar exercise in Britain by *Management Today* came up with eight companies that had achieved, alone among the nation's 250 largest, more than 17.6 percent return on invested capital over a decade and had never fallen below 13.2 percent. Their core businesses were defense electronics, out-of-town shopping, discount supermarkets, health care, pest control, and building products. Two of them, the Beecham drugs and foods to toothpaste and cosmetics business, and the brilliant BTR conglomerate, were multimarket. But they were no exceptions to the rule.

Like the single-market firms, they are marked by the absence of flashiness and the presence of solid common sense. All eight, like the American thirteen, had built their profitability primarily by exploiting the potential of well-understood markets. As in the United States, so in Britain: high achievement can be realized in low-growth markets and hot technologies alike. Actually, the core business that year after year provides good and growing profits in response to careful and continuous nurture has one supreme advantage over the runaway growth market—for example, the personal computer in its heyday. Products like SmithKline's Tagamet drug or Beecham's synthetic penicillins generate vast profits but are desperately hard acts to follow. A boom market always creates the what-to-do-for-an-encore syndrome, superbly solved by IBM when it belatedly grabbed the PC opportunity; but what comes after that?

Ambition does more than provide the kind of desire that makes former chairman Frank Cary rate IBM's chances of repeating the past ten years' profitability performance as 100 percent, or that underlies Sir Owen Green's belief at BTR that, having grown from $220 million of sales to $5.6 billion in a decade, "we can continue for as long as we choose to continue." Translated into numbers, into targets, ambition provides the mechanical driving force of these far-from-mechanistic businesses. For the British bunch, however, ambition has produced one visible difference from the Americans, taken as a whole: in the sunset circumstances of the 1970s, any British manager worth the name had to look outside the domestic market—and all six of the nonretailers in the *Management Today* article consequently have heavy international presence.

Evidently, a business like the building-products business, with

94 percent of the British plasterboard market, hasn't much left to harvest at home (note, again, the monopoly achievement). For such a company, North America is a powerful magnet. The attraction isn't so great in reverse. But most of the American thirteen already have global operations, and in an increasingly global world, would-be U.S. Supermarketers will have to widen their vision even as they retain their narrow concentration on high service at low costs—and with rich reward to the investors.

It sounds paradoxical that, thanks to their superb cash generation, these companies have tended to provide that abundant reward more in higher dividends and less in exceptional stock market performance. Those who find that disappointing should reflect on one final lesson of the Fine Thirteen and the Excellent Eight. Isn't that how capitalism (and Supermarketing) are supposed to work?

9. BLUE BLOODS, AND SHOTGUNS AND PICKUPS

Selling rat poison? Or prune juice? Marshmallows? Antacids? Then go West, or East, young marketer, to Grand Rapids, Miami, Salt Lake City, or Atlanta—those being, according to an article in *Fortune* magazine, the respective prime U.S. markets for these products. It doesn't say whether Grand Rapids is also the rat capital of America, which is a logical assumption. And there's no apparent reason why Atlanta stomachs should reach (or retch) for the Pepto-Bismol more than those in Savannah—which holds the gastronomic (or gastric) lead in monosodium glutamate and meat tenderizers (again for no apparent cause).

Illogical or not, that's the way things are. And it provides the way out of many a marketing dilemma. According to Thomas Moore's article, S. C. Johnson and Son, facing a static 40 percent market share for its Raid insecticides, went for the throats of the cockroaches in Houston and New York and of the fleas in Tampa and Birmingham, all in due season. The result? Bigger market shares in sixteen out of eighteen regions; a 5 percent rise in national market guzzle; and food for thought for any company (which means almost every company) that is divided into sales or marketing regions.

If these divisions are purely organizational, rather than tactical or strategic, the company is certainly missing major market opportunities. Targeted promotion always makes more sense—if, that is, you can locate the target. Thanks to new technological wonders like computers and laser scanners, as *Fortune* points out, the targets can be picked up, and picked off, with an ease unknown to previous generations. An operation named Prizm divides neighborhoods into forty-odd groups under such redolent names as "Blue-Blood Estates" and "Shotguns and Pickups" (the latter vehicles, incidentally, being a bull market in the Southwest). Advertising agency Ogilvy and Mather has the same message; it operates its marketing smarts on eight profiles of different U.S. "nations."

Using this concept state by state, the brewing giant Anheuser-Busch frothed up its national market share from 22.6 percent to 36.7 percent in only a few years. Note that the key doesn't lie in regional advertising, but in altering the whole marketing platform to suit specific conditions and tastes, season by season, product by product. That's how the whole marketing game has changed: place by place, season by season, product by product. And that's how the Supermarketers play the game: witness the progress of PepsiCo.

10. WHAT PEPPED UP PEPSI'S MARKETING

In the naked market today's hero company is quite likely to be tomorrow's—if not next minute's—bum. Take Coca-Cola and Procter & Gamble, respectively fourth and eighth in *Fortune*'s January 1986 list of America's most admired corporations. In February

351

of the same year, *Business Week* included them in another, less honorable roll: that of "marketing powerhouses" that had "stumbled"—P & G with old toothpaste and new disposable diapers and orange juice, Coca-Cola with the "ill-fated" introduction of New Coke described in Step One, section 1, of this book.

The roll of dubious honor is completed by Philip Morris, whose double stumble takes in beer (once a claim to marketing fame second only to Marlboro) and 7-Up. The stumbling powerhouse had put the latter up for sale, after years of losses that had mocked Philip Morris's marketing prowess, to the magazine's new hero: PepsiCo. Without question, the Pepsi people could parade impressive credentials ranging from the embarrassment of Coke to the Personal Pan Pizza. But so could P & G, Coca-Cola, and Philip Morris, in their long moments of undisputed glory. What grounds were there for supposing that Pepsi had some magic ingredient, more potent than its cola formula, that would avoid the dreaded development of feet of marketing clay?

The attributes that, at least for this season, work so effectively include:

1. Shooting from the hip, ranking speed of response over deliberation. To quote chief executive officer D. Wayne Calloway, it's "ready, fire, aim."

2. Strong belief in decentralization and insistence on its practice (in contrast to the top-down decision making said to stamp the P & G management style, all the way down to detailed questions of advertising and package design).

3. Heavy pressure on the managers, in return for their autonomy, to move fast and perform competitive wonders. *Business Week* quotes a consultant to this effect: "These are people who like to win. Virtually everybody is overworked."

4. Readiness to take investment risks. The 100 percent Nutra-Sweet formula for Diet Pepsi was launched without testing, "on the basis of a gut feeling that the time was right"—and sales subsequently rose by a quarter in just over a year.

5. Quick competitive reflexes. The magazine quotes the three new flavors of Slice with which Pepsi greeted the first two flavors of the Coke product designed to muscle into the soda-plus-real-juice market created by Pepsi.

6. Massive investment in advertising based on the use of celebrities: $460 million in a single year, a figure that grew by more than the increase in revenues, to promote products via personalities ranging from Michael Jackson to Marvelous Marvin Hagler.

7. Emphasis on a rapid flow of speedily produced new products. At the time of the article, Frito-Lay was testing some half-dozen new snacks to follow the success of the $150 million O'Grady's thick-cut potato chips. Their two years from lab to test market, though, had been shortened to six months for two newer products.

8. Continual close attention to markets: "looking, listening and learning." According to Calloway, "You hear a lot of conversations around Pepsi about what's going on with the consumer, what's going on at the supermarket, what the competition is doing. You'll seldom hear about internal things, like a controller's report."

One point leaps out from those eight: nothing in the Pepsi marketing magic is either novel or magical, and most marketing and management experts would come up with largely similar prescriptions for any company that wishes to hold its ground, let alone forge ahead, in the current decade and the next. Action before words; delegation of real authority to managers in the market; insistence on high performance from the devolved units; risk-taking investment; swift response to competition; heavy investment in telling promotion; innovative power; eyes and ears on the ground of markets; and total customer orientation. Throughout this book, the virtue of these virtues has been constantly stressed.

Indeed, any one of the three stumbling powerhouses could point to striking examples of some, if not all, of the eight virtuous qualities. Never in the whole history of marketing has any company made an investment in innovation that involved more risk than the launch of New Coke. Because it was rushed, and based more on gut feeling than convincing research, Coke was totally unprepared for the backlash that forced it to reintroduce its original formula as Classic Coke. While that bifurcation gave Coke more combined shelf space in the supermarkets, it left Pepsi as indisputably the biggest brand in soft drinks—and by early 1986 began to look like what might be called a mitigated disaster.

In other words, Pepsi's marketing looks like magic because some of it has worked like magic. By the nature of modern markets, there will be more setbacks like its Grandma's packaged cookies, which failed to become a national brand. As the marketing powerhouses square off against each other over vast tracts of consumer territory, from fast food to tortilla chips, soft drinks to cookies, each tract subdivided into increasingly complex segments, the result is the same for everybody: you win a few, you lose a few.

As *Business Week* pointed out, "Major technological breakthroughs are rare, markets change fast, and competitors can easily rip off each other's ideas." Such conditions guarantee flux. The pepped-up corporation can best ensure that its wins outweigh its losses by noting that the Pepsi Eight are in danger of becoming marketing clichés. Any idol company that degenerates into cliché management is measuring itself for a set of clay feet.

11. THE CLASSIC CASE OF IBM

This book began with two cases bound to become marketing classics, the turmoil into which two champions, in contrasting markets, had been thrust by the same competitive force: the pressure applied by a powerful rival. The story of the Supermarketers ends with the same two cases: Coke, as described in the previous section, still searching for the way (which may well not exist) to fight clear of Pepsi, and Apple, under its former Pepsi boss, back into good profits as it wrestles with the might of an IBM battling to keep a market dominance in personal computers once of old-Coke dimensions.

Yet the combative pressures of the 1980s leave nobody un-scathed, not even an IBM lording it over Apple. Like the former champion underdog, the latecomer champion has had to grapple with classic marketing problems in personal computers. IBM's amazing decision early in 1985 to drop the PC jr was as powerful evidence of unresolved dilemmas as Apple's one-week production shutdown at the same time. The events are intimately connected, since it was IBM's revamped jr, marketed with utmost belligerence, that helped build Apple's mountain of surplus.

IBM's classic conundrum started with cannibalization. With the original PC a runaway success in the higher price bracket, the temptation to head into down-market territory was irresistible. The difficulty of doing so without hurting PC sr sales, though, was obvi-ous and formidable. No doubt this explains why jr appeared with cheap features like a rubber keyboard; the strategem kept the new baby away from Little Daddy, all right, but also kept away the customers—in droves.

When a chastened IBM bit the bullet, it took, in *Fortune*'s words, "brilliant moves . . . to strengthen its product line, including its one weak link, the PC jr." But that fortification, along with aggressive pricing, cannibalized like crazy. In the retail market, jr overtook sr, but at a heavy toll on profits. With the down-market jr and up-market AT model both having dire difficulties, Philip Es-tridge, the father of the PC, moved swiftly from much-praised divi-sional hero to unsung corporate staffer.

Even if IBM had decided on a policy of *reculer pour mieux sauter*—coming back later in force with a better differentiated, deadly weapon—the morals would have been the same. First, no strategy, especially not this one, makes economic sense in modern markets if the trade-off for the economic benefit is a sacrifice in product attributes.

Second, don't expect lightning to strike in the same place. The rapid and unpredicted triumph of the PC must have encouraged IBM to think that its almighty brand would repeat the runaway success lower down. When jr flopped, the price cut and promotion blitz then thrown at customers tarnished the brand image while destroying the economics of the venture. That mistake in turn must have helped the IBM clones to halve its market share.

All the above, of course, is hindsight: Nobody could logically have foreseen the PC surge, or the jr flop, or the retreat. Yet it would be utterly wrong to conclude that there were defects in the original idea of setting up Estridge away from the organization and shibboleths of IBM's center. That was brilliantly right. But the perfect setup for a crash launch of a wholly new product in a wholly new market may be disastrous when consolidation takes command. You simply need a different kind of hero, and of heroics. To put it another way, the Supermarketer had better be prepared for change at all times, for all times, and everybody's markets are now subject to change—often with precious little notice.

12. OMNIPRESENCE OF CHANGE

That omnipresence of change is a cliché of the 1980s. Yet the full significance of what has already happened in the naked world market, let alone what is going to happen in the period to the 1990s and beyond, has only started to sink in. The first certainty is that there are no certainties—and anybody who doubts that need only look at the forecasts that predicted oil shortage and price escalation forever.

What actually happened, the crumbling away in the oil market, is a powerful and maybe ominous demonstration that the basic law of all markets will never be suspended: what goes up must come down. If what's rising is a price, sooner or later the higher cost will choke off demand, encourage substitution, and create a mounting surplus. With equal certainty, that glut will press harder and harder on prices until—presto!—it's no longer Yamani or your life.

But the law doesn't apply only to prices. Lovely, soaring profits eventually have the ugly effect of attracting competition, so that even a superb computer company like Digital Equipment finds its market

356

share receding inexorably, to the point where it can no longer take recession in its stride. Instead, it suffers severe decline in profits. If that sounds painful, look at the slaughter that affected weaker firms, as IBM's PC took its inevitable lion's share of a market where far too many kittens had been making their small fortunes.

Even big Apple, having hired its first-ever marketing supremo, had to solve some vile problems as it fought back against IBM, striving to sell the make-or-break Macintosh marvels without undermining its vital business with the almost immortal Apple II. When a market breaks, as have both Apple's and Sheikh Yamani's, those engaged have to remember one thing above all: the process is ineluctable. Once the basic economies of the marketplace have asserted themselves in this way, they can't be overturned.

Hence the truth that you can fix all of the markets some of the time, but none of the markets all of the time. The textbook answer to these dilemmas is that the company should establish so clear a marketing superiority that it is invulnerable—offering the highest perceived value at the highest price. The paradigm of this approach is Caterpillar Tractor. Yet, as noted, it made losses for the first time in its history because of recession coupled with inability to match the fleetness of foot of Komatsu, its once far tinier Japanese competitor.

The tragedy is that the superior marketer may build so superior a market share and saturate the market so efficiently that the company has nowhere to hide when recession strikes. The only course is to recognize that, one day, marketing's law of gravity will affect every business, and that the force bringing the law into play, as likely as not, will be international competition. The global transportation revolution is basic here, but so is the new technology that allows, for example, unskilled Asians to assemble and export high-tech products.

To make matters worse, currency movements make it impossible to predict exactly where the most cutting competition will emerge. In early 1982 the joker in the pack was the United States, whose currency had fallen so heavily against the deutsche mark that exporting suddenly became fun for American corporations—and much more profitable. That challenge passed, but in 1985–86 the dollar was down again—and the yen so far up as to threaten Japanese prosperity. With its inefficient domestic economy and total need for imported raw materials, Japan has no option but to develop still more highly competitive export industries.

Since most Western economies will also be trying to export more (if only to eliminate their energy deficits), you can bank on tough competition for as far as the eye dares to see. So how does the poor marketer manage? Actually, much as he or she was forced to manage from 1973 on.

1. Seeking higher added value first, rather than higher volume, by optimizing prices and reducing costs.

2. Going for specialized world markets rather than domestic commodity ones.

3. Taking all microeconomic opportunities you can find.

4. Developing as the main management strength the ability to compete—the crucial factor in today's markets.

Even for the best-placed companies, with the enormous boon of a rich market virtually to themselves, sooner or later somebody is likely to try muscling in. The Supermarketer of the 1980s and 1990s must become brilliant at repelling boarders and must learn to seize opportunities, but without being an opportunist. For this is a situation where it's essential to . . .

1. *Take a long-term view.* Don't jump in and out of markets and businesses, but aim to build a business that's good not just for this management generation but for the next, and the next. Having made up your mind on a market, show the utmost tenacity in sticking to it through thick and thin. By and large, in this effort to build long-term businesses. . . .

2. *Grow internally.* Many growth companies starting in the stock market make acquisitions. But the Supermarketers know that buys designed to get you into a new business area never work without

a great deal of sweat supplied by the buyer, and reckon that it's cheaper to build on your existing strengths—as Sears Roebuck, in its greatest days, did by adding stores to mail order. But in old and new businesses alike. . . .

3. *Go for the largest attainable and profitable market share.* Be less interested in short-term profits than in pushing up your share of viable markets in the belief that long-term profits come from market strength. This means, of course, knowing enough about the market to have an accurate picture of what your share actually is. But that's no problem if you understand the necessity to. . . .

4. *Spare no effort in getting all the information you can about the businesses and markets in which you're interested.* The amount that can be learned about competitors, without industrial espionage, is amazing. It's also amazing how many firms are ill-informed about themselves, let alone other firms. That makes it far more difficult, among other things, to be sufficiently alert to. . . .

5. *Follow the leader.* Being first isn't always best. When other people do the pioneering, you can learn their lessons at their expense, strike while the iron is hot, and have a target to aim at: the pioneering Number One. Which means, of course, that you must have confidence in your ability to. . . .

6. *Develop new products and services.* That has to be the prime aim of competition—with no nonsense about development being the task of engineers or some other separate group. Everybody in the business must be deeply involved—with the people at the sharp end, where the customers are, calling the tune. Don't rest until the offering meets all market needs. Which, of course, means *never* resting, and, even more important, you can then afford to. . . .

7. *Compete on everything except price.* In export markets (essential because exporting builds volume and lowers unit costs), heavy price cutting is often enforced. At home, where things should be under better control, do all in your legal power to maintain prices —if possible, premium ones. Only a fool, goes the doctrine, charges less than the customer is ready to pay. If prices crumble, that robs you of the profit benefits you should get if you. . . .

359

8. *Concentrate on strengths.* Search exhaustively for some asset you have that the competition hasn't, and that you can exploit to gain the upper hand. It might be high-volume, low-cost manufacture. It might be the best sales backup in the business. It might be top quality. Or some combination of the above. Your strengths should provide the USP—the Unique Sales Proposition—yours and yours alone, which convinces the customers to buy from you and you alone. That's the strongest way to. . . .

9. *Build a customer franchise.* The paying customers will come back again and again if they trust and like what you provide. The classic case in big business is IBM. Other American firms have had no trouble making products that are better than IBM's. But customers ignored them, by and large, because the IBM name was reassuring—and rightly so. With a strong customer franchise you can safely proceed to. . . .

10. *Minimize risk.* Obviously, you can't avoid risk—that's life. But the business ideas that make Supermarketers rich are ones that are certain to succeed, provided they execute the plans well. One risk you'll never avoid is that you might do something badly. Leave that as little as possible to chance. Thoroughness and painstaking deliberation are essential, as is conservative finance; but, paradoxically, care and caution must be allied to quick reaction, speed of foot, and daring. Once you decide to move, and once everything is ready, move very fast. One of the key principles of competition, in fact, is that of continual reaction to changes in the marketplace, to whatever the opposition (closely monitored, of course) is up to, wherever it competes.

This ten-point guide to competitive success, by no coincidence, fits exactly the methods by which the Japanese companies have achieved what have truly been wonders of marketing. To produce premium products at lower cost than anybody else is a fabulous achievement in itself. But to use such abilities to crack strange market after strange market, in which you don't speak the language, and in which neither the buying habits nor the practices in any way resemble your own—that has to rank as the supreme demonstration of Supermarketing in our time.

The lesson for management is that strategy must at one and the same time be grand and limited. Whatever its resources and scale, the company of the 1980s and 1990s has no option but to specialize in intelligently selected markets in which it can hope to capitalize on its special skills. Yet the number of major business sectors in which any company, however great, can afford to miss out in the conditions of the 1980s is limited as well. Too many missed businesses, and a company is somebody else's potential purchase.

For all that the sovereign importance of establishing a stranglehold on the prime market or markets is inescapable. Do that, as the Supermarketing companies do, and at best the company will live happily and profitably ever after. At worst, the purchaser, hated or welcomed, will be forced to pay through the nose.

Note, too, that in an era when victory has been expected to go to the big battalions, market after market has been scooped by the relatively small. From now to the end of the century, the old, across-the-board markets that made corporations mighty will no longer hold sway. The emperor is as naked as everybody else in marketing when the specialties are so infinite. This has made Supermarketing a game anybody can play, with one supreme proviso: he or she must play it superbly.

To summarize some of the important points I've mentioned in Step Twelve:

1. The first question a winning company must answer is how to build on and sustain its market success.
2. Marketing triumph is always a hard act to follow—and even harder if you insist on doing the same act.
3. If you hold mastery in the marketplace, never, never let go.
4. You must regularly and formally review the key activities that generate costs or income to find new ways in which either or both can be improved.

361

5. In marketing, you can get away with one whopping error, but seldom with two—especially if it's the same error.

6. Even old firms can achieve new marketing marvels by combining high product values with something easier to obtain: high ambition.

7. Develop acute knowledge of acutely defined markets to win the high returns that separate the winners from the also-rans.

8. You can afford conservatism—if you exploit your strengths fully to sustain a strong and leading position in a desirable market over long and highly profitable years.

9. You must vary your marketing place by place, season by season, product by product—because that's how the markets are changing.

10. Put action before words; delegate; demand performance; take risks; respond swiftly; invest in promotion; innovate—these are the winning market formulas, *if* you also keep your eyes and ears on the markets and the customers.

11. No strategy makes any sense in modern markets if the trade-off for the economic benefit is a sacrifice in product attributes.

12. Whether your operation is large or small, specialize in intelligently selected markets in which you can hope to capitalize on your special skills. That's how the big battalions have been and are being beaten in the naked market.

Selected Bibliography

ABEGGLEN, JAMES C. *The Strategy of Japanese Business.* Cambridge, Mass.: ABT Books/Ballinger, 1986. From a Western insider, a true picture of the realities of Japanese competition—inside Japan —and its shattering consequences.

BARRIE, G. JAMES. *Business Wargames.* New York: Penguin Books, 1986. The naked market is a kind of war; and it's highly advisable to learn what lessons real warfare can teach to marketers.

CAVANAGH, RICHARD F., and CLIFFORD, DONALD K. *The Winning Performance.* New York: Bantam Books, 1985. From the folks, or the firm, that gave you *Excellence,* this McKinsey study provides usable insights into what separates the marketing sheep from the goats.

SELECTED BIBLIOGRAPHY

DRUCKER, PETER. *Innovation and Entrepreneurship.* New York: Harper & Row, 1985. Every work by the master is must reading for the marketing minded; but in a time when entrepreneurial innovation is crucial, so is this book.

GRAHAM, MARGARET. *RCA and the Videodisc: The Business of Research.* New York: Cambridge University Press, 1986. Since failure teaches more than success, this perceptive account of one of America's biggest marketing flops is highly instructive.

GROVE, ANDREW. *High-Output Management.* 7th ed. New York: Random House, 1985. How the world of high-tech marketing looks from the inside—to the eyes of one of Silicon Valley's top managers.

KOTLER, PHILIP. *Marketing Management.* Englewood Cliffs, N.J.: Prentice-Hall, 1984. The universally recognized textbook of marketing: a practical and inclusive guide for marketers by a guru who knows all the ropes.

LEVITT, THEODORE. *The Marketing Imagination.* New York: The Free Press (Macmillan), 1986. By the most consistently provocative and inspirational marketing guru, even if the inspiring ideas are themselves inconsistent—but, then, so is modern marketing.

MAJARO, S. *International Marketing.* Winchester, Mass.: Allen Unwin, 1982. A highly instructive exploration of international marketing, which for some companies and countries has become the only kind of marketing there is.

MCCORMACK, MARK. *What They Don't Teach You at Harvard Business School.* New York: Bantam Books, 1985. The author may not know much that Harvard Business School doesn't, but what he doesn't know about negotiation isn't worth reading.

MCKENNA, REGIS. *The Regis Touch.* Reading, Mass.: Addison-Wesley, 1985. The lessons of marketing as taught by Silicon Valley's leading public relations wizard offer low-tech wisdom to marketers of any kind.

OHMAE, KENICHI. *Triad Power.* New York: The Free Press (Macmillan), 1985. Not the easiest read: but no international strategist can afford to ignore this Japanese expert's views on evolving world markets.

PINCHOT, GIFFORD, III. *Intrapreneuring.* New York: Harper & Row, 1985. A remarkable tour de force, combining excellently researched cases with acute observations of what actually happens to corporate entrepreneurs—instead of what should happen.

PORTER, MICHAEL C. *Competitive Advantage.* New York: The Free Press (Macmillan), 1985.

————. *Competitive Strategy.* New York: The Free Press (Macmillan), 1982. Both these books home in on the fact that competition is the dominant business mode of our times, and explain how to sustain the superior performance that competing requires.

RODGERS, BUCK, and SHOOK, ROBERT L. *The IBM Way.* New York: Harper & Row, 1986. A former marketing supremo at the greatest marketing company gives a simple, gung-ho account of how IBM goes about its customers' business.

WILSON, AUBREY. *Aubrey Wilson's Marketing Audit Checklists.* Maidenhead, Berks: McGraw-Hill Book Company (UK), 1982. A step-by-step, area-by-area method to ensure that no stone is left unturned in the marketing endeavor, which is how it should be.

WINKLER, JOHN. *Pricing for Results.* New York: Facts on File, 1984. A practical and profitable guide to the use of price as marketing weapon—which is, of course, what price should be used for.

Acknowledgments

This book grew out of my association with and writings for *Marketing* magazine, admirably edited by my long-term friend and associate, Tom Lester; I am deeply grateful to him and to his excellent colleagues. I also owe a debt of thanks and enlightenment to the many sources mentioned in the book, notably John Winkler and his book *Pricing for Results,* Gifford Pinchot III for his *Intrapreneuring,* John Thackray (the superb U.S. correspondent of *Management Today*) and, among several invaluable publications, the *Financial Times, Business Week, Time, Fortune, Management Today,* and the *Harvard Business Review.* I have had kind and efficient assistance from Anne Ferguson and Annabella Gabb; and I owe most special thanks to Anne Leguen de Lacroix and June Barber for unstinting and excellent help. The book would not, of course, have been possible without my many contacts with the men and women who manage the marketing of the companies I've mentioned—and many I have not. It has been a privilege to observe them in the most exciting business times that I (and I expect they) can recall.

I must also thank the publishers for permission to quote from the following books: *The Winning Performance* by Richard F. Cavanagh and Donald K. Clifford (Bantam Books); *Iacocca* by Lee Iacocca (Bantam Books); *The Regis Touch* by Regis McKenna (Addison-Wesley); *Marks & Spencer: Anatomy of Britain's Most Efficiently Managed Company* by K. K. Tse (Pergamon Press); *Pricing for Results* by John Winkler (Facts on File).

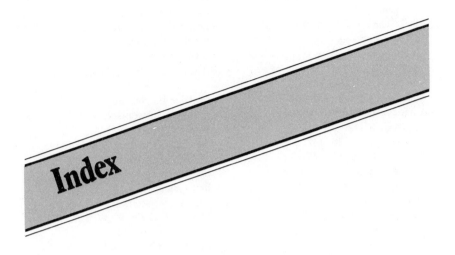

Index

INDEX

370

Dexter Brent and Paterson
(advertising agency), 199, 201
Diet Coke, 6–7, 23, 270
Diet Pepsi, 352
Differentiation of products, 25–28
and effectiveness of advertising,
188–89
Digital Equipment Corporation
(DEC), 88, 285, 286, 356–57
Direct marketing, 202–203
Direct-response advertising, 209–11
Distalgesic (painkilling drug), 243
Distillers Company Limited (DCL),
19–22
Diversification, 246–73
through acquisition, vs. launching
from scratch, 253–54
adequate return on capital and,
246–48
concentrated care for each
segment in, 129–31
concentrated units in context of,
252–53
effectiveness as only justification
for, 258–59
evaluating acquisition prospects
for, 264–68
as inadequate object, 28–30
increased market pace and, 261–64
management of explosive growth
from, 260
merger failure rate, 255–58
reliance on money vs.
management in, 292–93
reversing errors of, 309–11
strengthening core business and,
248–52, 270
targeting market niches and,
284–85
in "turbulent" markets, 270–72
Douglas Aircraft
DC-9, 115, 116
DC-10, 128
Dover (corporation), 346–48
Dow Jones, 346–48
Doyle (survey author), 180

DRI Europe (consultants), 143
Drucker, Peter, 112, 114, 259, 337
"Dumping," 217–18
Dunbee-Combex-Marx (DCM), 110
Dunkin' Donuts, 113, 286
Dunlop Rubber Company, 311–13
Du Pont Corporation, 115, 118, 249
Duracell batteries, 249

Eastern Airlines, 296
Eastman Kodak, 2, 22, 31, 39–42,
86, 144–45, 205, 206
Economies of scale, *see* Scale
Edsel cars, 100
Efficient management, 331–33
Egan, John, 163–64
Eicoff, Alvin, 209–11
Eight Entrepreneurial Truths, 112–15
Electra aircraft, 127, 128
Electrolux, 335, 344
Eli Lilly, 11, 156, 243
Epson Computers, 287
Ericsson, L.M. (company), 161, 162,
346
Esch, Horst-Dieter, 305–306
Esmark (conglomerate), 238
Estridge, Philip, 355, 356
Ethics, 213–18, 223–40
of financial inducements to
increase sales, 215–16
of governments, 213–15
of how to deal with misfortune,
239–40, 243
of intelligence gathering, 228–33
"management by semantics" and,
233–39
predatory pricing and, 217–18
in promotion/publicity, 183, 213
relative costs of dishonesty and
honesty, 223–24
theft of secrets and, 216–17,
227–28
value for money and, 225–27
European Economic Community
(EEC), 217
Eveready batteries, 22

373

INDEX

INDEX

INDEX